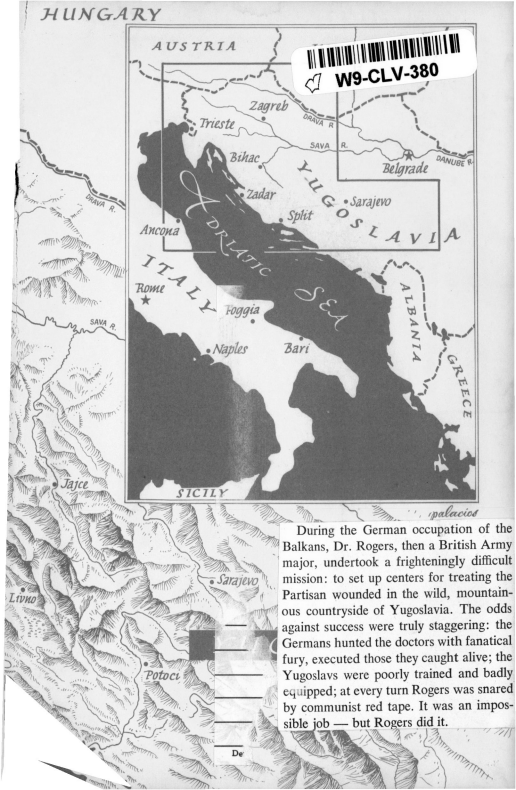

HUNGARY

AUSTRIA

Zagreb

Trieste

Bihac

DRAVA R.

SAVA R.

Belgrade

DANUBE R.

Zadar

Sarajevo

Split

YUGOSLAVIA

Ancona

ADRIATIC SEA

ALBANIA

GREECE

ITALY

Rome

Foggia

SAVA R.

Naples

Bari

SICILY

Jajce

Sarajevo

Livno

Potoci

palacios

During the German occupation of the Balkans, Dr. Rogers, then a British Army major, undertook a frighteningly difficult mission: to set up centers for treating the Partisan wounded in the wild, mountainous countryside of Yugoslavia. The odds against success were truly staggering: the Germans hunted the doctors with fanatical fury, executed those they caught alive; the Yugoslavs were poorly trained and badly equipped; at every turn Rogers was snared by communist red tape. It was an impossible job — but Rogers did it.

GUERRILLA SURGEON

Guerrilla Surgeon

By LINDSAY ROGERS

DOUBLEDAY & COMPANY, INC., GARDEN CITY, N. Y., 1957

AUTHOR'S NOTE

I wrote this story of some of my wartime experiences in Yugoslavia a few weeks after coming out of the country in 1945. It was written in Ceylon, in the space of a fortnight, without the help of any records, for records I had none.

There has been some slight rewording and minor amendment to the writing, but the story remains as I wrote it ten years ago, and the opinions expressed are those I held when I came out of Yugoslavia.

Many of the names in the book, both of places and of people, are "conspirated" names, adopted during the fight to mislead the enemy. I have made no attempt to distinguish between real and assumed names, for I frequently did not know which was which. The conspirated names appear in the story because I still do not know the real ones.

Bill, being what he is, quickly found the attraction of a very good Scottish lassie and now he and his family live in N.Z. Ian also married, lives in Seattle, and Vic's whereabouts is unknown.

By Lieutenant General the Lord Freyberg

VC., GCMG., KCB., KBE., DSO.

This book by Dr. Rogers is the War story of a New Zealand surgeon serving with a British medical unit. The story starts in North Africa and takes you to Sicily and Italy. Dr. Rogers was not satisfied with life in a medical unit behind the lines and he longed for adventure. He joined the Jugoslav Partisan forces and moved with them, first to Dalmatia and to Croatia and then to Bosnia and Slovenia.

A revealing insight is given into the life of the Partisani, of whom there were only 300,000 Jugoslav Partisani out of a total population of sixteen million. You will read about many strange people—the Chetnicks, the Otashi and the Donerbrands. Dr. Rogers is critical of the British propaganda efforts and in this he makes a case—he feels that the Partisani could have been educated up into being pro British because only five per cent of the total population were Communists and only ten per cent among the Partisani.

This book is well worth reading because it tells the story of a theatre of war that is little known and which was certainly more primitive and at times more brutal than any other that we took part in.

You will find lots to shock you—grim stories of torture, rape and murder. Had I read this book without my background knowledge of the author, I should have thought it was an over

dramatized story; but I should have been wrong. I know
Dr. Rogers as a very competent surgeon, and from my knowl-
edge of the Partisani, with whom we had great trouble at
Trieste, I know they had admiration and affection for Dr.
Rogers which amounted almost to worship.

My dealings with the Partisani, in May 1945, when we
snatched Trieste from Tito's grasp, were difficult, to say the
least of it. The Jugoslavs resented our being there, and carried
out operations against the civil population of Venezia Giulia
which were really acts of war. Short of fighting them, we could
not restrain the Partisani's violent ways, indeed, they behaved
exactly as described by Dr. Rogers in this book. The climax at
Trieste came, when I was obliged to get really tough with the
Jugoslav Commander, who was a well known Russian-indoctri-
nated Communist. But the whole attitude of the Partisani
changed when they realised that I knew Dr. Rogers.

I confidently recommend this book as an exciting and real-
istic story, and a valuable contribution to the history of our
lives.

BERNARD FREYBURG

Norman Tower, *Windsor Castle*
11th June, 1956

CONTENTS

GUERRILLA SURGEON

Pushing aside the double-blanket blackout, which covered the operating-theater doors of the 15th Casualty Clearing Station, I came into the daylight and started walking to the mess tent for breakfast. It was one of those hot Tunisian days, and already at 7 A.M. the far escarpment shimmered, and the lorries were streaming along the road toward the Mareth Line, leaving a cloud of dust, thinning out, like a trail of smoke, behind them.

The "Old Man" was standing by his bivouac, hanging his towel over the ridge pole; he dived inside, and later emerged, complete with forage cap, red tabs on his stockings, riding stick in one hand, and notebook in the other.

Our tracks toward breakfast converged, and after the usual short greetings he looked up and said, "Would you like a free day, Rogers?" "Too right," I replied. I needed one, I thought, after the hectic days and nights of work at Gabes.

He took his pipe from his mouth, flicked his riding stick under his arm, and, turning to me with a half smile suffusing his cyanotic jowls, said, "Well . . . it's high time I did some surgery anyhow, after all I am a gynecologist; so you disappear for the day, but don't get into trouble!"

Colin, a tough Canadian, decided to come along, too. Within an hour, with our packs on our backs, and a couple of tins of bully rattling beside two canisters of beer, we were walking along the track to the main road for Tunis.

We got a "hitch" in a three-tonner, as far as Medinine.
There the driver, a real Cockney (it did your soul good to listen
to him) said, "Sorry, chum, bus stops 'ere." Out we jumped
almost into a military policeman's arms, neither of us, as
usual, with identity cards or movement order. Fortunately
just as we jumped, a jeep swung around the traffic island,
driven by an officer who stopped when I hailed him.

"Can you give us a lift along the road?" I asked. "Certainly,
jump in. How far are you going?" And the military policeman
just stood and looked.

Colin quickly replied, "Oh, we're going to site an R.A.P.,"
and as he said R.A.P., I noticed the officer look up at the
badges on our caps which proclaimed the unit.

So away we went, leaving Medinine behind. Slowly the
traffic thinned out as we approached the low hills sweeping
toward the coast. Away to the south where the New Zealanders were a few heavy shells were bursting and the sound
fled down the valley to meet us. I could see Colin's interest
quicken at each new burst, and he grabbed his pipe from his
mouth and stuck it into his stocking. Then we swerved around
a corner and over a small saddle to see, just ahead, a couple
of ammunition trucks going hell for leather. "Bad spot, that,"
said the officer, and hardly had he opened his mouth when we
heard the whine of shells, then a terrific explosion, a burst of
flame, and the trucks had gone up in smoke.

I felt a trifle uneasy, but the officer didn't seem at all perturbed, for as we reached the trucks, still exploding and burning, he remarked, "They've been shelling everything coming
over this saddle for a couple of days." He ran the jeep under
the cover of a small wadi and we went over to the trucks to
see what was left of the men. Nothing tangible remained.
Colin picked up a man's forage cap, and a portion of an arm,
but it was wise not to linger, so into the jeep again and away.

No sooner had we started than the officer turned to us and said, "Where are you chaps going? There are no gun posts further forward except the Germans." "Yes," we replied, "you're right. We're just going to this next saddle to find a suitable position for when we do advance."

The jeep stopped, the officer said good-by to us, and in a moment he was gone.

In the sudden silence we realized that a bird was singing somewhere.

"We must be near the line," said Colin. We stopped for a beer and lay down on a bed of desert irises. I laughed, watching him trying to open the can without losing even the froth.

There seemed to be a good deal of firing in the distance, but where we were there was no sign of war. No burnt-out trucks along the verges, no abandoned dumps of ammunition, no wayside crosses made from broken butter boxes; just peace, and a bird singing on the wing. The beer flowed down all too quickly and then we regretted having finished one can so early in the day, for beer was hard to come by. Regretfully we started on the road again. Heavy bellies and the sleepy drowse of bees and hidden insects slackened our pace considerably. Ahead the road climbed to a low saddle between two hills, and the long slope made the sweat drip from brow and armpit. Colin tried to tell me it could be as hot as that in Canada, somewhere on some mythical peninsula he knew, where they grew grapes and tobacco in the open. But I had heard all this Canadian stuff before.

The strange thing about the road was the peace of it all. We reached the saddle and I suggested that perhaps the German lines were down the other side and we must be more careful. "Oh, they're miles ahead," said Colin, "and we must get closer to have a good look." However, we agreed to climb the steep hill on the side of the saddle and view the surrounding country from a safer aspect.

We started uphill over the stones; here and there a purple iris looked up before being shriveled in the noonday sun, here and there a lizard lay asleep, or blinked his eye on the hot rocks, slowly being rejuvenated after his long winter's rest. Colin was in front, and I could see the sun gleaming on his brown skin, so brown was it that, when he told us one day in the mess that he was descended from an Iroquois chief, we suckers took it all in. Now it burnt like old brass in the sun and I could watch every rippling muscle tighten and relax as he swung from rock to rock.

The top of the hill was just ahead, so I shouted to him to keep his thatch down. Once there, we both lay down flat, breathless and saturated. The purple scars on the distant mountains to the south were flaming at noon; and beneath, on both sides, stretched undulating country slashed with scarlet watercourses and pimpled by gray-green heaps of scrub and desert grass. To the north shone the sea, a streak of turquoise against white clouds now forming and dropping heavily to the horizon.

I suggested another can of beer, seeing we were at our goal, but as we opened the rucksack, a shell screamed over our heads. Then another, and another; we watched them fall in the British lines behind us, saw the puffs of smoke from the German batteries in front, and realized that we were betwixt and between the guns in a very unhealthy position.

The firing ceased, and I wanted to descend at once, but Colin said, "We've come to see a barrage from a grandstand seat and why leave it? We're safe enough."

So we slid down a little between two large crags, and there, sheltered for an hour, like umpires at the tennis net, we watched shells volleying over. It was interesting at first, and

then not so interesting, for we spotted a German observer on
the hill opposite doing the same thing. I recalled the Old
Man's instruction, "You won't get into trouble, Rogers!" And
at that moment a shell landed almost at our feet. Stones and
muck everywhere; then another and another. We slid down
the hill like lizards and luckily found a small cave and crept
inside. "Rock of Ages," drummed through my brain and I
pictured the St. Andrew's choir far away in Dunedin droning
it out.

Evening found us walking slowly along the road toward
Medinine. We had seen the Mareth Line and didn't want to
see it again. Now I began to think about the surgery that had
piled up in our absence, for we would be late home. How was
Sandy, the Old Man, coping? Over the second ridge and well
out of range we slackened pace. Colin pulled his pipe from his
stocking and lit it. I found a cigarette; talk came more freely.

We talked of this one and that. How Brownie was hitting
the bottle and losing heavily at poker; how the Old Man
wasted a hell of a lot of time modeling perspex from shot-down
aircraft, and how Jamieson was no good, never did a tap of
work, and needed shooting anyhow. And MacTavish, why
wouldn't he leave the desert and go to base for training as a
surgical specialist? He had done plenty, and was well fitted
for the job, and so on.

Then as the escarpment grew bolder and blacker toward
evening, we talked of the future. Somehow we both felt that
to be with the Eighth Army in Italy would be a tame affair.
There would be hundreds of American and First Army surgeons and the activities of the old 15th C.C.S. would become
limited and circumspect.

Anyhow it was due to break up. The Old Man had applied
for leave to England on compassionate grounds; Ken Herd-
man, my anesthetist, was due for a base job, and many of our

boys would surely go home after so long in the desert. So the old order would change and the 15th be no more.

Then Colin, taking his pipe from his mouth, turned to me and said, "Rog, I hear there are some British officers working in Greece with the guerrillas in the mountains."

"Where to hell did you hear that?" I asked, for rumors like this sailed over the desert's vastness with every evening wind.

"I heard it from a chap in Gabes. He's O.K., Rog. It's the goods; couldn't we get a job there?"

"Perhaps we could," I replied.

There and then, on the road home to Medinine, we decided to go to Greece. As it turned out, we neither of us got there. But the urge for a change got me, at least, to a neighboring country and a change which turned out to be a good deal more than I had bargained for.

Meanwhile the months passed; operating day and night, trailing up the front line past Mareth, Wadi Akarit, Souse, Karoan, and finally Tunis.

In quieter moments "the betwixt and between" on the Mareth Line was not forgotten and the vague aspirations for Greece became crystallized as we met the men of the First Army and the American Army. For the old 15th had made its glory, and our casualty clearing station, which since 1941 had toiled or raced up and down the desert tracks, had also made some history. More than that, it had cemented together our men, smoothed them out, and made them more understanding of one another. Finally we realized that in the future we would be infiltrated by new men, new officers, a new Old Man, and all the goodly fellowship would be lost as are the grains of sand in an empty desert.

We trekked down to Egypt for the last time. The battle for the North African coast had been won, and before we went to "rest and refit" at Sidi Bish, the grateful army authorities sent us to Amaria Transit Camp, a ghastly place a few miles along the coast from Alexandria. There we applied for without success for a "dangerous mission" to the Balkans.

However, the next day Colin was transferred to the 63rd General Hospital to undergo training for his grading as surgeon. So we parted, but not before a terrific party at the Union Club and elsewhere later in the night. That is army life. Friendships made, to be broken; faces seen, then lost; personalities dinting you, only to rebound into obscurity.

I escaped to Cairo for a few days on the pretext of gathering some equipment directly from the base medical stores. While there, the first person I called to see was my friend Colonel Buttle at the 15th Scottish Hospital. Every desert surgeon knew Buttle and his den in the cellar of the 15th Scottish. He was a man whose efforts far surpassed ours in the field, for by his efforts and his organization more lives were saved than by any other group of surgeons, and the blood he collected at No. 5 Transfusion Unit poured back life into many thousands of soldiers lying on the sands of Libya, or in the tented hospitals of the desert.

He was a grand chap, always ready to push aside his work and talk to us from the field of our experiences, always willing to help us unofficially with little pieces of equipment, or to lend us literature, the latest from the scientific world, and ever ready to come to the front and see us at work, and advise us on the new antibiotic drugs he brought with him. Incidentally he was one of the best looters I have ever known. He knew just where to find abandoned German and Italian scientific equipment, taking it back with him and utilizing it in his own laboratories for our benefit. And did he find it!

He was seated at his desk writing a letter when I walked in, a huge desk always untidy and covered with hundreds of open papers. He rose and explained to me that he was trying to compose a letter to the army authorities about some rifles the "Wogs" had stolen from his men's barracks, and which the Army held him to be financially responsible for.

"Be damned to them!" he said as he tore up the letter. I sat down beside him and we began talking about the new penicillin. How much could he let me have (privately, of course) and how much of this and that? Tea came in and with it a message for Buttle that the O.C. of the hospital would like to see him for a moment.

Buttle rose. "I'll be back in a minute; just start tea," he said, and went out. I poured out a cup, and then another and another, for it was good and hot. Still Buttle didn't return. A quarter of an hour passed and my eyes were vaguely wandering, when suddenly I saw right in front of me a letter, and all the upbringing and the manners in the world fled.

My Dear Buttle,
   It is our intention to drop medical stores by parachute into Yugoslavia in the near future. Do you think that blood could likewise be dropped . . . ?

Yugoslavia! There came back to me a book read long ago called *My Balkan Log*, by Abrahams, my old chief from Dean Street Hospital in London. Yugoslavia was to me a mere name in the First World War. Yet here must be a cry from Macedonia for help. If medical stores were wanted, then surely surgical help also.

When Buttle came back, I duly apologized for reading the letter placed almost under my nose, and then I asked him more of it. Not a word; he was like a clam.

I left the 15th Scottish determined to go to Yugoslavia, but where was Colin? Where could I find out about the job? What section of the vast Middle East housed the Yugoslav Department? What was happening there? A thousand queries flashed through my brain.

Early next morning I walked down to that vast block of buildings known as Middle East H.Q. Often I had watched hordes of officers leaving its barbed-wire precincts, and had wondered exactly what they all found to do. I still wonder. I recall having lunch at Bir Hacheim with a French surgeon in charge of an advanced surgical unit. After an excellent lunch Colonel Dubac and I were talking about our respective armies, and I remember his pointing the finger of scorn at me and saying, "Why, in the French Army we have only five base officers to one in the field, but in the British Army you have thirteen." I couldn't contradict him.

Just inside the barbed wire was a green-painted office where you showed your famous identity card and stated your business. I found my card, showed it to the sergeant, and said, "Where is the Balkan Office? I want particularly the Yugoslav Section." He looked at me and in a hushed voice replied, "Oh, sir, it is not here but at M.O.4. . . . I shall send a messenger with you."

We arrived at Rustum House, where I dropped the messenger, rang the doorbell, and entered. After a great rigmarole and more showing of identity cards, I was eventually escorted up the stairs to the room of some major.

He did not rise to greet me, but sat idly playing with a pen or flicking the flies from his baldish head. He was wearing a kilt which must have been extremely hot. Eventually he raised his head and asked my business. Very briefly I told him that I wanted to volunteer for surgical work in Yugoslavia.

While he was slowly taking that in, I surveyed his room. A huge map of Yugoslavia on the wall covered by little red, green, and yellow flags; a desk littered with papers, and in front of him a map of the Dalmatian Islands over which he had doubtless been browsing on my arrival.

He looked up at me, and in a rather pained voice said, "I have no idea of anything of that nature in Yugoslavia." Liar! I thought, but said to him, "No idea at all?" A few moments silence then he added, "None whatsoever."

"Well, it's a good map of Yugoslavia you have on your wall, and a more detailed map of the Dalmatian coast in front of you, anyway!" I retorted. He ignored this remark and a pained English silence ensued momentarily.

"Very well," I replied, "I have wasted my time. Good morning."

I trundled down the stairs, signed the exit book, and went out into Cairo's hot, stinking streets. I would go to the New Zealand Club, have a few beers, and work it off somehow, I thought. However, when I was about five hundred yards along the road, I heard someone running after me. I turned and saw a dripping orderly panting along toward me. He caught up and called, "Sir. Will you come back with me, sir?" And that was how I joined the staff of M.O.4.

First I had to learn a little of what was going on in the Balkans, and above all to choose the two boys who were to accompany me. Great care was necessary, they had to be absolutely fit physically, for we would be at times living under difficult circumstances, and, most important, temperaments should be compatible.

It was Colonel Buttle who recommended Bill to me. He had been a Royal Army Service Corps driver in the transfusion unit and Buttle thought highly of him. "Mind you," he said, "he's had no medical training, and is a little slow compared with your team in the desert; but I'm sure he's a good chap." That was enough for me, and a meeting was arranged. His Scottish voice appealed to me immediately. It was so like home, so different from the strained English accent I was used to hearing. His helpfulness in doing little things, his eagerness to come, and above all his frank admission that he knew nothing whatsoever about surgery, but was keen to learn, made me accept him.

Next day Bill brought along to me another Scot. This time a sergeant from the R.A.F. called Ian. He was from Edinburgh, and had been a physical-drill instructor in civil life. During his R.A.F. career he had been a parachute instructor, which would be of immense value to us later on. He was fighting fit, with a good physique, and though he also knew nothing of surgery, like Bill he would be easily trained and quite adaptable.

Then I went back to school again. I began by having lessons in the Serbo-Croatian language from a tutor, but made little headway. I was sent to the Sabotage School, and there saw how to blow up trucks, telegraph lines, bridges, railways, and everything else of use to man. Next I was detailed to the Commando School for Defence and Silent Killing. I didn't mind the first part of it, but over the second I pointed out that after all I *was* a doctor.

Then came the School of Photography and the Escape School, run by the famous Jaspar Maskelyne. Finally I had a course on Balkan history, a subject almost completely unknown to me.

Equipment was the next problem. The Medical Stores Department of the Middle East was extraordinarily obstructive and difficult in handing out any equipment at all. The colonel in charge had little time for these secret outfits, and what he called "side shows." Judging from his accent and his obstructive capacity, I sensed that he had spent many years in India. However, I did manage to drag something from them, and with the tools I had looted from the desert we were fairly well equipped. Buttle as usual came to the rescue and slipped in many a little thing for us, and gave us a good supply of the sulphonamide drugs.

PART I

Vis

Arrival by Night

We arrived by night. It was one of those autumn nights, cold and crisp, with the clouds scudding across a half-lit moon.

A few hurried good-bys to the British naval lieutenant who had delivered us so far, and then we tumbled into a small canvas boat which nosed its way toward the island of Vis, shrouded in the mist of the Dalmatian coast. The fisherman who met us couldn't understand our Serbo-Croat at all, and attempts at conversation soon lapsed. We landed in a small bay between rocky headlands, and with many *"Maria Madonnas"* he helped us to carry our few stores ashore. So we stood at last on free Yugoslav territory.

Late that night we reached the town of Vis, in Partisan hands, and we saw for the first time the Dalmatian Partisans, among whom we were destined to work for many months.

We saw the Red Stars on their Partisan hats, their cosmopolitan uniforms, some German, a few British, but mostly ragged Italian. We saw, scrawled across the gray walls of stone buildings, *"Zivio Marshal Tito,"* *"Zivio Marshal Stalin,"* and then we realized that we were working now for a different army, with a different philosophy and an outlook different from our own. The great scarlet Hammer and Sickle slashed across the town hall brought us for the first time near to our Russian ally, and the Red Flags that broke into life from dead flagpoles with every gust of wind waved a new idea and a new ideal across our essentially British outlook.

A British officer came toward us. Even in the gloom of the
night you could tell that he was British. His walk and his
high gum boots, his beret and his riding trousers, and his face
half lit by a smile of welcome placed him miles apart from the
guerrillas. He took us to a house, and told us to get some sleep,
for in the morning he would take us to the chief doctor of the
island, and thereafter we must make our own way.

I tumbled into my sleeping bag on the floor, Bill's gentle
snoring keeping the room alive; the warmth of the last rum
played around my inside, and with it a feeling that at last,
freed from the routine of orthodox army life, we could start
on our own work, do as we pleased, without odd colonels
and brigadiers poking around, without forms galore to fill
in, without everlasting orders from some Old Man. These
thoughts gave such satisfaction that plans for the future
tumbled across my consciousness in profusion, elbowing each
other, jostling and squeezing for a place in the scheme of
things, until, overwhelmed, I went to sleep.

Morning; and Ian woke me with a cup of tea. Then I looked
at the dirty floor where we had slept, Bill still snoring beatifi-
cally, the window full of dust, and outside the tramp of marching feet down the cobbled street.

After breakfast, consisting of the bully beef and tea we had
brought with us, we emerged into the narrow street already
full of Partisan soldiers hurrying toward the stone wharf,
where, during the night, stores had been landed. A rough-
looking crowd of Balkan brigands, they looked—rough, and
tough, too, for each carried a Sten gun, and at least two grenades swung from his belt. Few were in good physical condition,
some were shaved, and a few actually had gold braid on their
arms. A Partisan girl—"*Partizanka*"—passed us, walking up the
lane with a Partisan boy. They were singing, and singing cheer-
ily, too; we stopped to listen, but they turned the corner,

leaving behind them the rhythm of a melody we were never allowed to forget.

We turned down toward the wharf—just a stone wall at the end of the small harbor. Lying alongside were three fishing boats unloading what looked like British mines and boxes of Sten guns. We wondered where they had come from in the night. Then someone came up to us and spoke. "Zdravo, drugovi?"—"How are you, comrades?" But we, who had learned Serbian from a Chetnik, did not understand Dalmatian, so we just stood and gaped.

It was all so new and different, quite unlike the war we had known. We watched a guerrilla saluting an officer with clenched fist; he raised his hand and said, "Zdravo," and passed on. A fine rain wreathed the hills behind in obscurity. We stepped into a doorway to shelter and then noted Pears, the British officer who had met us the night before, as he came toward us.

He took us to meet the chief medical officer of the 8th Corpus, Dr. Zone. He appeared to have no rank and nothing to distinguish him from the crowds of Partisans who passed in a never-ending stream along the cobbled road, each with a case of arms on his shoulder. Zone, an elderly Pole, wore an old Italian uniform, and over his back swung a small haversack with a red cross painted flamboyantly on it. He carried it as an infant carries his first schoolbag, preciously and grandly, a treasure, a badge of learning, and over his other shoulder swung another small bag in which he kept his papers.

Through his thick glasses he peered at us, and welcomed us to the Partisan forces saying, "No matter how hard you work there will always be more to do." He suggested we should come with him to a temporary hospital already established on the island, and there start work immediately.

A sentry stood at the door. Passing him, Zone invited us

into a side room, a kind of mess, conference room, commissar's political room, and staff room rolled into one. He took from the sideboard a jug full of dark *prošek* wine and poured us each a glass. I gave him a cigarette and then we sat, sipped, and talked.

We told him that we would fit in with whatever he suggested and that our organization would endeavor to supply the island with all its medical stores. When things were better, we would arrange the evacuation of the wounded to Italy, where a Partisan hospital was already being established.

As we talked, another man came in, Dr. A. He was actually in charge of the patients. Zone asked us to go with him and he would show us the wounded and the hospital equipment. We followed him upstairs. There they were; thin and pale, in beds, true, but crowded together, the seeping smell of pus pervading the whole atmosphere. It was all so different from what we were used to; we just looked, and watched, and learnt.

Dr. A. then suggested that we operate on a fractured femur, already some four weeks old and heavily infected. So we went to the operating theater, the boys started unpacking our two cases of equipment, and soon everything was ready.

They carried in the patient and with him came a horde of onlookers—nurses, commissars, soldiers, and porters. It seemed as though anyone passing along the street had come in to see the British doctor.

Bill mixed the pentothal anesthetic and handed the syringe to Dr. A. to give. Then, for the next twenty minutes, I watched the worst intravenous injection I have ever seen given. He jabbed the needle this way and that, he bent the boy's arm over a bare piece of wood, and every time the boy moaned, he looked at him as though it was his fault. Every moment I wanted to take the syringe from him, but I managed to keep cool. Then at last he got into the vein.

I finished the job, put the leg into a Tobruk plaster on a Thomas splint, and gave instructions for him to have sulphonamide every four hours. We started the next case. Again the same procedure; not only did he fail completely to get the needle into the vein, but he seemed to disregard any pain he caused. The wounded were heaved onto the table like bags of chaff, bandages were ripped off regardless of pain, two patients out of four stopped breathing and nearly died, and every anesthetic had to be completed by the administration of chloroform.

It struck me as an impossible situation. When dinner came at 6 P.M., I felt that I had done my usual thirty cases instead of four. Slowly I walked down the stairway from the operating theater into the side room. Bill was with me, Ian having stayed behind to clean up. On the side-board was a full flagon of dark red wine; silently Bill took it and poured out two good glasses, one of which he slowly put down in front of me and said, "By Christ, that was bloody awful. Have they got no heart?"

An old man came into the room just at this juncture, a tall figure, in civilian dress, but wearing a Partisan cap. He proffered his hand, smiled, and said, "Say, guy, my name is Joe. I was in America twelve years ago, and can speak American."

"Say, Joe, I'm damned glad to meet you," I said. "Is there anyone else here who can understand English?"

"Yes, there's Zena, old Zone's wife. She will be here in a minute." Within a minute or two a small fragile woman, with hawklike Jewish nose, long, cigarette-stained fingers, black, scraggy hair, and a vitality which poured from her, came into the room. Every movement was quick and vital, every word accompanied by a flashing change of expression. She put out her hand and in perfect English said, "Major Rogers, is it?"

I produced a cigarette, we sat down again, and Zena refilled the glasses. Then we talked and talked, and I told her what an enormous amount of work needed doing in the hospital. I suggested that it would probably be better if Dr. Zone would give us a building for ourselves. We were a team, and Ian and Bill were both trained medical orderlies and anesthetists. (I thought to myself that no one could possibly be worse than Dr. A.) Perhaps they could give us two nurses, a few helpers, and someone who could translate until we learnt Dalmatian.

Her only reply was: "Wait awhile."

The meal was brought in, and as we were eating the door opened and another woman entered. What a striking character and face. We rose, and she came over and said in French, "I am Jela, the apothecary."

She sat down awkwardly and I saw at once that she was suffering from some disability. She rose and put down her Beretta repeating rifle in the corner and flung her little schoolbag on the settee. But she left her four grenades on her belt.

I hastened to pour out another glass of wine and offer her some food, but she refused all, and sat down looking at us, just taking us in.

What a fine commissar Jela was, and how much we were indebted to her later on. She was a Bosnian from Sarayevo and had been active in the "Struggle" since 1941. At first she had been a fighter, but the complete lack of vitamins, the poorness of scarce food, and the frozen winters had produced a peripheral neuritis, and now she could hardly hobble along. Her silvery hair, curly and crisp, fell down from under her cap, and around the lined corners of her eyes and at her mouth always played a smile. Her white, anemic hands with long, pinkish nails rested on the table, and we noted that Jela let Zena do all the talking while she did the observing.

The conversation was in French and English and when Jela wanted to say something privately she and Zena would speak rapidly in Bosnian dialect.

Then quick as lightning she threw this one at me. "*Majore*, what do you think of our Partisans?" That was a fast one so early in the game, but I replied, "Dr. Zone has treated us with utmost kindness and courtesy and if all are like him, then we will get on famously together."

"And, *Majore*," went on Jela, "what do you think of Dr. A. as a doctor?"

It couldn't be put off much longer, I supposed, so I replied, "Our techniques differ a lot, Jela, probably due to the fact that he learnt his surgery in the German school, and I in the British."

There was silence for a few moments after this and Ian came down from the operating theater and started his dinner. Still silence. Coffee was brought in, and with it came another woman.

This was Borga, the commissar for Vis hospitals. Zena introduced us and after she had put her gun in the corner, she sat down and began devouring her meal.

Borga resembled a cross between the frigid missionary type and an earnest schoolteacher. Her hair, jet black, was tied in a bundle behind her head, her cap fitted all skewwhiff, and she laughed heartily as some childless women do. A few odd black hairs stood out from a pigmented mole on her face, showing up a rather beautiful clear skin. She was one of these "friends at first sight" people.

The more the boys saw her the more they hated her, and the more I admired her. She asked, "Are your sleeping quarters satisfactory?"

"Not very," I said. "They are cramped and dirty, and perhaps better could be found for us." Out from her schoolbag came a notebook and down went our requirements, a typical commissar action. However, next day we had them.

After three days of surgical hell with Dr. A., Zena came to

us and said, "I have been appointed to work with you always and shall come and live with you and look after you. You are strangers here, you know, and do not understand Partisan ways."

So that evening the four of us walked back from the hospital, Zena pointing out the Dalmatian Alps across the sea, and the great Checknovitch Villa standing at the entrance to the harbor, and showing us houses where prominent fascists had lived.

A patrol of Partisan boys and girls passed us singing as they walked along the cobbled street. I asked, "Where are they going?"

"Oh, back to Bosnia, where the Germans are making a very fierce offensive," said Zena. "Yes, they leave Vis in small boats, in the middle of the night, and steal in the darkness across to the mainland where they are met by other Partisan bands and then start fighting again. It's awful in Bosnia now," she added. "No food, no clothes, no guns, no bandages, no doctors, and everywhere isolation and death."

We looked out to sea across the U-shaped harbor. The stars were shining and the water gently lapping against the stone wall, so gently, like the washing of a baby, so peacefully, that our pace slowed to its rhythm until finally, just before our house, we stopped and looked across the water to where the Checknovitch Villa stood.

"Ah," said Zena, "I asked Zone today if we could have the Checknovitch Villa for our own hospital, but he said, 'No . . . it is too exposed to E-boat attacks and air raids.' But," she added almost wistfully, "it is such a peaceful place and the summer sun shines across the bay and flames the harbor like a sweeping spirit, lapping the edge and turning the hills beyond into gold. . . . I did so want the Checknovitch Villa for us."

"Then you have asked Zone for a hospital of our own?" I queried.

"I was glad to," she answered, "for I know what that place and Dr. A. are. I have worked in a cow byre, in a pigsty, but that was in the mountains of Bosnia. Here things are different and we could make them so much better, couldn't we?"

We opened the gate from the harbor road into our new house, and saw in the windows the reflection of the fire in the front room. It had been the house of a wealthy fascist, since, of course, deceased, and now it was our own home. Yes, it was comfortable, clean, and pleasant, so much so that the rigors of the Partisan life seemed far away and hard to understand.

The fire burnt brightly and we all sat around, while Bill as usual produced the flagon of Prošek, and, glasses in hand, we slowly sipped, discussing the day's work. Bill Pears came in to speak for a moment about stores, then told us that the German offensive in Bosnia was going hard for Tito, and he thought that the Germans would soon attack the islands and we must plan a way of escape.

Jela came in, flinging her cap on her chair, the fire glowing kindly on her hair as if it were of gold. She placed her gun on the table beside her. No one spoke; all were thinking of Tito in Bosnia and the winter's fast approach. Bill Pears and Zena were smoking and tipping the gray ash on the hearth, Jela's eyes had died, and Zena crossed her knees and rested her little head on her hands. I was not yet used to the Balkan gloom. Maria, our cook, from the back regions suddenly started singing "Partisani Nasa." It awoke us, a flame leapt in the fire, and in a moment we were all singing, singing and laughing, for the Germans were far away and the night was fair.

Zena turned to Jela, and said, "Sing, Jela. Sing some old Bosnian song." Jela looked at me, as she did many times after-

ward. Her face saddened, the lines deeped, her voice strength-
ened, and she sang the song of the Montenegrin mother who
lost seven sons at war. Verse followed verse, and then silence.
As the fire died and Zena wiped away the tears, we felt that
now we were Partisans too, for we felt as they felt. We would
share as they shared, and would fight as they fought, and if
necessary die with them.

CHAPTER 2

Ian and the Partizanka

Even though the island of Vis was in Partisan hands and safe,
yet we were not free from daily Stuka attacks. They would
come at about 5 A.M., circle over the little town, then scream
down from a great height, and just above the houses would
drop their bombs and rise again. Bill and I used to watch for
them every morning as we dressed, and then lean far out the
window with our tommy guns and let fly as they turned; of
course to no avail. Still, it did us good to have a shot at them,
for they knew the wounded were coming to Vis and what they
wanted more than anything was to bomb the hospitals.

It was hardly light one morning when they came. We heard
them a long way off and wondered if the wounded had been
taken from the fishing boats yet. Down came the bombs,
crashing into the stone-built town. It lasted only a few moments, but in those moments they caught the old hospital
where Dr. A. worked. We dashed along, but to little purpose.
Most of the wounded were killed. Feverishly all morning we
tore away the fallen masonry and there, lying under it all, was
poor old Joe, the American. We got him out and laid him on a
stretcher. He turned his ashen face to Bill and said, "Say, you

guys are the goods." He died a few minutes later; far, far from Louisiana, where he had spent so many happy years.

By the afternoon most of those alive were in our hospital and we worked far into the night. At midnight old Zone appeared with Borga, the commissar, and asked me to come into the conference room and have a glass of wine and a rest. Bill and Ian and Goyka, the theater nurse, went on cleaning up, ready for the next case. The air raid was the chief topic. Dr. A. escaped, for he was not yet up from his bed in a nearby peasant's house. Just as we were finishing the wine, Borga reached for her little commissar's bag, took out a notebook, and began: "*Majore,*" she said, "it has come to the notice of the Partisans that your boy Ian is paying attention to the Partizanka Goyka."

"Not to my knowledge," I said.

"Well, that is so," said Borga, "and under Partisan law it is not allowed. It must cease."

"In the British Army, and that is what we are in," I retorted, "there is no interference in what a soldier does after his duty hours; it is his own business. But, seeing that it is straining relations, I shall speak to Ian at an early opportunity." Whereupon she and Zone rose, gave the Partisan salute, and went out into the night.

Trouble had started. I didn't blame Ian in the least, for Goyka was a charming girl, with long flaxen hair, deep blue eyes, and a merry wit. Curious, I thought, how Borga and Zone had found out, when I had seen nothing. I would have to speak to Ian. Then I too got up, drained the glass, and went back to the operating theater.

In the morning I called Ian and told him of the commissar's talk and told him in best army parlance "to pull his finger out." He blushed and said he would.

But love is never discreet. The very next day I saw furtive

glances between them, and innumerable little trips to the sterilizing room, where Goyka worked. What really worried me was not so much Ian falling in love, but how the commissar had found out. Who was watching us? Who reported it to the commissar and why were we watched?

As the days passed I forgot about it all in the rush of work. One evening Ian and I were walking home together after a long day's work. It was one of those clear autumn nights when the stars shimmered in the smooth waters, and the sound of fish jumping fairly echoed across the harbor. We had been silent for some time. In a hesitant voice Ian said, "Excuse me, sir, but I want to marry Goyka."

I stopped and sat down on an empty ammunition box lying near the sea wall. Then I said to Ian, still standing, "I understand, Ian, completely, but could you not just wait a little?"

How could he wait? Next day the commissar called again and beckoned me into a little courtyard by the operating theater. I knew what was coming and when it came I said simply, "My dear commissar, I just cannot prevent young people falling in love, and I am pleased, for I, too, like Goyka, and if permission were to be given for them to marry, then Goyka would become a British citizen, and I would make the necessary arrangements for them to go to Italy and hence to England."

The commissar was silent for a time, then, turning to me, she replied that the penalty for love in the Partisan Army was death. Tito had said so. Both of them would be tried and sentenced.

This seemed a trifle melodramatic, but the look on her pale-skinned face was set, a look we were to know better later on. Her eyes were blazing, and I quickly saw that I must retreat if the situation were to be saved.

So I assured her that I would speak to Ian and have it

stopped, if that was what they wanted. "Yes," she answered. "That is what we want." Then she turned coldly and left.

That night I called Ian to my room and told him the situation. He sat with his head in his hands for a long time. Then he asked if he could take Goyka away in the first British naval craft, for she too was frightened.

"Frightened?" I asked, "of what?"

"Very frightened," was all Ian said; he rose, turned on his heel, and walked off alone up into the hills.

Next evening Goyka disappeared. All that day I had felt something impending. It was a very busy day, for many casualties had arrived by night from the Bosnian campaign. Ian had been morose, and the starlight had gone from Goyka's eyes. At six o'clock Ian came and asked if he could go home, and I at once said, "Yes." She was sent away and put in the front line of attack as punishment. We never saw her again; somewhere in Bosnia is Goyka's grave, somewhere in the mountains. I heard months later that she died willingly, fell in the mud, her cap falling from her head and lying with its Red Star still gleaming against the snow beyond. The gentians will be bluer there, and the crocus more golden, and the nightingale's song will be sweeter near where Goyka lies.

CHAPTER 3

Winter on Vis

Winter was coming quickly. The coast was taken and was being slowly closed by the Germans. The wounded were getting fewer and fewer. More and more of the brave boats that left the mainland by night sailed into the shot and shell of E-boats. So the day's work would finish earlier and in the

evenings we would gather around the fire, talking and singing.
Jela would sing too, but always the sad songs, for she had seen
much. How well do I remember such an evening. Jela had just
finished singing and silence reigned. Zena was smoking a
cigarette and letting the ash fall unheeded to the floor. Bill was
sitting gazing into the glow of the stove and Ian, still downcast and morose, was enveloped in Scottish gloom. Jela's song
was cut short; her fine soprano voice had suddenly died, as if
by a memory, for she had been singing an old Herzegovinian
song, a tragic reminder of the terror and battles over the water.
The lamp had been put out for the lack of fuel and the
shadows twisted as the sea breezes eddied down the chimney.
I looked across at Zena, and saw her dark face buried in her
hands, a tiny handkerchief hugging her nose. Bill got up to
bring in the parting glass of wine, and I turned and laid a
gentle hand on Zena. She looked up, wiped her eyes, and said,
"I wonder will our children always sing such songs?"

Yes, conquest and corruption, slavery and persecution, tragedy and suffering have always steeped this land. That day and
every day we saw it, and ever night as we spoke, we knew that
our place was not here in the shelter of the islands, but over
there, beyond the snow-covered Dinaric Alps, over there where
the enemy ring was tightening, the Chetnik menace engulfing,
where thousands of peasant boys and girls were fighting and
waiting, wondering when help and liberation would come.

Jela would often sit in silence, then, turning to us, she would
say, "Oh, *Majore*, in Lika are three thousand wounded Partisans with no doctors, no bandages, no help. . . . Won't you
go?" Zone would tell us of the wounded starving in Bosnia,
starving and lying in caves on the mountaintops or deep in the
forests where no light ever comes. Mola, a Partizanka, would
tell us how in Stvria the wounded were being killed by the
Germans and the Quisling White Guard, the Domobranci. No

Partisan could get to help them, for twenty enemy divisions were there, more than were fighting the whole of the British and American armies in Italy. The fishermen who came by night told us how the coast was clinched in the grip of eight German divisions.

We listened, and every day when we walked along the shore to our hospital, now half empty, we would look across at the snow gleaming from the Alps, gleaming above the blue coast line so far away, yet so close in our thoughts. Secretly, in our hearts, we all decided we must leave and cross the sea and make our way to the center of things. But how?

More snow fell, creeping far down the mountainside, and our casualties increased again as German patrol work became difficult. We received a strange variety of cases. They had few clothes, poor food, no boots, and winter had begun to take its toll. Cases of frostbite began to appear, at first a few, then more until, with every boat that came in, more than half would have gangrenous feet owing to frostbite.

While in Sicily I had met a Dr. Malan, and he had told me the same story of the Balkan winter. In Albania hundreds of Italian soldiers suffered from frostbite and he had found that by injecting local anesthetic around the main artery to the leg they had improved if the process had not gone too far.

I tried it, but with little success. In a vain hope I tried injecting into the nerves where they came from the spinal column, but again with hardly any success. Case after case came in, many extremely ill, so thin from toxic absorption, so worn out by exposure that many died, but many we saved by plasma transfusion and amputation.

We often wondered what would happen to them in later life. How could they again take their place in the struggle for Balkan existence? Or would the new hope fight for them as fearlessly as it fought the invader? Many of these *drugovi* had never seen a doctor, for now the snow was falling, and the doctors, few as they were, couldn't get about as they did in the summer months. Some who had seen doctors had been treated by the old method of guillotine amputation, only for sepsis and often death to intervene. Many of these amputations were so terribly short that a future artificial leg was an impossibility, many had the bone protruding about two inches from the end of the stump and would need further amputation. It was all so tragic; especially when we recalled that some of our colleagues waiting in base hospitals in Italy or in field ambulances had been doing little work, or in some cases no work at all, for weeks on end.

Day by day we were inundated with tales of unbelievable escapes, of tremendous heroism, and undying patriotism for the new ideal. Even the youngest seemed filled with the new religion.

One morning, just before we had our coffee, they carried into the operating theater a young Partizanka. They placed her gently on the table as we were sitting at the end of the room waiting for the coffee to cool. She started singing, singing so softly. I can remember her song even now. . . . "Teško Je Zaboraviti Tebe," . . . an old Bosnian love song. She was recalling her home and her lover; we listened as Zena translated. "It Is So Hard for Me to Forget You." Sweetly, over her face, and under her hat, for she was still wearing her Red Star, came a smile. I went over to her and asked her what was wrong? "Oh, it's only my thigh," she replied. Gently we lifted the blanket, cut off the bandage from the gangrenous wound, and from the upper end poked the bare bone. I let the blanket fall again as Bill prepared the anesthetic. He bared her arm to inject into the vein. She asked what he was doing. I replied that we were just going to send her to sleep while I operated on the leg. "Oh no," she replied. "Keep the anesthetic for those who need it. I'll just sing." She burst into a flood of song, then, as she went to sleep, her song died.

One day a British brigadier came to the island, and with him our opportunity, for he fell and twisted his ankle and came to us for medical attention. As he looked around our hospital and saw us at work, I told him of Lika and how much we wanted to go to the mainland. "Can we go?"

"I suppose so," he replied, "provided you get someone else to take your place here."

That was enough. We didn't pursue the subject any further lest he change his mind. Who he was we never knew, but that night a message went off to Italy. "Please send relief to Vis. Rogers."

PART **II**

Dalmatia and Croatia

CHAPTER 1

From Vis to the Mainland

The bleak winds whistled up the harbor; waves dashed over the rocky wall and lapped the road beyond. The German Stukas came over the island no more, and the far coast line, once so blue beneath white clouds, was lost in scudding darkness.

Zena knew our secret and had a warm coat made for me from her blanket. Ian and Bill packed up a few surgical stores. Night after night passed. Then one day, when the drizzle hung low over the island hills, and the leaden water made no sound except a gurgle as it ran from flooded pools, Jela came to us, with no coat on, and two guns over her shoulder. She stopped and said, "*Majore*, I give you this gun, for you leave tonight. Away up the Dalmatian coast you will be met by a Partisan patrol and taken to Croatian Headquarters."

I took the gun, an Italian submachine gun, and put it over my shoulder, feeling awkward carrying an implement of death. But later I became very attached to it. Jela and I walked home. Zena was full of tears. Maria, the cook, prepared a little farewell dinner. When we were all gathered, Bill brought out the wine for the last time, and we sang "Partizani Nasi," then sat down to sardines done in white oil, and *bourac*, as light as a feather. We knew that from now on little food would come our way, let alone *bourac* and *prošek*.

Admiral Velebit, of the nonexistent Partisan fleet, came in

and gave us our last instructions. Then Bill Pears opened the door, having just heard that we were going. He asked if we had permission? Did the British Mission already in Yugoslavia know? And so on. I replied, "Yes, it's O.K."

He laughed. "You bloody Kiwis, you get away with anything!"

We carried our stores to the wharf. It was dark, almost mysterious, this flitting in the night. We seemed shrouded in an island spell, with only Jela and Zena standing on the wharf to say good-by. Two Partisans had just joined us, Ivo and Voyasin. We stumbled aboard a small fishing boat; the engine started. Looking back, I saw tears falling and mingling with the rain. Then all was lost in the darkness.

Bill produced a flask of rum and we drank in silence, then went below, down the three steps, and crouched in about two feet of headroom. The smell of hot oil and petrol fumes was appalling. We stopped. The fisherman in the stern directed a red lamp to the shore three times. Then came an answer, the engine started up again, and we headed into the open sea. I was nearly asleep when I heard "*Stoj!*" The engine stopped. We drifted. I thought momentarily of all the German E-boats stationed at Sibenik. Then we started again. I felt I must have some fresh air, so I crawled from my bunk and went to the stern. The night was clear now, so clear that I could see the black smudge of Vis to the south and the black rim of the sea away north. The steersman was crooning an old Dalmatian fishing song and I could see the other man, up in the bows, watching for E-boats and mines. I slept in spite of the lice which swarmed in the smelly rug covering me.

When I awoke, the engine had stopped, and both men were whispering in the stern. We were quite near an island, under the lee of a little promontory. I heard the sound of many engines and there, passing us in the shadow, were five E-boats, foam at their bows and phosphorescence in their wakes. I waited for the crash of machine guns, and wondered if I should wake the boys. Then a bright flare shot into the sky to the east, and the boats swung away toward it. We waited. The fishermen started talking again. Bill emerged from below, sensing that something was wrong. More rum all around. The engine started again and we headed north.

At dawn we reached the island of Kornat, threading our way past German lookouts on the promontories overlooking the narrow channels. Suddenly we turned into a little cove, which narrowed until the boat seemed hardly able to squeeze through on each wave that swelled between the cliffs. We reached a tiny landing stage at the foot of a great overhanging cliff. There we lay and hid all day, sleeping and eating and trying to keep warm.

In the evening we sailed again, threading our way north among the islands. We met a larger craft, which we boarded. A Partisan patrol boat from Dugi Otok, and headed for the mainland. We were now a long way north of Vis. It was early morning when we reached the shore where the Partisan patrol was to have met us, according to the admiral. But the only person there was an old fisherman, bowed and rheumatic, who could neither understand us nor tell us where to go. We landed our stores, and Voyasin, a medical student from Split, went to a nearby village and found us a house to rest in. Soon we were asleep, relaxed and glad to be in Dalmatia.

About two hours later Voyasin woke us, saying that this was the village of his ancestors and that he had found relatives already. All day long we were taken from house to house, and when they found we were doctors (for by this time Bill and Ian had been promoted to doctors too), we were besieged by requests for help. There had been no doctor here for over three years and the need was great. In every house hidden stores of fine Dalmatian wine were produced and at each one we sipped before going on to the next.

At 4 P.M. Voyasin announced that his relatives had asked us to share their poor dinner with them. Chickens had been killed, the aged cow milked, and small salted fish had been unearthed from a hidden barrel. However, I thought it much wiser to have a long walk by the coast first of all so that we could do justice to their efforts.

Leaving our box of instruments and what poor equipment we had outside the house, we started off along the road which ran parallel to the sea. It was cold and bleak, the clouds had crept down the mountainside, and a chilly, raw wind swept from the tops down to the gray Adriatic beyond. Vineyards lined the road, uncared for and unpruned. Stone fences were in a tragic state of disrepair and the countryside deserted.

Raw drizzle began to block any view we had, so again we turned and made our way back to the village. Somewhere in the gloom a few bursts of machine-gun fire broke the silence and we could hear motor transport in the distance. As we passed the first stone houses at the entrance to the village, a small boy came running toward us. Voyasin stopped him, to find that German troops had already entered the village at the other end. We thought of our precious box of materials lying in front of the house and the meal already steaming on the stove awaiting our arrival. Gone, and on our first day in the country! Firing had already broken out at the far end of the village. As we started to retrace our steps, we saw three trucks coming toward us. We jumped over the bridge on the main road, deep into the water, and hid under the friendly girders.

None too soon, for we had hardly time to realize that the temperature of the water was not much above zero when the trucks thundered overhead.

In less than half an hour flames lit the sky, as house after house was burnt down. Someone was screaming through the gloom of approaching night, pistol shots and submachine-gun fire echoed up into the darkened hills, and the cold, dank water soaked our clothes, cramping our limbs.

By nine o'clock it was obvious that the Germans had come to stay, for we heard them walking up and down the road. Orders were being shouted and we could see the glow of the dying fires from each side of the culvert.

At ten we decided to creep up the stream. Up in the darkness of the Alps, I thought, we would find some Partisans and eventually reach the 19th Division.

The water dripped from our clothes, and gradually the warmth of walking and struggling in the dark gave us new life. Eventually we found a road, so, leaving the creek, we started climbing upward in the night. The rain was steadily pouring down and thoughts of the hot meal which was to have been ours produced hunger pains deep down in the chilly vitals. None of us spoke.

Suddenly, in a sharp bend of the road, we heard machinery. We stopped, listening and peering into the darkness, and saw a low shed with a gleam of light. As we came closer it was apparent that this was a flour mill, with a water wheel going full blast. Pushing open the door, we went in. One Dalmatian was standing at the hopper pouring maize into the mill, and from the other end issued a steady stream of maize meal, coarse and moldy-looking, for the maize had been hidden in caves for months and was carried at night to the mill and then taken away before morning light came.

He greeted us suspiciously. Luckily he knew Italian and we soon made it clear who we were and why we had come. We lay down on some bags, wet and cold, and he took the tallow lamp and disappeared into the darkened loft of the mill, returning with two full bottles of wine. It warmed us up inside, so that the wetness and the discomfort were forgotten. On those bags of corn we lay down and slept, only to be wakened by hordes of lice which quickly took possession of body and soul.

At daybreak a Partisan soldier came in, wet, in rags, unshaven, and dirty-looking. He likewise sat down on the bags and promptly took off his ragged Italian uniform and methodically stoned the lice with which they were crawling. The Dalmatian peasant had a long conversation with him in a language unknown to us, and then he told us that the soldier would take us on.

So out into the dripping morning, along mountain tracks until about eleven we reached a peasant's house. We were left standing while he went inside, only to be followed out immediately by a young commissar, aged about twenty-one, who spoke good Croatian and asked us if we were Germans or spies.

I explained our mission to him, but it seemed to be all in vain, and without further ado we were taken up to the loft and the door locked and barred on us. Well, at least we could get dry, so off came our clothes, and we curled up in the straw and again sleep rescued us.

I awoke at dusk, went to the window, and looked down the mountainside to try and get my bearings in case an opportunity for escape should come. However, the door was unlocked and a Partisan approached with a large bowl of polenta, made probably from the corn ground in the mill down the road. The porridge was hot but tasteless. We wolfed it down and then came a large stone jug of wine. Evidently they didn't want to starve us. Darkness came and we could hear people coming and going outside, and through the chinks in the door heard some kind of discussing going on below.

At 8 P.M. I was summoned downstairs again, and found a conference headed by the young commissar. Again the interminable questioning and my apparently unsatisfactory replies. However, in the meantime I noted a wireless transmitter on a small table at the back of the room. I asked the commissar to wireless Tito for our release. Finally I gathered that that was impossible, as the batteries were flat, but he would send a courier to H.Q., 19th Division, who could get in touch with Tito. In the meantime we must remain prisoners.

Next morning was fine and sunny, as far as we could tell. The only Partisans left were a cook and one to guard us, complete with machine gun and hand grenades. However the others returned at 4 P.M. and through the window we saw another prisoner, ragged and unkempt, wearing the badge of the Ustashi, or Croat Quislings, on his cap. His wrists were tied together with copper wire and over his shoulder hung a small haversack such as Italian soldiers carry.

After the evening meal I was again taken downstairs and saw this bedraggled man still with his wrists tied with wire, standing between two guards, both with pistols and grenades in evidence.

The commissar asked me if I knew that he was a Ustashi? "No," I replied. "I have never seen a Ustashi before."

"Then why do the British support the Chetniks and the Ustashi?" he queried.

"I did not know they did," said I.

"Do you know the terrible massacres they conduct and their awful atrocities?"

"No, I don't."

"Then look in his bag and see," he said.

Stepping forward, I took the bag lying on the table and opened it. At first I thought it was a bagful of shelled oysters, then on looking closer I discovered that they were human eyes. I left it open. "Now why do the British support such people?" He was baiting me, I could see, so I sat down, a little sick, and waited. "He shall be shot," the commissar said, "and you can go upstairs and tell your companions what you have seen." In less than ten minutes we heard the door of the house open and then, in a minute or two, the firing squad. All this had a sickening, depressing effect on us and sleep would not come until long after midnight.

Next morning we heard some new arrivals, and after breakfast we met another commissar, who informed us that he was to take us to H.Q., 19th Division. After a final hunt for lice we started again.

CHAPTER 2

A Hard Life

Was it a mule, a horse, or a donkey? I was filled with shame when she passed and I found that it was a woman. What poverty; what a burden to bear after bearing the burden of motherhood; what a life to keep alive, and for what purpose?

The Dinaric Alps are high, and the road was long. At night we climbed and climbed; some days we would rest in a peasant hut; some nights we would sleep in the open. The commissar seemed to have legs of iron and the stamina of an ox. We reached the snows. The cold winds whipped our ill-clad bodies, for by this time we had given away a lot of our clothing. We missed our food; only two bites a day and that of polenta (this time of beans stewed without salt). Our tired tempers began to fray, and I wondered whether we would ever come to those three thousand wounded.

One night, just as it was dusk, we approached the main German highway. We were to stay with a small sabotage group in a village which had been burnt to ashes by the Germans as a reprisal against the group. But they were still there. We opened the door of the only remaining house and in that small room were about twenty Partisans. Most of them were young men from the mining districts around Sarayevo. We smoked Herzegovinian tobacco and drank a little *rakija*. Then came the inevitable question. "When is the Second Front coming?" How often had we been asked! Sometimes with just a slight tone of a sneer in the question; sometimes with a feeling of misgiving; but mostly with an earnest desire for good news; news that would bring relief to the tired soldiers. By this time our answers were all prepared.

"Well, it is not really the Second Front that you mean; it is the Thirteenth," and one by one I recited the campaigns we had fought. Then I followed it by saying that we did not know; but we, like them, hoped and prayed for it soon for the sake of the world. But we were still prepared to leave the decision to the great Allied leaders, Churchill, Stalin, and Roosevelt, and questioned not their decision.

British propaganda had been very bad. The Partisans knew little of our campaigns in Egypt, Libya, or Tunis. They knew nothing of Eritrea, of Norway, of the fight and Battle of Britain, or the bombing, or our casualties. They did not know that we alone faced fascism in 1941, and they conveniently forgot that Russia had collaborated with Germany. Our Navy was unknown, and our air fleets, which then, in 1943, were unseen, also remained unknown. But in bright contrast was the Red Army—the "Rdeča Armada." To them it was the one fighting, triumphal bulwark against fascism. Every victory was punctuated by immediate celebration; every general was known and his name sung by every mouth, and pictures of Stalin hung from every brigade headquarters. The Red Army would save the world while Britain continued to play politics with the Chetniks and Mihailovich. That was always a bitter pill to swallow. Already we had seen enough of the Chetniks'

work, and had read captured German battle orders relating to
movements of Chetnik battalions under their command. We
had seen the cliff over the Kerka River where the Chetniks
threw two hundred Partisan soldiers with their hands tied
behind their backs. We had seen the burnt-out homes, the
empty pastures, the healed wounds of peasant women whom
Chetniks had mutilated. "Surely the British authorities must
know," we asked ourselves privately. They showed us captured
British arms allegedly dropped into the Chetniks. Then we
had to explain away the American film which glorified the
Chetniks as the main fighting force against the terror of
fascism in Yugoslavia. We had to explain why the British were
dropping in agents to the Mihailovich leader of the Chetniks,
and into the Partisans at the same time; and in that burnt-out
house before those Bosnian miners I felt a trifle dishonest in
my defense of our power politics.

Not only did they ask about these things, but they asked
about living conditions in England, particularly in mining
towns. And we fell into the trap, for we told them about the
improvements in living and working conditions that were
slowly yet steadily sweeping the mining areas. Carson, my
operating-theater orderly in the desert, was a Durham coal
miner, and from him I had learnt much. We told them of
mining conditions in New Zealand, and the wage level. Then
they told us that for years in these mines in Bosnia they had
been paid the equivalent of five shillings weekly, and these
mines were owned by British capital. They told us of the
intense fight to live, of the economic desire on the one hand
toward family limitation and the open prejudiced hostility of
the Church on the other. No wonder they risked their lives
daily in the struggle for a new and better country. No wonder
such a flame had been kindled and had swept the tinder of
the country in a burning desire for a new federation, a democ-

racy that should give to them just the right to live. How could we not sympathize with them?

The hours sped during these discussions, and when we opened the door to go to our sleeping quarters, it was already 3 A.M. The moon shone crisp on the frozen snow, and we stepped down the stone steps, slipping and sliding until we reached the bottom. A Partisan led us to another burnt-out house, where one room remained. We climbed the stairs, opened the door, and got a blast of foul air as from a heat furnace. The stove was red-hot, and every available inch of floor was taken by some sleeping form, Partisan or Partizanka. Even on the table two were asleep. Ivo woke some up and they squeezed together to make room for five extra. I counted thirty in that room not sixteen by eleven feet. We stripped off as much of our clothing as was practical and lay down. We couldn't move without moving our next-door neighbors. I noticed that Ian chose a nice Partizanka to sleep alongside. I lay down in the stench and heat and could feel Ian already making advances to his neighbor. I gave him a kick as a reminder. But Scottish blood is strong and I became dimly conscious of his advances becoming more practical in nature. I administered another rebuke. Bill was steadily snoring on the other side. Ivo, who had been placed next the red-hot stove, was so suffocated he had opened the door and gone outside. Johnny, as we called Voyasin, was, like me, watching the play going on, in fear and trepidation. Suddenly the Partizanka got up, dashed outside, and left Ian. She came back and got under the blanket again, evidently relenting and feeling sorry.

Next morning we rose early to watch the sabotage technique. With a young commissar we climbed a high, craggy hill just over a saddle from the village, and there beneath us was the narrow winding road—the great supply route of the German Army in Yugoslavia, the route from Split to Zagreb. We hid

behind stones and watched. A German control post was just
beneath us. We could see the soldiers walking in and out. A
motorcycle detachment would arrive, dismount, and disappear
into the house where they were quartered. We scanned the
road. It twisted and turned in and among the mountains like a
great sinuous river, now disappearing around corners, now
reappearing higher up. Even as we watched, a German convoy
came speeding down the road. The commissar seized the
glasses and watched. First came a few motorcyclists, then two
small tanks, then a couple of infantry-carrying trucks, and
finally the convoy of empties bound for Split for stores. In the
rear came one tank and a few cyclists. We noted it all down on
paper. Then we went back to the burnt-out village. Our comrades by this time had sallied forth with Italian machine guns,
mines, tire busters, and electrical firing apparatus. Away up
the road we made our way to where the cover was good and
the turns were steep. A large mine made from unexploded
American aircraft bombs was laid in the road, and the place
carefully camouflaged. Then away on the other side of the
corner another mine was laid and concealed, electric wires con-
necting them to the chargers. The group dispersed itself
among the rocks on either side of the road and waited. They
let the patrols, whose job it was to keep the road clear, pass
by unheeded. Then came a signal from the spotter telling us
that the convoy was coming. Tire busters were quickly spread
on the road, and then we waited. The first motorcyclist passed
up the road; just before the first tank reached the farthest
mine, it was blown up. By this time the convoy had passed
the rear mine and it too was exploded, thus blocking all escape.
Several of the tire busters had blown the tires off the trucks
and already the bullets from Partisan machine guns were singing through the air. The Germans started to reply, but our fire
was so dispersed they searched in vain for any one spot to

attack. One tank was already on fire. A Partisan crept down from the rocks and threw a Molotov bottle at another and it burst into flames. With machine-gun fire echoing up and down the valley the Germans faltered. The Partisans pressed closer, from rock to rock; another truck was in flames. Their rear tank was backing and trying to escape through the partially blown road. I watched a small Partisan boy leap down, and through a halo of fire throw his grenade at the tank track. Then something hit the petrol tank and it exploded into flames. Two trucks had escaped from the front of the convoy and were roaring up the mountain road. In all the confusion I heard a wounded man cry like a trapped rabbit. I leapt down to him, but he was dead. The valley was full of smoke and the stench of burning oil. Another truck burst into flames, the soldiers leaping from the floor where they had been taking shelter. They fell like ninepins. Suddenly from down the valley came the roar of the German patrol. No more damage could profitably be done and already Partisan fire was thinning out as the main group moved higher into the mountains. Three stayed behind to hold the Germans. We climbed higher and higher out of range, crossed the hill into another valley, and stopped. The sound of firing had ceased, and only the hills hung heavy with smoke.

After working with this sabotage group for a month we eventually reached the headquarters of the 19th Division and met the colonel. I asked to speak to him alone, for I felt that some slight protest should be made about our detention and the fact that no patrol was there to meet us and make the way easy. I asked him first if he had known that we were coming. "Yes," he replied. "I did." Then, with a touch of what at that time I considered just indignation, I told him what I thought. His commissar, a most likable man (whom we met many times afterward), pointed out to me that I had yet to learn the

difficulties of Partisan life. For even though they had heard
from Tito's headquarters that we were coming, yet it had been
impossible to meet us as they were surrounded by the Germans
and had been fighting ever since.

I saw how foolish I had been and at once relented.

The divisional headquarters was situated in a farmhouse,
and the colonel, a quiet young Bosnian, gave us his bedroom
and thus heaped coals of fire on my shoulders. We went to
the room and lay down on the floor and I told the boys what
had taken place at the interview. We all felt ashamed, and just
as we were discussing it, the colonel came in with an Orthodox
priest, a Montenegrin. He asked me if I would be so kind as to
see a sick girl, his niece, who was living in a house about seven
miles away. I was pleased to do anything to make amends and
we set off walking along the road. He spoke English fairly
well, having been in America some years. Although it was
winter, the road was hot. The stones were large and difficult
to walk over and we made slow progress. But time passed
quickly, for he told me much of Partisan life and particularly
of his own life. He, with his brother, his brother's wife and
child, had escaped from Montenegro and had come to this
isolated spot when the Germans occupied the Montenegrin
country. Compared with Montenegro, Dalmatia was a poor
land. No water despite the snows and the rains, for it all
soaked away in the limestone swallow holes. Village water was
collected by large concrete floors which drained into underground tanks. There was no soil. In the little depressions, or
jame, as they were called, the peasants made small patches for
cultivation. Soil was carried from far and near. Animal dung
was brought, and there, in these quarter-acre plots, they eked
out an existence.

Life was hard here. He told me that almost 80 per cent of
the country's primary wealth went to the three large towns

and stayed there, and that, as long as the old system of politics remained, there would be no hope. I asked him what the Greek Church thought about the Partisan organization, which at that time I thought to be a communist organization. He assured me that it was not communist, but that the whole essence of the movement was a peasant rebellion. The German occupation merely fomented the existing troubles. Not only had it fomented them, but the inflammation had spread like an acute erysipelas until the whole country had accepted the infection and was burning at fever heat.

So the miles passed and we came to the house. It was a well-built house for the country, two stories, with a separate building for the cattle. He knocked at the door. It was opened by a comely woman, her brown eyes burning with hope. We went in. The floors were carpeted (the first I had seen since our arrival) and the house was clean, good, and wholesome compared with the usual peasant's house. We climbed the stairs and there met the child's father, who told me the medical history. Before he had gone far I realized that the child had Pott's disease, or tuberculosis of the spine, and the whole tragedy of our impotence became strikingly real. We went into her room.

There on a real bed with white sheets lay a small, fragile, beautiful girl of sixteen. Her hair was done in plaits tied with blue ribbon, and she wore a bed jacket of beautifully worked lacy wool. She smiled, and I went to her and took her thin white hand in mine. I felt the perspiration on her fingertips. I sat beside her and talked to her, and told her why we had come to Yugoslavia. As she listened her brown eyes deepened and deepened, and I noted her rapid breathing, and saw the pulse beating through the thin skin. We examined her and found that she had a marked spinal deformity and associated tuberculosis of the chest. What could I do or say? I gave a few

words of encouragement through the Partisan priest, and then
with the mother and father we went into another room. I
spoke vaguely about operative treatment. . . . "But where,
Doctor?" they asked. I mentioned diet. . . . "But we have
nothing except beans," they said. I spoke of the necessity for
complete rest. . . . "But what can we do if the Germans come
and find her?" they said.

I tried to assure them that they would not harm her, for
she was a small child, sick and beautiful in her tragedy. They
said nothing, knowing better than I the ways of the master
race. Finally, feeling a hypocrite with every word that came
out, I spoke vaguely in general terms, as one does in such circumstances. Yet what could they do but watch her die?

The mother brought in tiny glasses, and *rakija* tinged brown
with the minutest flavor of burnt honey was served. I returned
to the bedroom to say good-by to the girl. She turned her
head on the white pillow. Two days later I heard that the Chetniks came down to the village where we had been and they
took over the two-storied house as their headquarters. They
found the little girl, so white and beautiful in her sheets; they
stabbed her to death and threw the body from the second-story
window to the parents beneath and shot them a few minutes
later.

We reached the divisional headquarters and I found that
during my absence the commander had given us each a bottle
of captured Italian Sarti, a small handkerchief, and two packets
of Ustashi cigarettes. I thanked him, and began to think that
the sooner I really learnt the Partisan ways the better.

Next morning Bill, Ian, and I went for a walk of explora-
tion to see an old ruined Turkish fort. The colonel had told
me that within a few days he was sending his wife, who was
nearing her term, to her village of Kerenitsa, and he wanted

us to be with her in case anything should happen en route. So we went for a walk this morning. After about an hour's toiling up the stony valley we saw some peasants hurrying down the other side, driving little flocks of sheep—about fourteen in each group—with them. As we watched them, a German shell landed only a few yards away. More shells landed, exploding among the rocks and throwing up debris far and wide. We crouched lower still and watched the hill they were coming from. We saw three peasants running now, leaving their flocks to follow them. We saw figures moving on the skyline. Then came the sound of machine guns from the opposite side of the valley as the Partisan patrol opened fire. Luckily this turned the direction of the fire from our quarters, and we dodged down the valley. By eleven the firing had ceased, but a patrol had come in, and from the information received it appeared that we were completely hemmed in. The Germans had begun a general squeezing process from the west, and we were forced to move.

As soon as it was dark we left. The colonel provided me with a horse, but it was so cold I gave it to Bill to ride. We trudged over the mountains again all night long, nothing to eat, absolute silence, and just at dawn we stopped in a patch of wood and there prepared some ersatz coffee. The colonel came to me and told me that he regarded the position as very serious and he wished us to go on ahead with his wife so that she should be safe.

For the next few days we pushed on with a gay kind of commissar who had a great red triangle on his sleeve. We called him Y.M.C.A. Joe. By this time we were getting hardened to night walking and the days passed quickly enough. We met various Partisan patrols and stayed with them, sharing what they had, which even in 1943 was little enough. A piece of bacon fat here, and a crust of corn bread there, and everywhere a welcome. Each day we heard the sound of distant firing from patrol activity, and in every little patrol we found plenty of German loot. But, oh! the need for things to conduct a war with! No boots, no socks, no vitamins, no overcoats, little ammunition, poor, obsolete guns, no pistols except captured ones. Everywhere such deep enthusiasm and such a burning belief that one day freedom would come.

We left the colonel's wife at Kerenitsa. I heard later that she too was killed. We passed through the dead and terrible town of Udbina, where not one roof was left, not one dog barked in the snow-covered streets, not one wisp of smoke reached to heaven—a monument to Italian occupation. A few nights later we reached the commissar's house, and, to our amazement, found it to be in telephonic communication with Croatian Headquarters.

The commissar said that he would ring up and let them know that we had arrived and that they could send a car for us as it was only some thirty miles away. We listened to the conversation. The *drug* (comrade) ringing up shouted, "*Devedeset*," "*Devedeset*," then again and again. Getting no reply, he would turn the handle frantically; "*Devedeset*," "*Devedeset*." Then someone else would get on the line and we would hear a muttered obscenity, and so on for about an hour with no result. We were so foot-weary and tired we lay down on the floor and slept.

There was a terrific crash in the dark. I awoke and snatched for my gun, Jela's gun, and waited. Then I heard a truck maneuvering in the yard. Presently up the stairs came the sound of heavy feet. I wiped my eyes and into the room squeezed a huge man, well armed, followed by three others. The commissar introduced us. The huge man, Dr. Novosell, asked us to start right away for Plitvice. I said that we were very tired and was it really necessary? He muttered something about Heinkels and Dorniers and I dozed off again. The four newcomers were soon stretched on the floor of the room, which already contained about fifteen persons and a red-hot stove. Added to this, the truck outside kept its engine going all night for fear of a sudden German attack. It was a wood-burning German truck and very difficult to start in the intense cold.

At odd moments we slept, but I was glad when morning came. We washed, said good-by to the commissar, and climbed into the truck. Dr. Novosell sat on cushions while the other Partisans and a few peasants were herded in at the back, standing and lying on the floor. This surprised us, for we imagined that all class distinction had gone in the common fight. But no; it was always first- and second-class even among Partisans.

Now we were in Croatia and the road climbed through low mountains. It led through narrow valleys, and everywhere we saw stark destruction. Every village burnt; churches burnt with just broken crosses remaining; hospitals bombed to pieces; schools burnt, and not an official telegraph line in existence. The destruction of the enemy sneered at us from every turn, and every village had its group of newly dug graves with their crude crosses to mark the onward march of German culture.

We passed Babin Potok, climbed the saddle, and dropped down into the valley of Plitvice, with its eleven hanging lakes. Snow covered the ground; there was no sound except the chugging of our engine; every waterfall was frozen hard, a series of great icicles tying lake to lake. The trees hung their branches and wept too; only a few pale hellebores pushed above the snow along the roadside. It was a journey of extreme danger. With cliffs on one side of us and high banks on the other we swung and skidded and slipped our way down the valley. I hesitated to think what would happen should we meet something. Village after village we passed, roofless and snow-covered. Suddenly we lurched around a corner and saw, standing by the lake, two large two-storied wooden houses— our destination, the Croatian Command of General Gossjak.

Dr. Novosell told us that there was a British officer living there in one of the houses, so we asked if we could see him first. I felt that we should make some kind of report, for already months had slipped by and presumably no one knew or had even the faintest inkling where we were. The truck stopped; we stretched our tired, frozen legs and jumped from the truck. A Partisan sentry met us and Dr. Novosell told him to take us to the British Mission. He led us to the far house, and as we went up the stairs we met the officer coming down.

He welcomed us; we sat down; he gave us some refreshments, and, best of all, some clean clothes. He told us his name was Reed, Owen Reed, captain in the Intelligence. I said that my name was Rogers, in the Medical Service, and that Bill and Ian were my "boys." I felt that the conversation flagged a bit; there was something not yet said. Was it stupid British reticence, was it a remnant of officialdom, or what was it? Finally out it came. He had had no word of our coming from the British Mission at Jajce. (I hadn't anticipated that he would have, considering our manner of departure.) He had had no word of what we were to do, and as the Yugoslavs were extremely difficult about strangers in their country, he was considerably embarrassed by our arrival.

I sat by the stove and told him what I thought would pacify him—that I had the approval of a brigadier to come here. However, I found out it was the wrong brigadier. No wonder he had given permission so readily. There was another at Tito's headquarters who was not so charitably disposed to adventurers. But after an hour by the fire his English officialdom disappeared; his two boys began arguing with mine, and he suggested that we make our camp in the meantime in an adjoining room and that evening he would take me to see the general.

I asked him his civilian occupation and he told me that he was an actor. My opinion of the stage rose daily, and throughout all my stay in the country. Despite the difficulties at first it was always Owen Reed who spoke the most sense, who bore the burden of hostility without weakening, and who remained our wise counselor and friend.

CHAPTER 3

A Meeting with the General

The snow crunched under our feet and in the half gloom I saw the silent lake below us. Reed went first, showing me the way. We crossed a little makeshift bridge between two houses, then climbed the hill a little toward a blaze of light. Evidently the general wasn't afraid of night bombers in his valley fastness. At the door we were halted. Ivo, my interpreter from Vis, who had come with us to make the talking easier, spoke to the sentry. Then we were shown upstairs and into the general's room. He greeted us just a trifle coldly, I thought, but I put out my hand and he shook it grudgingly. Then he turned and introduced me to Colonel Terric and to Colonel Elia. Terric, I gathered, was the general's adjutant, and Elia the officer in charge of all the technical side of the Army.

We sat down and Ivo began a long harangue about how we had been sent at Jela's instigation, and with Tito's permission and approval, to help with these three thousand wounded in Lika. I noted a slight raising of the eyebrows at the figure but let it pass. Ivo then told him of our work on Vis and our many adventures on the road up. Owen Reed and I sat dumbly watching the show and quickly sensing a certain amount of hostility. Terric, the small, dark-eyed, rather theatrical adjutant, asked some questions about stores and told us how short they were of medical equipment. Could we do anything to relieve the situation?

I replied that we would do everything in our power to get matériel dropped in by parachute as early as possible, and said that we would like a hospital of our own, for our technique was slightly different from that of their own doctors and nurses, and this led only to confusion. The general quickly interposed, "But cannot you train our nurses in your ways?"

I replied, "Yes, we could, but I still think a British hospital as a unit will enable us to do better work."

During the conversation I quickly took in the general's room, for it apparently served not only as a staff or command room but also as his sleeping quarters. A large map of Croatia hung from the wall with strategic points marked and a line drawn around certain points which seemed like German concentrations, for they all seemed to be in the valleys. On the floor were two Montenegrin rugs, clean and new, while a half-finished game of chess, equally disposed between the blacks and white, stood on the table.

While Ivo, who was always excellent at these interviews, was doing all this talking, there was a continual accompaniment rising in a louder and louder voice from below—"*devedeset, devedeset, olloa, olloa, devedeset, olloa, olloa.*" I wondered how the hell the general could put up with that all day long and why he didn't get the telephone exchange moved somewhere else.

The interview ended as coldly as it had begun. The general said that he would communicate with the chief of the medical staff in the morning and also with Marshal Tito's headquarters, and in the meantime, would we kindly stay in the house of the British Mission.

I rose with Owen. We bowed our way out and fumbled downstairs.

Once in the cool air (and it was cool after the superheated *glavni stab*, or headquarters), I felt freer and easier. I was getting used to the suspicious, cool welcome now, and was learning to take them.

The silence was broken by Owen, who cheerfully remarked, "Well, regard yourselves as under house arrest, anyhow!" And we were.

Next day the snow trickled down in fine dust all day long. At 3 P.M. I got so sick of being inside (about ten of us in the room) that I said I was going for a walk. Who would come? Bill and Ian and Ivo came, but at the door we were met by two *drugovi* with submachine guns and grenades who followed us and told us that we couldn't move beyond the house. This annoyed me. So I dispatched Ivo over to the *glavni stab* to see Colonel Terric and to ask if we could not even go for a walk. Permission was granted, and we walked down the road along the frozen lake's edge, returning as darkness fell. Somewhere (it seemed just over the mountain) we heard spasmodic firing which the guard said was a patrol operating near Babin Potok.

Three days passed and then I received word to go to the *glavni stab* again in the evening. The whole atmosphere had changed. A cordial greeting and smiles from all, coffee was handed around, and we quickly saw that word had arrived about our activities. I asked Elia straight out, "Have you heard from Tito's headquarters?" and he replied, "Yes, it is all right, and tomorrow the general wishes you to go around some of the hidden hospitals with the chief of the medical staff, stay in them and see how they work, and then come back and report to him how they could be improved."

This didn't suit us at all, for we had not come to make an inspection, but to work. However, it was a start and we felt satisfied.

CHAPTER 4

Surgery against Odds

Next morning we left with a Partisan major whose name we never could say but who knew a few words of almost-forgotten English. He was so keen to relearn that we called him afterward "Kako Se Kaze" (What Do You Mean). Back up the valley we trudged in the deep, soft snow, through the village of Babin Potok, and then down the Otocac road. Evening came and we found the medical headquarters in a tiny village on the mountainside. Here a room had been prepared for us, and after kicking the snow from our boots we climbed the stairs and threw off our wet clothes. The room was in a peasant's house and the first thing that caught our eye was a large poster. "Kill that louse, it spreads typhus." This pleased my eye greatly, for evidently the doctors of Croatia were far ahead of those in Dalmatia in their concepts of public health and in the value of the poster. Alas! It was all shattered when I went to the lavatory. Just a hole in the floor of the upstairs veranda over which one squatted. The excreta fell below into the yard where the fowl and flies puddled around in it. What it must be like in the summertime I could not imagine.

Colonel Boravic had the best room in the village. He was obviously an ill man, thin, with deep lines where once he had been fat; pale skin and pale lips and nails, scraggy hair where once a large mop had grown, and thick clothing to keep warm in spite of the almost intolerable heat from a huge stove. Exertion distressed him, and he had obviously lost his fire, his drive, and his interest in the Partisan guerrillas who at that moment were guarding the snow-covered passes and mountain-tops against the Chetnik and Ustashi patrols.

He spent the time showing me some photos of forest hospitals, some in caves, some in log cabins, and I quickly noticed how different he had looked earlier in the war. Now it was almost in vain to try and stimulate his interest in our work, or to speed up starting a hospital for us. He asked the usual "Second Front" question, and told me of the vast stores the Russians were going to pour into Croatia when they came. I told him of my talk with General Gossjak, and how he had asked me to go around some of the hospitals and report to him on their condition, a thing I could not do without Boravic's knowledge, and a thing I resented even being asked to do. But he waved his hand and said, "Ah! You don't understand the freedom of Partisan life; we all criticize one another, for by doing so we achieve something better." I tried to picture the same circumstances in the British Army but couldn't.

Next day we started away over the snow-covered mountains with just a courier to find the villages of Turnavic and Turiansky. The path led up a long, forested valley deep in snow. We trudged and puffed and blew as we dragged our feet from newly fallen snow two feet deep. Our bellies were empty save for a small meal of polenta in the morning. We crossed the saddle to enter another valley, all the time getting deeper and deeper into the forest. Boravic had told us that the hospitals would be expecting us, but, as usual, no one had heard of us or what we had come for.

The first collection of wounded was hidden in a peasant house and the adjacent cowshed. Indeed, only a makeshift partition separated the cows from the wounded. The doctor was an elderly man of Jewish faith. He showed us around his small group of wounded. Just to see them, the pale, toxic-looking faces in the evening gloom, their thin hands veined with blue streaks, the fractured femurs lying with back splints, and ankles with pressure sores, made us anxious to get to work and try to help. I recall a Partisan boy (he couldn't have been more than nineteen) lying on his side. He had most of his buttock sloughed away because of pressure sores, or what is called "decubitus." The raw area was stained deep yellow with acriflavine and the whole buttock showed not one healthy portion healing.

I asked about a few cases, but the old doctor, who had done his utmost with nothing, explained that he had been a gyne-cologist in Zagreb and that he knew little of war surgery.

Every bandage was threadbare, for all were washed at least ten or twelve times until they rotted and fell into dust. There was no soap, and almost no instruments with which to work. We went into a little side room which was really the hayloft, and he told me his troubles.

As we were speaking the wounded started singing, singing as though all the world were happy and the battle already won. It was this absolutely indomitable spirit which was the miracle of Yugoslavia. The appalling suffering these boys and girls stood with fortitude amazed us. Why did the world not know about it all? Why were more materials and more help not forthcoming? Why was the press of 1943 silent in the presence of the greatest and most heroic sacrifice made against the evil of fascism? The song ended in the glorious "Na jurish"—"Let us fight."

It was nighttime. The snow had frozen, and a fresh courier took us again over the mountaintops down into a hidden vil-lage lying around the bottom of one of those deep *jame* with no outlet. Dr. Novosell was there to meet us and took us to a peasant's house where we slept the night. Here we met Dr. Kayfesh, later stabbed to death by the Chetniks while defending my wounded. He was a grand chap, Kayfesh; one of the two surgeons of Croatia, young, energetic, well informed, full of energy. In the long evenings we would sit around the stove talking and arguing of techniques, or various splints, or methods of resuscitation. And then, as the fire grew dim, he would tell of his work in the early days of Partisan life, when things were not so organized as they were then.

He had been to the Medical School of Zagreb and after the German occupation he stayed on in Zagreb working in the large hospitals, sometimes operating on German soldiers; sometimes operating on civilians, and all the time, every night, leaving Zagreb with a load of medical material on his back— stolen, bought, or otherwise acquired. He would slip out of the town through the German lines and reach the country. There, at a rendezvous, he would be met by a courier and would hand over his precious medical supplies and then make his way back into the town and get ready another lot for the Partisans. He did this for months, until one day he received word that the Gestapo had caught the courier, and his life was in jeopardy. That night he made his last trip and never went back, for he joined the Partisans in a new role, that of surgeon to the Croatian Command.

We watched him operate. His technique was good and he believed as we did on the non-closure of all war wounds. He did not approve of the Thomas splint, but, like all Yugoslav surgeons who had come under the aegis of German teaching, believed in Dietrich's method of treatment for fractured femur or perhaps Whitman's plaster-cast technique, both of which British surgeons like on principle. The plaster cast, though handy for the immediate evavuation of patients, produced appalling pressure sores under guerrilla conditions and Dietrich's method produced no extension of the fragments, which accounted for the vast number of shortened limbs we saw. We got him to adopt extension with pin for all fractures of the lower leg, thus preventing the shortening and the angulation we noticed so often.

We watched Dr. Novosell do guillotine amputations, and saw with horror the painful dressings which followed, but no amount of persuasion could get him to attempt the flap method, the defense being the incidence of gas gangrene. We pointed out the method of secondary suture of the flaps when all danger is over, but off the legs came, often when the only indication was the presence of crepitus owing to air having been carried into the wounds with the missile, or often owing just to local gas-forming organisms.

Perhaps the thing our team rebelled against most was the lack of consideration for the wounded. This was almost universal. They would be left lying on the operating table for half an hour in the freezing cold while a conversation was carried on, then a huge dose of camphor in oil would be given to counteract the "heart failure." Dressings would be ripped off these huge guillotine stumps and if the boy groaned the retort was, "What! You a Partisan and can't bear that!" Needles, elephant size, would be used for intravenous work where a much smaller one would have sufficed and the intravenous work was usually bad, so that we saw many painful swollen arms afterward. It was this extreme callousness which made us angry at times.

We worked at Turiansky for a time, and then I went again to the *glavni stab* to make the promised report to the general. But first I called on Boravic and read it over to him. We talked about this lack of gentleness and he freely admitted it, saying, "Yes, they are tired and have suffered so much themselves,

they have forgotten how to be gentle; it is the Partisan life."
Unfortunately every shortcoming was attributed to the "Partisan life." Despite all this the work that was being done with
nothing at all to do it with was a great achievement, and the
nursing done by untrained peasant girls equaled, and was in
some cases even better than, our own.

It was agreed that we should take over this collection of
wounded in the Turiansky area and that Dr. Kayfesh should
be transferred nearer to Zagreb to work as a divisional surgeon.

Two days later I was at the *glavni stab* and there talked for
a long time with Colonel Elia about all I had seen and had
already communicated to Boravic. Elia agreed with me, telling
me that many times they heard about the brutality of certain
doctors. But I must remember what they had gone through
and remember it was the "Partisan life."

I liked Colonel Elia. He was a young man of thirty-five
and had served for two years in the Spanish Civil War. He
escaped to France and then spent the next two years being
starved and maltreated in various concentration camps. It
was there he developed tuberculosis, which accounted for the
deaths of thousands of these idealists, and only in 1938 did he
again reach his native country, filled with the vision that there
was only one way to help the suffering world, and that was to
sweep away the old and to force in the new. Some months
later Elia went on a mission to Slovenia, and while passing
through the mountains was ambushed and killed. Many of the
best in Europe have fallen in this struggle for the new world.

I saw Owen Reed and arranged for medical stores to be
dropped in by parachute near Turnavic as soon as the weather
moderated. He showed me a rather snooty message from
Brigadier Maclean about my arrival in Croatia, wanting to
know who gave permission for me to come at all. We let it
rest there.

Back at Turiansky there were few admissions owing to the deep snow, but hardly had we started again when a courier arrived with a note from Boravic asking if I would go to a medical conference to be held at Glina in five days' time. Glina was up near Zagreb on the Karlovac road. How we were to get there I just didn't have a clue. However, we said we would.

The day for leaving came, with about eight feet of solid snow lying on the ground and still falling. We just looked out and went back again. Four days passed, and then came a break of fine weather and away we went—Novosell, Kayfesh, Ian, Bill, and Ivo. We left Voyasin and a Dr. Premaru to look after the wounded, who by this time had all been fixed up. It took a hard day's work to reach Boravic's headquarters. Novosell, who was a very heavy man with great blue jowls and who was short in the wind, hardly made it. He sank so deep with every step, and the mass to lift was so great, I wondered whether he would die of acute heart failure before we arrived there.

I left Ian and Ivo with Boravic and next morning left on skis for Plitvice. The road was alleged to have been cleared from Plitvice to Glina for a truck to take us. At Plitvice I found Owen Reed the same as ever—a breath of British friendliness, a stimulus to my dormant intelligence, and a generous giver of new clothes, socks, and comforts.

Early next morning I wiped the steaming window with my hand and saw on the road the truck that was to take us about one hundred miles to the conference. Two *drugovi* (comrades) were busy stoking up a fire they had lit under the engine—I suppose to warm it up. Two more were shoveling great masses of pine blocks into the truck, for it was a German wood-burner, and three more were trying to tie four sets of chains over the wheels with pieces of telegraph wire. It all filled me with the greatest confidence. By eleven o'clock, after great shouting and instructions coming from all the bystanders, the engine burst into life, and the fire was rapidly scraped out from underneath. By noon we moved off, about twenty in the truck. We swung perilously around the hanging lakes and the cold wind, raw and bitter, cut through my ragged and torn clothes. Many times we ran off the road. Many times we pushed and shoved and dug the snow away while Boravic got angrier and angrier with the unfortunate driver, who did wonderfully well, considering the roads.

That night we slept at a small village in some straw spread on the floor of a *gostiona* (pub). Novosell, as usual, had the best seat in the truck and at odd intervals pulled out some salami, which he ate in great ravenous bites while we just salivated.

Next night we reached Sluin and by this time there were about fifty people on the truck, commissars and *bolničarke* (nurses), *drugovi* and peasants, officers and doctors, all going to the conference. We had two meals a day, usually of polenta, and hot coffee, which Bill always managed to procure from somewhere. The cold was biting through me, and Bill's nose, always long and thin, was permanently lengthened by a frozen drop.

We reached Glina the following evening. The truck roared down the main street and nearly skidded through a great plate-glass window, then stopped, never to start again, at the Omladinski Dom (Youth Hall). We had a great meal of bacon and potatoes, then Bill and I were taken to our billet, which was the house of the town's wealthiest doctor. A real town house, but full of knickknacks on the tables and great allegorical pictures of "The Birth of Croatia" on the walls, reminding me vaguely of passages from the Book of Revelation. The artist who conceived the allegory must have lived in

a warmer Croatia than we had experienced, for the nymphs
who danced in sylphlike attitudes around the new-found king
couldn't have stood the Croatian winter as we found it. Despite the knickknacks and the great fancywork pillow bed the
lavatory was only slightly better than the peasant ones we had
already experienced. But it was pleasant to be in a civilized
house again even for a few days.

That night the conference opened. The first speaker was the
leader of the local "Liberation Committee," who welcomed us
to his town. Then followed the leader of the Anti-Fascist
Council, who gave a long political talk on the future of the
Democratic Federated Yugoslavia. Colonel Boravic then
spoke on the ideals of the conference and made fitting reference to the British help they had received, at that time still
small. He also brought up the "Second Front" story, which we
had heard so often. General Goyko Nickolic, chief of Tito's
medical staff, then gave a long talk on army planning and the
battle of Banja Luka. He was an able speaker and obviously a
good administrator, whatever his professional qualifications
might be. He welcomed us to his country and spoke of our
work in Vis. I followed with a short address, very badly translated, but replied to the Second Front story by telling a little
of what the British medical services had done on the various
fronts. Colonel Elia now appeared on behalf of the Croatian
Command and spoke with great simplicity and honesty about
the condition of the medical services in Croatia.

Speeches, speeches, speeches; they are the world's best
talkers and the world's best audience, for every little while
someone quite spontaneously shouted, "*Zivio Marshal Tito,*"
and the whole audience replied, "*Zivio Marshal Tito.*" Then,
not to be outdone, another voice shouted, "*Zivio Marshal
Stalin,*" and the great hall resounded again to "*Zivio Marshal*

Stalin." Poor old Churchill didn't seem to be included in the galaxy at all.

At the end, about midnight, they showed a British propaganda film of the Teheran Conference. Stalin got about twenty minutes of "*Zivio*-ing" while Churchill got about one minute. It was painfully obvious to us how little they knew or were told of our war effort and how sympathy swept in a great tide toward the Slav border.

Next morning at eleven the surgical part of the conference started and Novosell opened by advocating the "open technique of war wounds." This was a complete reversal of his own practice and was done solely to oppose his opponent, a Dr. Finderle from Susak. He spoke on and on, advocating the Dietrich method of treating femurs (this was for my benefit) and then about the dire need for more and more medical supplies, and suggested that now that I, a British doctor, was here, perhaps things would change and they should get some recognition for the great fight they had taken part in against the invader, and so on. . . .

I then spoke at length about advances in surgical technique in the Eighth Army and brought out that not only was immediate treatment important, but also a long-term view of the case. I stressed the need for better amputations, more traction for fractures, and finally the use of new drugs, the sulfa drugs and penicillin, when they became available.

Kayfesh spoke next and told of the difficulties in technique owing to lack of materials. Lack of anesthetics, of disinfectants, of bandages, of instruments, and of vitamins. . . .

Just at that moment a Heinkel came over and bombed the town. The meeting quickly broke up, and as we clambered onto the truck (a new one) and started off toward Topusko, the German tanks came in the other end of the town.

We reached Topusko that night and the conference started all over again. Dr. Finderle, obviously an able surgeon trained in the Italian school, attacked the Thomas splint and our method of fracture treatment, saying that the Thomas splint meant inevitable bedsores, hopeless difficulties in nursing, and complete failure as far as Partisan warfare was concerned, where immediate and urgent evacuation of the wounded was the almost weekly or even daily rule and not the exception. And so it went on. At 2 A.M. I crept out of the hall after waking Bill up, and we tumbled into our bed of straw and fell asleep.

Next day more Heinkels and Dorniers and tanks came, so we moved on again and reached Sluin. It was a bright sunny Sunday, May 1, the greatest days of the communist calendar. The town was full of Partisans and Partizanke; peasants in their national costume, commissars and officers in gold braid, and children rushing from one excitement to the other.

Bill and I wandered into the square after lunch, for the conference was not due to start until evening. We saw an old woman selling roast pork and bought a roast for 120,000 *kune*, for we were very hungry, and had had enough of polenta. With the pork we sat down on a curb and saw ahead of us the Roman Catholic church with bell tolling and battered shelled crucifix on the tower. Bill was a Catholic, so I suggested that we go in and have a look.

We opened the small door to hear the monotone of the priest. We had not expected this, for it was 2 P.M. We sat down to get accustomed to the gloom, and there, clad in a lace stole, was the priest going around the Stations of the Cross, gaudy golden Stations, followed by about twenty elderly women, three very aged men, and ten small children. We waited in the cool and then went outside. The square, which we had left half empty, was now full. Three thousand *drugovi* and *drugarice* in their parachute dresses of yellow, green, blue, black, and scarlet filled the square. All were fully armed with Sten guns and grenades. Children darted in and out of the crowd. On the stone dais was a huge photo of Stalin and Tito, and from the platform a commissar was extolling the virtues and the victories of the Red Army. *"Zivio Marshal Stalin"* shouted its way to the skies; *"Zivio Marshal Tito"* echoed down the valley. How different from the Stations of the Cross!

The evening was memorable, for Nazor the poet appeared. He was given a tremendous ovation as leader of the Anti-Fascist Council of Croatia, and a great welcome as the national poet, who, with Tito, had suffered and marched in the dark days of the great fifth German offensive. He spoke so kindly, so beautifully about the Partisan doctors. He told us of his own experiences with doctors, and how in the fifth offensive they had sacrificed their lives that the wounded might live. He spoke about the motives which draw men to the profession and which, unfortunately, seem to die as they grow older. He spoke as a father of his people, about the cruelty of man to man, and then he spoke of the new world to come and the hope that burned in everyone's breast—the hope of eternal peace.

The night drew on, and at midnight the chief of the Public Health Services spoke. He was a man of great vision and understanding. He knew his country and its needs, and one by one he took the causes of the Balkan medical tragedies and showed the way to conquer them. I looked around the audience. More than half of them were asleep—asleep while such truths and such plans were being discussed. The war was a short war in comparison with the eternal fight against disease: He talked of typhus and lice, typhoid and latrines, tuberculosis and housing, endemic syphilis and arsenic, rickets and feeding, nephritis and exposure, rheumatism and clothing. He ended by saying, "Diseases can be prevented and finished, not in the new world to come, but now, if we will." His speech will live in my memory for many a year.

Thus ended the conference, and we all tumbled back into the truck and set off through the snows to Plitvice. For me it had been a great success, for I was able to judge more clearly what was needed and how urgent was the need. It revised my opinion of the Partisan medical services, for I saw men of vision and men of ideas behind it all, striving against tremendous difficulties to make things better; no books; no periodicals; no contacts; many of the doctors unqualified medical students; many of them country practitioners; and I wondered how would we have got on had these difficulties been ours. In the Eighth Army we never had the enemy on all sides of us, all the time; we were never at a loss to evacuate our patients to safety from bombing and throat-slitting; we always had a "Q" Department to furnish our every need, and the more I thought of it the more I felt proud to have been caught up in this cleansing fire, this great struggle against the inhumanity of fascism.

CHAPTER 5

The Trip to Bosnia

Hardly were we back again at Turnavic when a courier arrived with a note from Colonel Elia to say that word had been received from Marshal Tito that he wanted me to come to Bosnia. This was indeed an honor that our work had been recognized by Tito's headquarters, but I was a little dubious about making the move without British sanction; for, though we had lived entirely with the Partisans ever since we had been in the country, and never in a mission, yet I was still under the control of the brigadier attached to Tito's headquarters. I went to Plitvice and asked Owen Reed to wireless the British Mission for authority to move. This he did and in due time it came. I decided to leave Bill and Ian in Croatia to await my return, for we were to start out by captured German staff car in which there was only one vacant seat. Moreover there was still very thick snow and it seemed needless for the boys to undergo further hardship.

I arrived at the *glavni stab* early one morning, and, accompanied by Colonel Terric and Colonel Cryovlich, we started forth. After we had left, I saw that Terric had been elevated to the rank of major general and was resplendent in a new uniform with much gold braid.

The road climbed steadily to Babin Potok, where I was to pick up an overcoat, but snow was falling fast and the overcoat was not there, so we carried on. Hardly had we started when suddenly the front of the car suddenly disappeared into a huge snowdrift about twenty feet deep. Only with the greatest difficulty could we clamber out and find the light of day again. Terric stood for a moment in his beautiful new high boots and new golden uniform surveying the scene. "We shall walk," he said simply. So we started. Mile after mile in the snow, and I began to start dysentery. This held us up, but Terric never complained, and indeed he helped me in every possible way. In the evening we met a *kola* (wagon) and I just lay down on the snow-covered woolen rug, too weak to crawl underneath. That night we stayed in a peasant house and continued the next morning at the first streak of daylight. I began to lag behind, and when we arrived at another peasant's house, it was obvious to Terric that I couldn't keep walking much longer. Another *kola*, and off we started. That evening we crossed the saddle and made our way into the *polje* (plain) to Kerenitsa.

There we stayed. *Rakija* was produced and also some milk, which helped a lot. Next day again in a *kola* with Terric and the colonel walking behind, until the snow got so deep and soft the horse could not get through it. So I had to walk. I could hardly put one leg in front of the other, and at the foot of the hill before the climb to Udbina, with night already on us, I just stopped dead. Terric made a hole for me in the snow and covered me with his new jacket. Then he and Crylovich left to look for help in Udbina. I soon fell asleep and about an hour and a half later they returned, having found nobody in the dead town. They helped me up the hill and in the dark laid me down in a bombed-out house with snow so deep that half the windows were covered. Disappearing again into the town, they combed it until they found a small outpost of Partisans. With their help they came back and carried me to their house. It likewise had no roof, but tarpaulins had been slung across the eaves and in one corner of the room a bed had been prepared for Terric and a stove was roaring to keep them warm. Terric gave me the bed, and with half a bottle of *rakija* I fell asleep, Terric sleeping on the floor alongside me.

The next morning the snow was so bad we could not even venture outside. During the day a few Partisans arrived and danced the *kola* (cartwheel) dance in the next room to keep warm. The music supplied by a piano accordion repeated the same melody over and over again, and as I lay, half dozing and half waking, its rhythm and repetition almost drove me mad. But it was so cold and they had to keep warm, and, after all, I was lying under a thick woolen peasant rug, so I dropped off to sleep again.

We ate bacon fat and drank *rakija* again copiously. That seemed to fix my innards well, for next day I felt much better—

the bleeding had ceased—and we started to walk down to the area near Mazin. Terric's new uniform with its bright gold lacings was showing signs of wear already. By this time I knew that he had been appointed Ambassador to Moscow, and he was worried about his appearance.

We reached a peasant house near Mazin and here whom should I find but my old friend the colonel of the 19th Division. He still had some Sarti, and as we threw down our sweaty, dirty clothes and washed in the copious hot water, his commissar, Y.M.C.A. Joe, brought us food and drink. I always liked that commissar; indeed, all the Bosnian and Croatian commissars seemed to be different types from the Slovene ones we met later. We rested there for two days, and then, with a large guard, we set forth on foot to cross the Knin–Bihac road.

The battalion (of twelve) left about two hours before us to see that the way was clear, and all we had with us was one courier. We climbed over those low hills, a biting wind driving the snow hard into our faces, and just as we were approaching the road, we found a Partisan soldier, the back of his head almost blown off. His companion was weeping copiously. He had, it appeared, stopped walking for a moment to have something to eat, and was slinging off his Sten gun when the trigger guard slipped and about three bullets shot up across the back of his head. I did up the boy's head with a first field dressing (British) and just at the critical moment along came three peasants with a horse. So they slung him over the horse and carried him back to the division headquarters.

That night we crossed the Knin–Bihac road. For hours we stood in the snow just above the road watching the German patrols come and go. They would enter the patrol hut and we would see fresh smoke rise from the chimney as they stirred up the fire. Then the relieving patrol would issue forth and start

along the road. When it was dark we crossed—the whole battalion—not more than five hundred yards from the patrol
house. We walked all night and hid in some scrub during the
day, for a courier had returned to tell us that a German and
Chetnik patrol was searching for us. Next night away again,
and I recall that about 2 A.M. we met an ammunition train
of peasant women going in the opposite direction. Over each
one's shoulder hung the colored peasant bag and in each bag
was one shell and one cartridge for their mountain gun. None
of them wore a coat or boots—just the bullock-hide slippers
the peasants were forced to wear. Silently they filed past, a host
of old women, hooded by their black *rute*, backs bent with age,
tired feet, yet marching on for liberty.

Two days later—Martin Brod. We rested there in a house
built on an island in the middle of the river so as to catch the
water for flour-milling. Indeed the whole village was built on
little islands and every house seemed to have its own water
wheel. The noise was deafening. Water falling over the dead
water wheels, for there was no grain to grind. I slept a little
and was now feeling much better. About 6 P.M. we left again
on horseback, climbed the great hill, up the stony track, always
the black rim still above us, and then the summit, and we
passed into the valley of the Una. Down through pine woods
and oak forests to a Partisan patrol, and then on next day
toward Drvar, where Tito had his headquarters. Terric left
us in the morning to go south to the headquarters of the
1st Corps in Montenegro, so the old colonel and I and a
courier rode along the snow-covered valley. The country was
so barren I wondered how the peasantry managed to live at
all. Here and there a few dead maize stalks stuck above the
ground, but beyond that there was nothing. As we rode, heavy
firing broke out to the south of us where the Germans were
trying to come up to Drvar from the neighborhood of Livno.

PART **III**

Bosnia

CHAPTER 1

Arrival at Drvar

At last we saw the town ahead of us, nestling in a valley, with cliffs on its northern aspect, and above the cliffs the great Mount Yasekovac. On the southern side wooded hills, rising to two thousand feet, hemmed us in. Ahead we could see the tall chimneys of the two large cellulose factories, and as we drew nearer I saw two British officers walking in the snow, both of them with walking sticks.

When they drew abreast, I perceived that one had red tabs on his collar, and decided that this must be Brigadier Maclean. I saluted awkwardly, pulled the horse up, and introduced myself.

"My name is Rogers, from Croatia," I said. A long silence followed, during which time I deemed that my name was not exactly one of a *persona grata*.

"Oh," was the reply.

The Partisan colonel looked dumfounded at the warmth of greeting between British officers, but was polite enough not to mention it.

"You had better go up to my headquarters. You will find it in a peasant's house on the south side of the town." He flicked a piece of snow from his boot with his stick and they walked on.

I knew why he was like that, for I had come into the country rather behind his back. I started to construct my story as we rode on.

In the town the colonel left me, and with a courier I found the British Mission about a quarter of a mile from the main road. Dismounting, I gave the horse to the courier, kicked the snow from my boots and legs, and, opening the door, went in. There, seated before a game of patience, a curious thing in this hectic country, was a British officer. He rose to greet me; it was Randolph Churchill.

I asked him where I could wash, shave, and get some clean clothes. He directed me to another house nearby and there, beside a roaring fire, once again I became a British officer.

Evening came and the mess assembled. Maclean, whose previous war record was known to us all, and whose swift rise to fame as an undaunted soldier, as well as a diplomat, had doubtless brought him to the position he now held, occupied the head of the table. On his left was Andrew Maxwell; stolid, but a good chap, kindly and friendly and more communicative than his chief. Then there was Churchill, whose job I never fathomed, a signals officer called King, and a Major Clarke, who later gave me his horse a fortnight before the blow to Drvar came. I never had the pleasure of actually riding it, though it came in very useful for carrying stores.

It was a restrained and rather dull mess, quite different to the hectic rough and tumble of a casualty clearing station mess, where irregularity and crises break every army rule, and certainly quite different from Partisan life, where food didn't seem to matter much and rank held no inhibitions.

I interviewed Maclean that night. He thought that my entry into the country without his knowledge was "highly irregular" and let it go at that. I asked him why Tito had asked me to come, but he didn't know. I told him that I would see the Medical Headquarters in the morning and was glad to escape with no more said.

Next morning I went and found the Medical Headquarters

and interviewed a Colonel Krause, who told me that they wanted me to come to Bosnia and start a hospital here. But I said no; I was well content where I was in Croatia; I had plenty of work to keep me going day and night, and already we had made firm friends with the Croats. He hold me that Tito would like to see me that afternoon and that he would take me to him. So I left and walked through the township (burnt by the Germans a year before) back to the mission.

CHAPTER 2

Interview with Tito

That afternoon Krause and I rode down to the river by the sawmill in Drvar, and there, challenged by the sentry, we continued along the cliff bottom which flanks the river Una. Colonel Krause was riding a small Bosnian pony, deep bay, and I was lumbering along on a tall Slovene hack captured from the Germans some months before. For about a quarter of a mile we rode along the riverbank until we arrived opposite a place in the cliff wall where a great fault had occurred, leaving a cleft about three yards wide. There we stopped and gave our horses to a *drug* who stood at the bottom of a wooden ladder. We climbed the ladder, three flights in all, and then I saw for the first time that the cleft had widened into a cave, and there, built across the cave, supported by great roughly hewn beams of pine, was Tito's headquarters. Its windows looked across the valley of the Una, above towered the cliff, and beside the door stood a sentry caressing Tito's dog. He saluted Colonel Krause and we walked along the platform to the door. The sentry went in, then returned and beckoned

us in through the open door. I entered a room where, sitting
at his desk, was Tito.

He rose as I entered and we shook hands. Such a powerful
hand and so friendly the shake. How different from Maclean's
welcome. He motioned me to sit down and then talked to
Colonel Krause, asking him if I could speak Yugoslav. Krause
thought that my Yugoslav was too limited and he suggested
an interpreter, so Tito's interpreter came in and stood at Tito's
right hand.

Here was the man whose name had for months now been on
my lips and in my ears; here was the dynamo of Yugoslavia.
The metalworker who had electrified the country with his
spirituality, who had welded aggressive Serbs, undertrodden
Dalmatians, proud Montenegrins, primitive Bosnians, difficult
Croats, and intellectual Slovenes into one great unified fighting unit. Here was the man who, for his ideals, had been tor-
tured in King Alexander's prisons, who had schemed under
the nose of the Gestapo in Belgrade, and whose humanity and
kindliness had sanctified him in the eyes of his peasant army.

I looked at his rugged, strong face. Deep lines creased his
forehead and his cheeks. Yet this was not the face I had seen
portrayed in every village throughout the country. This face
was kindly in its strength; the merry blue eyes, which looked
at you with every word he spoke, his quiet slow speech, and his
facility in accepting me as a Partisan made me reject the word
"dictator" for "savior."

He handed me a cigarette, a Russian one, half of which was
tube and the other tobacco, and I started lighting it at the
wrong end. Tito laughed, leant forward, and said, "This end,
please."

He thanked me for the work the boys and I had done for
their wounded, and told me that Jela had written to him
about us. He asked me how I liked the Croats, and whether

I was happy working with them; then he asked me to give him my ideas of how we could improve the medical situation and the medical service.

I told him that the main needs were three. First, better food for the wounded. Second, evacuation to Italy, where they could rest in peace and without the constant fear of attack and murder. And third, the wider dissemination of modern knowledge in the treatment of war wounds.

"Yes," he replied. "I read your speech given at the Glina conference." I told him that I had had the idea of starting a medical school, where the students who were working as doctors in the brigades could come for a short period, and we could work together for mutual good. Yes, he thought that a grand idea. Would I come down to Bosnia and work here at Drvar?

"No," I replied. "I have a fairly large hospital in Croatia, I know the Croatians and like them, and now they know and understand me. Besides, the little equipment I have is in Croatia, as are my two assistants Bill and Ian, and my Yugoslav boys, Voyasin and Ivo."

Tito looked up at me, and with a half smile coming over his face said slowly, "I need you in Bosnia."

I said nothing for a moment, then looked up at him and said, "I greatly prefer Croatia." "Ah well," he said, "the need here is much greater, there will be more fighting here, and after you have seen our Bosnian hospitals, I am sure you will stay with us. I shall speak to General Maclean about it all."

Coffee came in, served in dainty cups and sweet with sugar. Tito leant back in his chair and spoke to Colonel Krause, who left us for a moment.

I looked out through his windows, curtained with parachute silk, and saw the dark hills on the other side of the valley; faintly I heard machine-gun fire and Tito turned and looked

out too. "You hear?" he said; his expression changed slowly
from one of paternal kindliness to that of the severe military
commander. "You hear?" he repeated. "There is too much
work here, too much suffering, too many dead, and we have
too few doctors."

He spoke then about the future and asked me about our
new Medical Service in New Zealand. I couldn't help wondering at the breadth of his information in these very trouble-
some and darkened days. I told him about our country and
its inherent wealth and great social progress; I told him of the
happiness of the people, and of the almost complete lack of
poverty. He asked about our educational system and our uni-
versities. "Yes," he added, "and we have so little."

The walls of the room were also covered in parachute silk
and behind his desk was a great map of Yugoslavia; a British
map, I noted. The room seemed small in comparison with the
man behind the desk; his vision was so large. The afternoon
had fled and as I rose to go the darkened valley outside caught
my eye in turning toward Tito. His thinning silver hairs caught
the last gleam of light and as we shook hands he said, "There
are three things that I want you to do. Help our wounded here
in Bosnia; ask, as only you can ask, that our wounded be evacuated from all over the country to Italy, and tell the world of
our suffering."

The door closed, shutting me from a great man. The Partisan sentry, just a boy, saluted us, and we climbed down the
ladder to where our horses were waiting. There seemed to be
nothing to say; it had all been said. I swung into the saddle
and slowly the horses walked back past the sawmill, then up
the road into Drvar, and thence to the British Mission, firing
still echoing over the hills in the night.

CHAPTER 3

A *Lithuanian Doctor*

I was to stay in Bosnia, and next day I spent the morning planning the new hospital. Colonel Krause told me that away up in the mountains above Tito's retreat was a partly built hospital in the forest. They would put it in order immediately in spite of the snows, and we could start work as soon as my boys arrived. I sent a long signal to Bari, asking for more stores to open the hospital, and later set out with Colonel Krause to visit a nearby collection of wounded.

We rode on horseback over the crisp snows and up into the mountains. He asked a lot about medical stores and told me that few had as yet been dropped by air. I couldn't understand this, for I knew that at the medical store in Brindisi there were hundreds of tons waiting to come in. I listened and said nothing. We met a peasant Bosnian girl coming down the mountainside singing. She passed us, stopped, and turned back to watch us riding up the stony path, for the melting snows had washed the track clean. Then I heard her sing again, sad and tragic, in microtonal intervals that were very strange to us. Krause turned to me and said, "Song is all they have left now."

The divisional hospital was ghastly. In one small room I saw sixteen *drugovi* lying on the floor, without mattress or blanket, all with active tuberculosis. In another room were three recently wounded, all with general peritonitis and the *facies Hippocratica*. All would die within a few days. They asked me to see an arm with a mortar wound in the biceps. A great deal of the muscle had been torn away, but the neurovascular bundle was intact. It was to be amputated in the morning. "Why?" I asked. "Well, it will go gangrenous if we don't," they replied. So I said to the German-Jewish doctor in charge, "For God's sake don't amputate it; think of the man's future." Ah!" he replied. "We can only think of the present." Next morning off it came.

We left after two hours. But those two hours showed me quite clearly that our path lay up the opposite side of the valley into the forest, where we could work in our own way and bring to these Partisans some hope for the future.

Two days later I went away eastward to another hospital. This one had moved on the average of every four nights, carrying all its wounded with it. The doctor, a Lithuanian, was a great chap. He told me that in civil life he had been in the administrative side of medicine and had never done an operation in his life. But here he was, in these Bosnian mountains, operating on every wounded Partisan who came in, and operating well. He was using plaster of Paris wherever possible, when he had it, and he followed with almost religious fervor the teachings of the Vienna surgeon Böhler. Böhler's book was his only personal possession, and when I looked at his instruments and his equipment, I was proud to have met such a man. We had a drink of *rakija* before I left to return to Drvar, and while sitting there with his commissar he told me how the Germans had come to his town a year before. They called on the mayor of that Lithuanian town, demanding food for a whole division. The people had nothing to give. "Well," said the German officer, "twenty-five hostages will be shot unless you produce it." And twenty-five were. That night one of his friends threw a grenade into the room where the German colonel slept. Three hundred were shot in reprisal. The doctor's daughter was caught and taken to the German brothel, and his wife was shot while attempting to escape to the woods. I asked how he escaped. He smiled and said that in the morning he was lined up to be shot with the mayor and other city officials. The machine guns opened fire. He was hit in the chest and fell to the ground. The person next to him, a lawyer, fell dead on top of him. All day he lay still, hardly able to breathe, and at night he crawled away to a friend's house, where he lay hidden for three days. Then by night he made his way to the forest and lived with the Lithuanian Partisans, and gradually made his way to Yugoslavia, taking about six months on the journey.

Now he was a fighter doctor, working among the *drugovi*, always, despite his tragedy, with a smile for them; always sacrificing himself that they could have more, and filled with that almost holy fire which drives martyrs to the grave.

As I crossed the snows alone toward the valley of the Una, the picture of that Lithuanian village was vivid before me, and the dark-skinned doctor lying among the dead. His journey down through occupied territory and his work among the wounded peasantry, filled with the same righteous fire as they in the fight for liberation, made me feel how little I had really done in this world struggle. I remembered some hospital messes in Cairo; I felt a little ashamed.

The snow was gone from the streets of Drvar. I looked up at the cliff where yesterday I had been with Tito. Above the darkened rim of Yasekovac was a starlit sky. The tired horse walked between the dead, bombed houses toward the British Mission, and as I turned from the main road I heard song soaring into the night, and something told me that these people would have victory with the new dawn.

CHAPTER 4

Hotel and Hospital Combined

The brigadier never had his breakfast with us; indeed breakfast was a dull meal. Randolph Churchill was never up, and Andrew had his somewhere else, so it meant that only the waifs and strays turned up for it. But this morning the brigadier did arrive, and, seeing me, he said, "Oh! Come down to my office as soon as you finish, will you?" I wondered what the hell I had done now. However, when I arrived he asked me when the hospital at Otocevas would be ready, for he would like me to take charge of a mission in the meantime. I asked, "Where?" "Petrovac," he replied. An American colonel had been in charge, but he had been called to Italy, and now that the snow was melting fast they hoped to be able to land some planes there to bring in supplies and someone had to be on the spot.

Next day I started riding to Petrovac, which lay over the mountains, past Ostrel, on the Knin–Bihac road. It was a grand ride. Once we left the valley of the Una and began real climbing, the view became superb—Yasekovac towering up on the right, mountains stretching away to the southern distant blue behind us, and the white, snow-covered slopes leading up to the green pine forests above us. Such a morning! I turned back and looked at the valley of the Una and the town of Drvar lying so peacefully below. A lark sang in the sky; not a sign or sound of war anywhere. I passed a Bosnian pony coming down laden with hay for the Partisan horses at Drvar, its sure feet stepping in the tracks made by some horse before it. An old woman followed it, a bundle of raw wool on her shoulder which she spun as she walked, spinning and singing to herself an old song from Lika to which the Partisans had put new words "*Druže Tito.*" It recalled to me nights we had spent in the peasant houses of Lika, coming to Plitvice. They would sing verse after verse, adding verses to suit the occasion. Many times Bill and I tried to capture its melody but couldn't. The old woman looked up as she passed, her tragic face lit by the dark blue *ruta* around her hair. Her fingers momentarily stopped the spindle, then she passed, singing to her horse ahead carrying hay for Tito's horses.

The track steepened and we entered scattered patches of timber. Just then I saw above me and coming over the pass out from the forest, a whole train of horses laden with hay, and as I was looking at them, down from the sky came a Heinkel. It swooped over Ostrel, and, sighting the peasants and their horses, in a second it was firing at them and dropping bombs among the horses. My own horse started at the explosion and jumped from the track into a few trees. I slid from the saddle and led it under cover, then lay down between some stones and watched. The horse train was in confusion. I could hear a horse shrieking and whinnying. It had been hit and had rolled down into a hollow. The peasants were shaking their fists at the plane, which had swerved away over Drvar and was now coming back again. Several of the horses had thrown off their loads, and when the peasants saw the plane swooping around to return, they frantically started to lead the horses back into the forest. But the plane was over in a moment. I heard the shrieking whine of the guns and saw another horse roll down the hillside. Then silence. The plane disappeared over the pass and the sun still shone above. I hurried up and reached the scene in about half an hour. Two horses were dead and a Bosnian mother sat sobbing in the snow beside her dead husband.

Down over the pass I saw beneath me the *polje* of Petrovac.

Far in the distance was the German airdrome at Bihac, whence the plane had doubtless come. Primroses were already in bloom along the roadside, and around a burnt-out house clusters of primroses and winter roses made a bright patch in the melting snows. From the *polje* below smoke rose from chimneys, and in the middle distance I saw Petrovac, the mosque jutting its tower above the white roofs.

It was late afternoon when I arrived at the military mission, to find that the American, Colonel Farish, had already packed up to go, for a British plane was due to land that night. For days about five hundred *drugovi* and Bosnian girls had marched backward and forward across the landing strip to harden the snow, and the R.A.F. sergeant had decided that the strip was ready for that night. I took over the mission and the colonel showed me the running of it. The main function was to receive stores dropped by parachute during the night, hand them over to the Partisans, and take care of any personnel who might drop. When it was dark, at 7 P.M., a wagon arrived and away went Colonel Farish. Later he was killed parachuting, I think in Albania. He was a good chap, and I wished he were staying, for I felt considerably more at home with him than with others of the mission personnel. He left some *rakija*, the first I had had for some time, and some parachutes for trading with, so that night I lay in bed with a drink beside me and a good book I found in the stores, and waited until eleven o'clock came. Precisely on time I heard our plane fly overhead toward the strip. Then silence, and I knew it had landed. Fifteen minutes later back again it flew, heading for Italy, some four hours away.

Next day the first thing I did was to get the mission cleaned. As usual the lavatory was appalling, so I had it scrubbed and disinfected. Then the rooms—and as I was so engaged the *komanda mesta*, the head of the village Soviet, came to

see me. He was an enormously tough-looking young man, a
Bosnian woodsman. He didn't like the British much; he told
me that he couldn't understand them. I poured out two *rakijas*
and produced some chocolate. We lit cigarettes and he took
up the book I was reading, Galsworthy's *White Monkey*. "Ah
yes!" he said. "I have read a book by that author translated into
Yugoslav. It was about an English family called Forsyte."
This opened my eyes, and I asked what other English authors
he had read. "Well," he replied, "I am reading now a big book
called *The History of the World*, by H. G. Wells." He asked
me if I had read any books by Yugoslav authors. Shamefacedly
I had to confess that I hadn't. Then we discussed airplane
landing and the control of stores, and just as he turned to go
he told me to expect that night about twenty American airmen
whose planes had been shot down. They were coming to await
evacuation from the country.

This was a handful, I thought as I looked over the shelf con-
taining a few comforts and stores. I rang up Drvar and asked
for confirmation. No, they hadn't heard of any U.S. airmen,
but they might have come from the north, in which case they
wouldn't hear. I asked for some stores and clothes to be sent
over. They replied that they had little enough themselves, but
would do what they could. I then asked if they would wireless
Italy and ask for some stores to be dropped to us as soon as
possible. Yes, they would.

Hardly had I finished when a courier arrived and behind him
some thirty American airmen. Most of them were completely
exhausted from days of walking. Nearly all had diarrhea, many
had extremely bad feet, none had any soap or other toilet
things, and most of them only had their big ungainly flying
boots, which were completely useless in the snow. We got
them a meal. They were struck a bit dumb when they had
beans served to them yet again, but it was all we had, so that

was that. We did have some good hot coffee, but before many of them had time to drink it, they fell asleep on the floor where they lay. The ones who were really ill were put into houses, but the rest slept on straw in an old hall.

Next morning I received word that more were coming and among them some escaped prisoners of war—two very ill. I sent a courier to Drvar to wireless the 15th Air Force and ask for food and medical comforts to be dropped from one of their planes, and at the same time to send over all they could possibly spare in the way of blankets and clothes. I took sixty parachutes from the underground hiding place and made the beds a bit warmer. At lunch time two wagons arrived with the sick boys. One was a New Zealander called Morrow. He had roaring pneumonia and the others had bad dysentery and were very dehydrated and worn out from their long journey. So we started a real hospital again as well as running a hotel. Almost straight away trouble started, for the American pilots were all well supplied with dollars as escape money, and they began swamping the food market. Then the peasants wouldn't sell to the townspeople or to me, and I had the Council of Liberation hot on my trail trying to get it stopped. I spoke to the American officers about it, and they replied, "Well, are we to go hungry?" But when I explained the situation fully to them, they gave me the dollars and we bought the extra food through the council itself.

Every day brought its problems. They all asked why a plane had not come for them and when it would come. How many would it take? I said probably twelve. There were now seventy waiting.

The only way to deal with them was to take down the dates when they were shot down, and from that list I made a roster showing who had priority in leaving. Typhus began in the village, and the next trouble was in getting them to have their clothes disinfested. This meant showering and waiting in a very cold building until the clothes came out of the disinfestor. The sensible ones made no complaint, but three said they weren't going to shower in this weather. So that needed fixing. On the whole they were good boys, but they were always hungry, they had no beds and no fresh clothes, and they had too much money.

One night the *komanda mesta* came again, and after we had been talking a while he told me that a very serious thing had happened. I knew in a moment—one of the boys had been caught with a woman. It had been reported to him, and he would have to report it to Tito's headquarters. I suggested that he leave it until I had found out about it, and over another *rakija* he agreed. I soon found the enterprising airman, a lad from Kansas. "Yes," he admitted, "it was all too easy. I was billeted by you in her house; her husband is a Mohammedan and away in Bihac. I slept on the bed and she used to sleep every night on a rug on the floor. She suggested one night the bed was softer, and so it was." The unfortunate thing was that one of her neighbors had come in in the early morning. Next night over a cigarette I told the *komanda mesta* that the woman was a Mohammedan and her husband was fighting for the Germans. "Oh!" he said. "That woman. She belongs to Hitler's 'Lonely Women's Corps'—but watch the airman." I had to, and he was lucky that sulfa drugs were available.

One of these boys had had a miraculous escape. He was just a kid of nineteen. He had dysentery badly when he came, so I got to know him quite well, and he told me his story. He was a tail gunner in a Liberator. They were bombing Maribor and had just turned to come back when the plane was hit. He felt the tremendous shock and the explosion, then turned to get his parachute, which was kept hanging in the fuselage near the turret. He walked along the fuselage and found that the rest of the plane had disappeared, and that he was sailing down in the tail. His parachute was gone, so he had nothing else to do but to sit in the tail and wait. Down to earth he sailed and hit the ground right way up. He walked out of the tail completely unharmed—I expect the only man who has ever done that.

The Americans were still briefing their pilots in 1944, in the event of their being hit and bailing out, to make for the nearest Chetnik unit. Indeed, some were even briefed to make for towns held by the Germans. We sent messages to the 15th Air Force telling them about this, but even so it continued for quite six months. Presumably someone read our intelligence reports—but who?

Morrow nearly had to stay permanently in Yugoslavia. Luckily we had some sulfapyridine, and with it he just managed to get around the corner. He had escaped from a German train near Maribor, and it would have been tough luck had he failed to make the grade, having gotten to the only landing strip that was working at that time.

Eventually planes did come, but not before the airmen had made four trips down to the airfield in the snow in the middle of the night. Then one night down swooped four planes. They all tumbled in and in less than twenty-five minutes were on their way back to Italy and home.

CHAPTER 5

The Russian Mission Arrives

Though the British Mission worked extremely hard and long hours, yet I always felt that their lives were wrapped up in code books and the pseudo-security of a safe territory. They lost much by being a mission, shut off as they were from personal contacts with the actual fighting Partisans. They did not see the daily heroism shining through the stark terror of the civilians' lives, nor the look of hope on the faces of the wounded. They did not share the long trudges through the snow at night or, what was more important, the zeal that burnt in everyone's heart for Tito and the liberation.

They were truly a little bit of Whitehall there in the mountains, almost like an isolation hospital, and we who worked outside appeared to be beyond their walls.

But the bridge between diplomacy and humanity is a narrow one, as was clearly shown when the Russian Mission arrived a short time later.

That was a great moment for the Partisans in more ways than one. The temporary air strip was crowded with Partisans in their nondescript uniforms: some Italian; some old Yugoslav Army in buff gray; and some light blue German uniforms taken from German dead. Thousands were there and the excitement was running fever-high. The official British Mission was there to meet them also, Brigadier Maclean in his battle dress with scarlet tabs, and the other British officers and men all in battle dress. If I remember correctly, one very important young man in the mission had his walking stick with him for support. Tito arrived with his staff; Tito in his unadorned uniform of gray modeled on the old Yugoslav Army style, the aging Dr. Ribar, General Arso Voyvanovich, commissars and colonels, captains and couriers, and a thousand *drugovi*. The plane came over the skyline and swooped around the field where fires had been lit to show the pilot the runway. Smoke curled up to heaven, bearing its prayer to the coming men of liberation. One circle, then the DC-3, piloted by Russian airmen, swept down the field, landed, and taxied to a standstill.

This was the greatest moment of the war for them. "*Zivio*

Marshal Stalin," "*Zivio Marshal Tito*" thundered across the plain; Tito and his staff started toward the opening door of the plane; thousands of *drugovi* pressed forward; suddenly there emerged the Russian general, and the whole multitude stopped and wondered. As he emerged, his decorations, great stars pinned across his breast, gleamed and sparkled in the sun. His sky-blue cloak caught the gentle breeze and fluttered like a banner across the drab green of the plane; his great shining top boots glittered like glass, and the gold peeping from the folds of the cloak blinded the *drugovi*. I watched Tito. Just for a moment he looked at his own plain clothes and then stepped forward. I could imagine their thoughts. Was this the *Rdeča Armada,* so splendid in the morning sun? The general was quickly followed by his staff officers, some in bright blue, some in red, but all so very splendid in comparison with the mud-spattered, stolen clothing of the Partisans. Great shouting and tumult filled the air. *Drugovi* rushed forward and kissed the pilot and as the shouting died and the captains and the kings departed, it seemed that the fate of Yugoslavia was sealed.

CHAPTER 6

Our New Hospital

Bill, Ian, and Ivo, leaving Voyasin in Croatia, arrived down from Croatia and together we left Drvar, crossed the Una by the old sawmill. We climbed the hill towards Ostrel. Halfway up we left the main Bihac road and turned into the mountains for another hour's walk. The snow had melted rapidly during these few weeks, and it wasn't until we reached the high *polje,* or plain, of Otocevas that we came on clumps of snow still lying. It was midday when we crossed the saddle into the *polje.*

Gentians in their thousands shone blue in the brown grass. Crocuses crept right up to the snow's edge, and ahead of us we saw the green forest where our new hospital was.

We crossed the valley and entered the forest. The great dark pines reaching up to the sky hid the sun from us, but in open glades the fresh green pine tips sheened the trees anew with the promise of spring. We turned from the track and followed fresh wagon marks on the new earth through the trees. Then, quite suddenly, we came upon our new hospital.

There it lay, silent in the forest, four log cabins hidden by the trees. The roofs were camouflaged with pine branches, and outside one of the cabins was a group of Partisans. "*Zdravo*," they cried. "*Zdravo*," we answered.

Suddenly, who should rush out from the door but our old friend Zena. "Well, I'm here!" she said. "And what a journey I had through the German lines to get here." She kissed us and led us inside. It was dark, for we had no glass for windows; there already, on homemade benches, were patients waiting for us. "*Zdravo!*" I said again, and went around to them all, shaking them by the hand. Then Zena led us away to a small hut which would be ours. Soon we had a meal of polenta and coffee; just the same as the old days, I thought, and there was a cook for us, too. Everything was grand. Zena sat with knees crossed. "Please, a cigarette," she said, and we produced many for her. She sat looking at us, and then a whole torrent of reminiscences poured forth. Do you remember this one and that one? Do you recall how we did this and that? Do you recollect the day the German planes came over and how busy we were? And so on.

Next day we started operating, and next day, too, we heard that many stores had been dropped for us at Petrovac. Some wounded arrived by night in *kola* drawn by oxen from Petrovac, some twenty miles away. Some arrived by day, carried by

Bosnian girls through the woods from caves and hideouts all around the district. Some had never been treated at all; others had been operated upon and required aftercare. More guillotine amputations. Osteomyelitis cases by the dozen, and before we knew it, we had our hospital full.

It wasn't long before the peasants began to come to us too. First in ones and twos, and then in dozens, until each afternoon was spent in handling outpatients and doing what we could for the civilian sick. Five years' surgery was piled up in Bosnia and there was work for months ahead.

Ian had left us to join the Balkan Air Group, and one night Vic Cameron, a London Scot, dropped in by parachute to take his place. Vic was a great hulking fellow, rather full of his own knowledge, and not so adaptable as Bill, but he worked very hard and very well. His one fault was that he made no attempt to learn the language, whereas to Bill the language came almost naturally.

Soon we had Balkan beams made and erected over the beds by the local woodsmen, and all our fractures were suspended from these beams and traction applied. Many we refractured and tried to pull out, so that the legs would be somewhere near equal length. I did a lot of plastic surgery, and covered many large raw areas with skin grafts taken with an ordinary razor blade. We soon ran out of Steinman pins for fractures, and used ordinary four-inch nails, and for our ligatures it was always the unraveled silken cord from parachutes. Gloves we had none; gowns we had none; and lots of the essentials, according to our standards, we did without, but somehow we managed well and nothing untoward ever seemed to happen.

One day General Goyko Nickolic came to visit us. The last time I had seen him was at the conference in Glina. He went around the hospital, looking at all the new things and asking us about our technique. Then, as we had a meal under the trees (a poor meal, that day, of stewed beans), he told me that twenty-five doctors would be arriving in a few days for a three weeks' course in surgery. Also a batch of Bosnian Partizanke to be trained in hospital nursing. We were working about sixteen hours a day as it was, but I knew that we would manage somehow. I had no textbooks for reference, no blackboard, even no paper to write on, but he said that it didn't matter. He rode away at 3 P.M. and I called my commissar, Borgo, and Bill, and we made plans for the future.

In three days they were all there and the hospital became a very busy place indeed. Most of them were from the brigades and many were as yet unqualified. All were most eager to learn, and I found them most receptive. At 6 A.M. we started with a lecture on surgical anatomy. It was curious, as the days went on, how much of the academic anatomy returned to me. But we dealt almost entirely with the practical side, limbs particularly, for the great percentage of war wounds occurs in the limbs. At seven we had breakfast, and then we went around the wards for an hour, picking out this case or that and using it as a text for our talk. Translating was very difficult, but Ivo did very well and it was surprising how quickly we got on and how little the language difficulty really mattered to people keen to listen. They used Latin freely when discussing medical situations, whereas we use it hardly at all. But I remembered it and quickly got into the way of phrasing my teaching in Latin. At 10 A.M., or whenever we were finished in the wards, we had a break, and then we started operating. Before every case we discussed what we should do and how, then one of them would give the anesthetic and I would operate or they would operate with my assistance. These were most instructive mornings and when lunch came, usually under the trees, discussions were continued until often the polenta and the coffee were cold.

In the afternoon three of them would come to our "Outpatients Department" and all afternoon we would see and discuss the cases that came to us for treatment. Much ground was thus covered, though it slowed up the work tremendously; not only slowed it up, but banked it up, too. Usually at 6 P.M. there would be the final lecture on some academic or theoretical subject such as the sulfa drugs, or shock, or blood transfusion, and so on.

Night would come and in the next room I would hear the work of the day being discussed and argued about until the late hours. We needed no stimulus in this work, for we were helping not only the wounded in our care but indirectly the wounded all over the country.

One day a Dornier came. It was early morning and luckily the fires were not yet lit. The great lumbering plane swept over Yasekovac almost at treetop level and searched up and down the forest for our hospital. This worried Commissar Borgo, because, he said, the Germans were sure to know that much medical material had come to us and they were very short of material. Not only that, but in their policy of total extermination they concentrated particularly on the Yugoslav hospitals, many of which had already been burnt to the ground, and the wounded murdered in their beds or burnt to death in the hospitals. This altered all our routine, for now it was too dangerous to have smoke rising from the forest during the day, so cooking and water heating for the operating theater had to be done at night. Every day now they came over, and every day the wounded grew more apprehensive. Bill and I made a plan for immediate evacuation, which would entail taking all the fractured legs down from their suspension beams and putting them in plaster.

One night a courier arrived with a note from the mission at the dropping field at Petrovac. Would I come at once? The mission had been bombed that morning and there were British casualties. Yes, the courier would wait for me with his truck. "Where?" I asked, for no truck could get near the hospital. "Oh! Down the bottom of the hill," he replied. Bill got a few things ready for me, I changed into warmer clothes, and, slinging the medical haversack across my back, went out into the night. Through the dark forest I stumbled with the courier, and then down onto the Petrovac–Drvar road. There, instead of a truck to meet me, was a motorcycle. And such a cycle! The first difficulty was that it had no lights.

I sat on the carrier and hung onto the rider like grim death. The road was all uphill, and a rough mountain road at that. Every five hundred yards we would plunge into the uphill bank or jump downhill and then have to drag the bloody cycle up again. My legs were all bruises and most of the bottles and ampoules in the haversack were broken, but on we went. Luckily the night had a half-moon, which showed the direction of the road. Many times I felt like saying, "To hell with the cycle; let's walk." But I thought of the chaps lying there and just held on tight. We reached the top. The track was slippery with thawed ice. We started down into the *polje*, and the courier turned off the engine and began free-wheeling. I managed to remonstrate. "Oh!" he replied. "I haven't enough petrol to reach Petrovac unless I free-wheel." We slipped and braked, we skidded and stopped, and when we reached the open road where the drops were much greater, I was too terrified even to ask him to stop. But we reached Petrovac. The mission had moved since the bombing and it took an hour to find where it was. One man had died in the meantime, and the other, a wireless operator called Price, was seriously injured.

I fixed him up for the night and stayed with him until he went to sleep and then one of the Partisans took over. In the morning I gave him a large dose of morphia and a small one of pentothal, and we lifted him onto a truck and started back again to the hospital. I kept him pleasantly anesthetized all the journey, for even to the fit and well it was a journey of much discomfort. The truck went as far as it was able to. Bill had sent down stretcher-bearers to meet us, and we carried him for the next three hours through the forest to the hospital. Late that night we operated and when he awoke he found himself with a great number of wounded Partisans and with three of his four limbs in plaster of Paris and his head swathed in bandages.

A few days after this I received word to go to a village called Drenitz, where there were some wounded. It was over Yasekovac mountain and about thirty miles away. By this time we were used to walking long distances.

I took Bill and one of my couriers with me to help to carry the equipment, such as we had, and left the medical school to run itself while I was away. It was a welcome break from teaching, and a welcome break to see the sun shining straight from its heaven and not being filtered by the forest. We reached the village in the evening and I stayed with the head of the village committee, or soviet. All the villagers came in during the evening to see an "Englishman." (Bill still loathed being called an Englishman. I had gotten over it.)

We found out that since we had left the wounded had been carried away to another district, for the Germans were very close and it was not safe to leave them there. We had a long talk that night about their troubles, and they told me how the Germans and Chetniks came one day and surprised the women at work in the patches of corn when the men were in the forest. They shot ten women who attempted to run away; they shot four children who ran with the women, then they took the remainder into the village and demanded food and *rakija*. The villagers gave all they had that was not hidden. Then the Germans went into every house and took what they fancied

and smashed everything else they saw. Finally they burnt to
the ground the houses of two known Partisan soldiers, and
took their womenfolk away, raped them, and killed them. This
was a common story of most villages in Bosnia.

In the morning the host escorted us up through the forest
and showed us a hidden underground bunker where food and
wool were stored. It was most ingenious. He pulled the branch
of a dead tree which was lying on the ground, and the whole
tree moved quite easily, disclosing beneath a wooden trap door.
This he lifted and we went down into a cave about a hundred
feet long by forty feet wide. It was moderately dry and filled
with boxes of food, dried beans, peas, maize, looms for weaving,
bottles of *rakija*, skins, and everything else the village possessed.
By noon we reached the bush railway which ran from Jajce to
Drvar, and we said good-by to our guide and continued our
way along the rail track, still fairly deep in snow.

About three we heard a plane in the distance near Ostrel
and heard bombs exploding. The Germans had been hunting
for days for the locomotive which was used to clear the line
with a snowplow. But it worked only at night and during the
day was run into the forest and hidden. We stopped and tried
to see the planes but couldn't. Then more and more bombing,
and I wondered if they had caught a pony convoy taking to
Drvar material parachuted in from our planes at Petrovac.

We had just entered a long cutting in the railway lines,
when suddenly we turned and saw the Heinkel coming toward
us at what seemed a very slow speed. It was following along the
rail track hunting for the engine. We were in the cutting with
no hope of getting under cover of the trees. The pilot saw us
and swooped lower, then the screaming of the machine guns.
But all went too high, for we had lain down in the snow. Evidently he had no bombs left, but as the tail gunner spotted us
we were showered with bullets. Bullets hit the snow with a

hot hiss and in that brief moment I was sure I was killed. One
moment and he was gone. I lifted my head and saw Bill lift
his head too. My God! What an escape. We just stood and
looked at the row of holes in the snow. "Let's get out of here,"
muttered Bill, and in case the plane came back we ran through
the cutting and hid in the forest beyond.

We heard him gradually fading into the distance and then
caught a glimpse of him flying over toward Bihac, so we started
again for home, but very carefully. A mile and a half from
Ostrel we found the engine belching smoke in a little siding
built off from the main line into the bush. The fires had been
lit when darkness and safety came, and we loaded the wounded
from the raid of the Heinkel into the van, went to Ostrel, then
carried them ten miles and began working as soon as we
arrived back at the hospital.

The next few days were days of peace. Beautiful sunny days;
birds singing above us; meals all outside in the shade of the
forest, and our only concern the daily visits of the Heinkel,
usually about eight in the morning and four in the afternoon.
Price, the wounded British wireless operator, was doing well.
The nurses were working like Trojans and Zena was happily
entertaining each new visitor. The higher the rank the more
Zena entertained. Every night I had two of the students in for
polenta and I was enjoying every moment of the twenty-four
hours.

We had penicillin dropped by parachute now and it had already proved its inestimable value in recent wounds, particularly open fractures, which we operated upon and then closed
by secondary suture some days later. Our underground bunker
had been excavated and was ready for the stores should we
have to evacuate, and we were searching for a good place for
another in which we could accommodate all our patients if ever

the need came. General Nickolic was a frequent visitor and seemed duly grateful, and patients were beginning to arrive from far distances for consultation and help.

Talbot, the correspondent from Reuter's, arrived one day, more dead than alive, with a courier, and I took him around the hospital and showed him the spot where our local gray wolf was lying with her young. He stayed for lunch and told me that in a few days there would be a great anti-fascist meeting in Drvar and advised me to come down for it. The mission was giving a party for Tito and was going to present him with a jeep for his exclusive use; on what roads I just didn't know, seeing that the Germans were all around us in about a thirty-mile radius. But all seemed quiet enough during those days of early 1944.

CHAPTER 7

The Anti-Fascist Youth Congress

I decided to go to the Anti-Fascist Youth Congress for two reasons; mainly because I wanted to go and listen to what was said, and secondarily I wanted to order some special stores through the Drvar mission wireless link.

It was a sunny morning and I left the forest and crossed the little *polje* toward the steep escarpment which fell to the valley of the Una. A few cows still grazed contentedly among the stones and trees of the *polje*; gentians and crocuses still bloomed, shining in the brown grass, stars cerulean blue. A fox started and ran away in front of me over the ridge, and the ground squelched and sprang as my new heavy nailed boots sank into the uncovered, saturated topsoil. A peasant boy in his white homespun socks and bullock-hide shoes went laughing up the *polje*, driving a few sheep, tall, gaunt-looking animals just lately taken from the winter housing into the fresh air. I wondered how long it would be before he was engulfed in the terror, and as the crest of the escarpment was reached, I sat down and viewed the valley before me.

It was all so like home. Why, here was Lochindorb in New Zealand, seen again from the Rocky Dome. There was the rushing river below, and there the dark peaks beyond, crisscrossing the horizon like a jagged saw. People's faces flashed before me, pleasant, contented, happy New Zealanders who had never known murder in their midst; had never seen burnt churches with blood running down the steps; who walked freely through the mountains, never listening for the coming steps of terrorists; who never heard the rattle of machine-gun fire echo down their valleys; whose bellies never sank empty and scaphoid for lack of food; whose cattle browsed contentedly and whose hens and chickens scratched around stable yards. Yes! It was a long, long bridge which separated us, and the bridge had almost caved in.

I looked down again and saw the two great chimneys of the cellulose factories, and just beyond the rising ground where the British Mission worked. I knew that if I hurried I should be there for breakfast, or a cup of tea at least. The track was very steep and stony—a real goat track—so, swinging my rucksack firmly across my shoulders, I ran down it and in twenty minutes was on the railway and walking sedately, as became a British officer, into town.

The mission staff had altered slightly. Major Clarke had returned from one of the outstations and he greeted me cordially and said, "A cup of tea, Doc?" and we had one. Then we spoke of this and that. John was a product of Eton and the Guards, a brave soldier, and a good chap. He was as friendly as the brigadier was aloof, and amused us all by his references to the uncouth Colonial Empire, of which I was a member and, at that time, the sole representative. He told me that he was going down to Montenegro shortly and would give me his horse and saddle if I needed them. What a gift! Not for me, really, for I found walking just as quick as riding, but to carry our equipment if the need came—it was too good for words. I thanked him and we sat in the sun on the hillside above the mission and began speaking about the future. He didn't seem happy about it at all. It was all too quiet for John. I told him of our daily German reconnaissance planes and he pricked up his ears and warned me to be careful, for they had long envisaged an attack on Drvar, and he asked what plans we had made for escape.

We had made plans, of course; it was the first thing we ever did when we took over a new hospital; but plans very different from the rest of the mission, for we had wounded to look after and precious stores to carry. On the other hand, we were high in the mountains and deep in the forest, so it was easier for us.

As we talked, the new intelligence officer came and sat down with us. He told me that should I care to come to his room he would give me an account, with the aid of a map, of what was happening elsewhere. So I left John and walked down to the office. As we reached his room, we met a wing commander of the Air Force and Ian. They were just leaving for Glamoc Air Strip to put it into order for dropping supplies, and suddenly, as we were speaking, a German plane swept over Yasekovac across my mountain home and down into the valley of the Una. We watched it. Straight up the valley it came, perfectly level. "He's taking photos," the wing commander said. Randolph had appeared and stood looking for a moment, then disappeared. The plane continued on straight overhead, never a bomb, never a shot, flying fairly low. It continued until out of sight. We turned to one another and the wing commander said, "Glad I'm getting out from here, boys. There's dirty work in the air." He and Ian turned to the door where their rucksacks were lying on the ground and their ponies waited, loaded with stores. We shook hands and away they went to Glamoc.

The intelligence officer gave me a good résumé of local affairs and then of world affairs. I could see that he was a leftist and wondered how he had got into this mission, which was predominately Old School Tie. This cleavage was more noticeable at meals when he and Randolph began arguing. Randolph couldn't argue without getting difficult. I well remember one evening when an American colonel, who tried unsuccessfully to establish an American mission at Drvar, was present. He was a wealthy company promoter from New York, and his brain was agile, cold, and matter-of-fact. The question of the theory of democracy came up. There appeared very quickly to be a difference in the American and the British conceptions of democracy, and Randolph took up cudgels. Gradually the room emptied, for we had all heard Randolph before. As he became more heated, the American colonel just listened quietly, and then, with shrewdness and logic, tore Randolph's argument to shreds. Finally, with dignity the American rose and said good night.

With the new intelligence officer it was different, for he was no match for Churchill's Parliamentary training, and I was relieved when the time came for us to get on our coats and start for the meeting.

We arrived at the huge hall about 8:15 P.M. They had converted the complete cellar of the burnt-out cellulose factory into a meeting place, and when we went in, it was as though one had stepped into a great theater held tense with emotion. The atmosphere was electrical and the hundreds of delegates from all over Yugoslavia, many of whom had walked for months to get there, were awaiting the arrival of Tito. As we entered they stood and shouted, *"Zivio Churchill, Zivio Inglesi."* I sat between General Popovich, the renowned general poet of the 1st Corpus, and Colonel Voya, the medical colonel of the 1st Corpus. Between the Russian Mission, on one hand, and the British Mission, on the other, was an empty space with a central chair, and here, doubtless, Tito would sit. On the platform in front of us was the Anti-Fascist Youth Council, about twelve in all, with a central rostrum for the speaker of the moment. Behind seemed to be thousands of *drugovi* and *drugarice.* Every moment the air was shred with *"Zivio Marshal Stalin."* Then *"Zivio Marshal Tito"* followed by *"Tito—Tito—Tito"* in never-ending crescendos. Then a new arrival at the door, a personality, perhaps a Slovene or a Croat who had traveled miles and miles for this tense moment. Thunderous greeting would shake the air as he walked to his appointed seat. And so the evening wore on and still no Tito. Every seat was filled and hundreds were standing at the sides. Boys of fourteen and fifteen with hand grenades around their belts and Sten guns over their shoulders; girls with long hair, and knives in their belts.

At 9:30 Tito arrived. There was a momentary hush and then a great tumultuous shouting, *"Zivio! Zivio! Tito! Tito!"* and as he walked to the vacant central seat with General Arso Voyvanovich, the rhythm of *"Tito! Tito!"* must have reached the stars. He tried to silence the crowd, but for the first time in their lives they now saw their hero, they felt his magnetism spread, seize and envelop them, and stretch far and wide to embrace millions who couldn't hear. *"Tito! Tito! Tito!"* For here was the greatest general, the idealist saint, the bravest hero, and the wisest politician Yugoslavia had ever known, the hero of youth, and the founder of the new democracy.

Tito rose and held up his hand. Gradually quiet and then

stillness, almost deathly peace, swept over the assembly, and he sat down. He had lost the merry twinkle in his eye. The lines seemed deeper and the expression stronger. His hair seemed whiter, and his shoulders broader, for here he was giving to youth the pledge of freedom and the new hope that forever they should be free.

A girl stood on the central rostrum, a Montenegrin, the president of the Youth Council. She looked over the vast assemblage and with her right hand swept her hair from her forehead. Her Red Star burnt above the dark hair and her left hand grasped the lectern firmly and boldly. She spoke in a soft voice, but one full of passion and strength; she spoke of the aspirations of youth and the call to its leaders for the new democracy. She told of the unequal struggle and the bitterness of the fight; she told of the simple heroism of those who had fallen. Applause thundered after every few words and I could see emotion surging over her as she looked down on the birthplace of the new ideal, the hearts of her fellow fighters. She told of the birth of the movement and the place Tito had taken in the fight, and she spoke of the burning need for unity among the ranks, not only now, when Montenegrin, Slovene, Bosnian, Dalmatian, and Serb were meeting together, but for the future; she painted with swift, powerful strokes the picture of the new Yugoslavia.

Tito rose from his chair and advanced slowly to the rostrum. I turned and looked back into that vast cellar, dimly lit by the red and smoking flares. In that mystic glow every face gleamed, every eye shone with a spiritual fervor. And from every side arose the tumultuous, hypnotic chant of *"Tito! Tito! Tito! Tito!"* All my New Zealand identity, my very roots were shattered, swamped in the sea of emotion. I sat bewildered, exalted, a Partisan among the Partisans.

In a low, clear voice Tito delivered his message. He rang

out a clear clarion call to defeat the invader, to stamp out
fascism forever, and to work for unity when the Federated
Democratic Yugoslavia would be, not a caption hanging
from every wall, but a state, a great state, taking for the first
time in the history of the world its rightful place among the
nations. He saluted his soldiers and turned toward his seat.
Amid the deafening applause were tears, tears shed in joy and
adoration for their hero; every face looked transfigured; every
soldier grasped his gun more firmly.

Speech followed speech. The Russian envoy spoke, but how
flat after Tito! He spoke in dull Russian and then it all had
to be translated into Yugoslav. After all, there is little difference in the language. General Popovich spoke and was greeted
by tumultuous cheering, for the poet-general knew not only
how to fight but how to speak. Then, on behalf of the British
Mission, Churchill spoke. He had learnt his speech in Croatian. Every word he had memorized and he delivered it in
striking contrast to the monotones of the Russian officer. Fire,
enthusiasm, and forcefulness punctuated every word, and
when he sat down he was given a great ovation. Then followed
many *drugovi*, telling of their exploits against the enemy. I
saw Tito smile when one *drug*—he could not have been more
than fifteen years at the most, complete with hand grenades
hanging from his belt and Sten gun from his shoulder—
mounted the rostrum unafraid, and told the story of how he
had blown up a train and finished by shooting the German
patrol which arrived on the scene.

I tried hard to imagine such spontaneous declarations of
loyalty in our own army. But we have not seen the troubles,
nor have we suffered as these people have suffered. At midnight Tito rose to go; he walked quickly toward the door
before most people realized what was happening, and then the
ecstasy faded, and in the afterglow as I walked back to the

mission I knew the power of youth; I knew the power of resistance and the fever of hope which drove them on. Yugoslavia would be free.

Before I left the next morning for Yasekovac, the brigadier called me to his room and asked me if I had made any plans for escape. I said I had, but why? He told me that there had been increasing German interest in Drvar and they thought that an attack was imminent. Should it take place, the mission would go to Potoci, where a place had already been prepared. I thanked him and told him that I would confer with the medical authorities, who doubtless had some plan, and would let him know what they advised about the evacuation of the hospital.

This I did. I saw General Nickolic before leaving, and he told me that another hospital was being prepared for me near Potoci, twenty miles distant, and that I would receive plenty of warning should the situation become at all serious. So I left Drvar and started with John Clarke's pony to climb the road up past the mill, and so on toward Ostrel and finally up into the forests and home.

All was well in the hospital and that afternoon in every ward I told them all the details of the meeting. In the evening the doctors gathered and we had a great dinner of beans and tea, followed by a rum ration under the trees, for it was summer now and the snows had gone. Long into the night we talked and above us flitted the small bats of the forest attracted by the glowing cigarette ends. Somewhere a nightingale sang and just as I was going to bed a fresh batch of wounded arrived. Bill and I looked them over and put them to bed, for all were old cases, and would be better done as teaching lessons at a future date.

There was among this group of wounded a thin, dark Bosnian boy about eighteen, for all the world like an unborn fetus.

In fact, we called him "the Fetus," though his real name was Boris. He had a large perpendicular wound of the back in the lumbar region, fairly deep. The bullet had removed the spinous process of the vertebra, but luckily his cord was undamaged, though he couldn't walk owing to lack of stability. His back muscles were gone and the huge raw area kept him in constant pain every time he moved. Fear of being caught made his terror worse, for he had been in a hospital the Germans had found, and all except him had been burnt to death. He had crawled into a drain filled with water alongside the building and had lain there while the building burnt itself down beside him.

He was an excellent case for medium-thickness skin grafts. So we cleaned his wound up with sulphonamide powder, removed a piece of dead bone which had kept the infection going, and when he was ready, we covered the complete area with massive grafts taken from all parts of his body. He was so thin that the actual available donor areas were small in comparison with the need. But we managed to split off enough skin to cover the raw area completely, and then applied a dressing strapped well down with elastoplast and carried him back to bed. With the aid of daily nembutal we kept him at rest for a week and then undid the bandages to find practically all the area healed and covered with fresh growing skin. In a fortnight he was on his feet. His gratitude was boundless and he followed us around like a dog. Poor old Boris! I met him months after with a group of wounded running from a German patrol. I had no time to look at his back; just time to grasp his hand. I often wonder what happened to him.

A fortnight after the meeting my commissar, Borgo (the best fellow in the world), came to me and said, "*Majore*, the news is not good; I think the German plane which circles over

us every day has found us and we will be bombed." He told
me that only that day a plane had circled overhead and
watched a group of peasants carrying a sick woman up the hill
and enter the woods. This was bad, said Borgo, very bad; we
must stop the peasants coming to us. I didn't want to stop my
flow of clinical material, for they needed help as well as the
soldiers, otherwise who was to populate the country afterward? But nevertheless, rather than prejudice our safety, I
decided to stop it for a while at least.

Next day we started transferring some of our surplus stores
to the hidden underground bunker, or cave.

CHAPTER 8

Quick March

It all happened so suddenly. I was in the operating theater
doing a simple case of piles. The students were gathered
around, with Colonel Voya of the 1st Corpus and General
Nickolic. The piles were third-degree, and I was explaining the
Gabriel technique for their removal. The windows were open,
for it was hot, and as I talked I was conscious of planes circling
overhead. I stopped talking and hurried a little. Some of the
students, with Voya and Nickolic, went outside to see what
was happening. Then down the bombs came. Not the long-
drawn-out wail of falling bombs in London, where they fell
from a great height, but a quick hiss, then a momentary stillness, and then the crash of the explosion. They kept falling.
The noise echoed and reverberated up and down the *polje*, in
and out of the trees. Everyone hurried outside into the forest.
I finished the operation quickly by tying up everything with a
clamp. Then Bill and I carried the still-unconscious patient

into the woods. The students were carrying the patients outside from the wards and Zena was directing operations at the
other huts. Luckily not one bomb hit the hospital and in five
minutes the raid was over. But it was enough. General Nickolic, who knew more than I did, immediately disbanded the
medical school and gave instructions to hide all the patients in
the forest. Then he disappeared and I never saw him again in
Yugoslavia.

All the afternoon Bill and I worked like Trojans, for all the
students had gone. We took down all the fractures on Balkan
beams and put them into plaster. Borgo organized the carrying parties. All those that could walk, or even crawl, left early,
taking food and water with them, and disappeared into the
forest with another commissar and a medical student. I never
saw them again.

The rest, completely bedridden, were carried away up the
mountain into the forest and with them went the Lithuanian
doctor, who had just joined me in the medical school, and a
few nurses. Then in the night Bill and Vic and I carried most
of the precious medical stores into our underground bunker.

Next day the hospital looked an awful shambles. Straw all
over the floor; pieces of old bandage lying everywhere; splints,
blood-covered and still with pieces of bandage tied to them,
were scattered on empty benches. Balkan beams stood empty,
like disused gallows. Vic took our own personal belongings,
treasured through many a previous retreat like this, and hid
them under some stones. When night fell, Zena, Bill, Vic, and
I, together with Borgo, had a meal in silence, wondering where
we should work next. I knew I would never have a school again
and that the peaceful days of Drvar were ended. Milica, our
cook, was terrified and wanted to start at once for Drvar,
where she had friends, but we persuaded her to stay, for it
would be safer for her, and a help for us too if we needed it.

Voyasin and Ivo were afraid of what was happening, for they also had been in many situations like this and knew what the Germans did to doctors and Partisans who helped the British. It was certain firing squad. We all oiled our guns and I dealt out hand grenades and ammunition. At 9 P.M. we had some *rakija* and went to sleep.

Next morning at six a great droning above woke us all. We rushed outside, fearing another bombing raid, but by the time we got beyond the trees where we could see what was happening the planes had passed. Then we heard bombing going on in Drvar just below and we knew that the long-expected attack on Tito's headquarters had come. I went back to get on some clothes and just as I emerged saw another wave of planes pass overhead. We watched them and saw descending from the sky hundreds of parachutists. Almost immediately came the sound of machine-gun fire and then another wave of bombers, each towing a glider.

We went back to the hospital and I ordered a meal, for we knew not what was in store for us. During the day Bill and I went into the forest and tried to find the wounded. We found the serious cases hidden and guarded deep in the forest; we did what we could and tried to find the walking wounded but could not. Price, the British wireless operator, was still fairly ill, and I did what I could to give him confidence. We returned to the hospital about 3 P.M., when a few wounded arrived. Four of them needed transfusion. Luckily we had hidden the blood in a deep hole near the hospital and we transfused them then and there in the forest, tying the bottles to the trees. We had no means of sterilizing anything, so we just didn't bother. I dressed them all, gave morphia, and sent them up into the forest. About 4 P.M. a courier arrived to say that there was a great battle going on in Drvar. Eight hundred German parachutists had dropped, followed by eighty gliders, all full of troops. The

British Mission had been heavily attacked and many were
wounded. Would I go down? I didn't know then, but later it
transpired that this courier was a Chetnik spy. I called Borgo
and Bill, and decided to leave Vic behind with Ivo, Voyasin,
and Zena and go down and have a look for them. We packed
a small medical kit and took with us some benzedrine tablets,
grenades, and our guns. The firing was still intense and wave
after wave of aircraft flew over every half hour or so. We left
the hospital and walked toward the escarpment edge. The sun
was shining serenely, but from the valley below smoke oozed
up, the smoke of battle. We lay down on the escarpment in
the sun, hiding under some rocks to wait for the evening. Aircraft passed so close overhead we could see the pilots. We lay
on our backs under scrub and fired at them. They were too
busy even to notice it.

Toward dusk we began descending into the town, coming
down just to the east of it. We passed a few peasants frantically
driving their three or four sheep ahead of them into the mountains. We passed one peasant's home completely wrecked by a
bomb; a dead woman lay scattered about in the mud outside
the door, while a child was crying within. Then another wave
of bombers came over.

The fighting seemed to be mainly on the low hills just
behind the cemetery. Already many houses were burning and
we could see the gliders lying along the flat of the river valley.
A burst of firing started from near Tito's *pecina* (cave) and
even as we looked we saw the old sawmill burst into flames.
The planes were heavily bombing the Partisan units to the
south of the town. They seemed to be using small bombs.
They would drop them, then circle and open fire with their
machine guns, then turn back over our heads for the Bihac
airdrome, about twenty minutes' flying time away.

The flames grew brighter as night fell. We reached the valley in the dusk. We met a few Partisans, but they knew nothing of the mission. We made our way up to where the old medical headquarters had been, but all we found were a smoking ruin and some dead Germans lying around. Luckily the lanes were worn deep and afforded good protection from the bullets which pinged past at odd moments.

Then we saw the British Mission. It was burnt to the ground and lying alongside were two German gliders. We met a Partisan who told us that in the morning he had seen two Americans running toward a house on the hill beyond Drvar. We made our way there and found a whole Partisan brigade waiting to go into attack. No, they had not seen the British. We searched all night, but not a sign.

With the first streak of morning I decided that it was much safer to get up the hill again, and we started climbing, climbing, climbing, pursued by a German patrol. Poor old Borgo found the going tough; he wasn't as fit as we were. The tracer still lit up the sky and German flares shot into the gray of morning, lighting the scene of desolation around them. All the firing seemed to be concentrated now in one small valley near where the British Mission had been. It looked as though the Partisans were beating them out of it. German fire was sporadic and lessening. As we watched, from out of the gray of the morning came the drone of German planes again, and down from the skies dropped parachutes with bundles swinging beneath them. More flares went up, giving the Luft-waffee the German ground positions, and ammunition came sailing down. Not only ammunition, but also mortars and mortar shells. Within ten minutes renewed and redoubled attacks came, and we knew that Drvar had fallen.

It was daylight. Benzedrine tablets helped us tremendously to get back to our mountain home, and when we returned

Zena had hot coffee waiting. She hadn't been to bed all night, waiting for us. We produced some rum. Then to bed.

About three that afternoon a commissar rode into the hospital area and told us that Marshal Tito had said that we were to go with the Fifth Brigade of the 1st Corpus, which would come along in a few minutes. I told him that was impossible, for I had about two hundred wounded in the forest hidden away and we were going there. "No," he said, "they will be all right; we shall look after them." But I was adamant and after he had gone Bill and I went into the forest to find the wounded. We arrived at the place where they had been the night before, only to discover that they had moved. Where we knew not, and it was useless to try and find them. So we went down again to the *polje* and found that in the meantime the whole brigade had arrived and Zena had packed up on three horses and they were waiting to move off.

During the day the Germans had captured Petrovac, and their tanks and heavy guns had taken possession of the Petrovac–Drvar road. A courier was sent to spy out the road and he reported that it was being constantly patrolled by tanks. But that did not in the least perturb Major Velebit (who was in charge of the evacuation of Tito's headquarters), and as evening came the long cavalcade started out across the *polje* toward the Petrovac–Drvar road. Just above the road we halted and lay down behind a stone wall, awaiting dusk. Below us we could see a constant procession of German trucks and tanks. The brigade seemed to be joined by more and more people coming up from the direction of Potoci.

Night came; one of those cold nights with darkened, ragged clouds fleecing across the moon. A dog was howling in the distance and behind the wall I saw that the *drugovi* were getting ready their Stens and their grenades. There was a movement and someone said, *"Tišina!"*—"Silence!" I noticed a patrol preparing to go down toward the road. Darkness swallowed it up. We waited. A few ponies pawed the ground anxiously, then one whinnied. I heard the boy smack its thigh and say, *"Hudič."* Then we all started to move down into the dark valley below us. Suddenly came the whirr of tanks from the direction of Drvar. Machine guns burst into action, then a sheet of flame lit the sky as a Molotov bottle was thrown against the tank's side. The Germans were stopped going up the road, for the flaming tank straddled it at a narrow bend. The valley was full of tracers now, and a flare shot up into the sky. The Partisans closed in on all sides. Bullets were pinging past as we descended to the fray. Another sheet of flame as a truck was hit. I heard the tanks behind trying to reverse and go back down the road. A truck had gone over the bank and was in flames. Now we were down on the road above the bend where the attack was still going on. Ponies were hurried across the road; ponies carrying pots and pans, ammunition and machine guns; a British Peat mortar in pieces, and more ammunition. Many had already crossed the road when our little team crossed. The firing ceased. Three trucks and two tanks lay smoldering, glowing red in the night. We could hear a truck and a tank careering down the road into Drvar and saw more flares.

There was no stopping, but up into the mountains on the other side of the road we were hustled; then along the mountaintops parallel to the Una below us. All night we walked; the moon fell and the black moving column seemed to me to have enlarged in the night. From where I knew not. I was very hungry and very tired, so I lay down for a rest under a stone just below the track and watched the single-file cavalcade pass. I thought I recognized some of Tito's staff but wasn't sure. Later I found that it was Tito himself passing in the night. I

dozed a little, then awoke colder and hungrier than ever, and
set off to catch them up again. About 6 A.M., in the coldness
of a rainy summer morning, we stopped and slept under
the trees.

Next night it was the same, but now the cavalcade was
smaller again. Some had left us during the day and gone over
the mountains. We reached a peasant house about four in
the morning and camped again under some rocks. Despite the
rain, which fell all day, I seemed to sleep well, sheltered under
the lee of a large rock. During the day we achieved a ration of
meat. Old bull, it was, in great hunks. We boiled it without
salt and solemnly sat down and gnawed it till it disappeared.
All night again on the march, and next day we hid among the
rocks and were told that we would stay there some days. So we
made ourselves as comfortable as we could. Zena was not
standing up to it too well, so during the day I made my way to
the divisional commissar and asked for a pony for her. "A
pony!" he exclaimed. "Is she a Partisan or not?" I pointed out
she was certainly a Partizanka but was a woman of poor physique and old enough to be his mother. But to no avail. She
must walk like everyone else. This was a bit tough, I felt, and
as I had been personally responsible for getting Zena here from
the shelter of Vis, I felt rather bad about it. Later during the
day I met Major Velebit and suggested a horse for myself, my
own pony being loaded with our medical equipment. He
looked at me knowingly and said he would send one. So Zena
got a pony, but, even so, the way was long and hard.

We rested for three days, hiding as well as we could by day,
and cooking our two pieces of meat in the evening. No more
planes arrived; Drvar was completely occupied by the Germans.
Our patrols brought back word that they had lined up four
hundred of the old people in front of the Partisan headquarters
and shot them all "because of the resistance." Girls were taken,

if found, and put into the German brothels for use until such times as nature or disease intervened. Then they were shot. The nurses' school at Otocevas I never heard of again. Perhaps it went the same way.

Late one afternoon we saw German tanks coming down the road on the bottom of the valley. There were three of them and three trucks going to raid a village for food. A Partisan patrol left immediately, Bill and I with them. We saw the tanks turn from the main valley road and head up the mountainside to a little village surrounded by crops of corn. They entered the village and soon after we saw smoke rising, and one of the Bosnian houses burst into flames. Then another house burst into flames and the smoke of destruction eddied its way down the valley, and, like the Una, dissolved into nothingness. Quite suddenly we saw one of the trucks turn from the village and start careering back onto the road. We fired. The truck stopped, one of its tires blown off. The Germans started jumping down, but too late, for Partisan bullets were singing across the little valley. Then bullets began pinging all around us and the village. We could see the little puffs of smoke. The Germans got their mortar into action and started firing blindly into the clumps of bushes on the hillside. The whole valley echoed and re-echoed with explosions. The tanks started down the hill, then the first one stopped. I watched some cattle stampeding and bellowing up the hill behind the village and some women running, driving a few sheep which had been browsing so contentedly in the open space above the houses. A shell from their mortar landed just below where we were; a terrific explosion in the confined space, while dirt and stones showered the scrub and hillside. Then another house started burning. We watched the thin column of smoke rise slowly and then burst into a great flame as the dried timber and shingle roof took hold. I heard Bill mutter, "The bastards!"

Suddenly the firing ceased, and in the summer peacefulness
the crackle of burning timber and the shrieking of some
women were all that reached us. Our comrades started coming
back to where we were. Sweat was dripping from under their
Red Stars and their hands were black and greasy from the
machine guns. Bill and I walked back to where we had been
lying under the rocks and lay down again. Zena and Ivo came
and joined us. Zena had her small handkerchief to her eyes.
She looked at me and said, "Did you hear the shrieking?"
"Yes," I replied, for we both knew what had happened.

Later four *drugovi* brought in five German officers; just boys.
They were Storm Troopers. Neatly dressed, clean-shaven boys.
One had blood oozing through his green tunic sleeve. They
stood, surrounded by a strong guard, outside the house which
the Partisan patrol had taken as their temporary headquarters.
Then a courier arrived at our rocky home and asked if Zena
would come over and help with the interrogation. I went with
her. We opened the door of the house and entered the living
room. Sitting at the table were our commandant and his commissar. Zena sat down beside them. I went to the side of the
room and sat down on a three-legged stool. The Germans were
brought in one by one. All their possessions were laid on the
table. A faded letter, a diary, a bottle of hair oil, some rubber
protectives, a postcard of a blond girl with a message of love
scratched across the corner; a photo of a group of young
officers in a training camp; a picture of an old lady standing
beside a farmhouse door. The commandant picked them up
one by one and handed the writings to Zena, who fluently
translated the German into Serbo-Croatian. They were mostly
simple love letters from home. The commissar started the interrogation. The official questioning took a bare five minutes.
I watched Zena. A holy hate burnt in her dark Jewish eyes.
When it was over she asked them:

"Why do you burn down our houses and our villages?"
No answer.
"Why do you take our young women to give them disease?"
No answer.
"Why do you shoot our old women and children and torture our couriers?"
No answer.

I remembered a courier patient of mine who had escaped from a German unit. He had been caught by a patrol and taken to a headquarters and asked about the movement of Partisan groups. He didn't answer. They struck him on the face with their rifles and said, "Answer, you dog!" He was only seventeen. They struck him again and again until he fell. He was pulled out and locked in a room. Next day the same thing happened. No answer. Then they tied his arms with wire to a beam above his head, and from his testes they hung a brick tied with copper wire. Gradually his bladder filled. The pain was terrific. A sudden spasm and the abdominal agony ended. His bladder burst and he swooned away. The next thing he recalled was a peasant lifting him down at night and carrying him into the darkness. Luckily I was near at hand and operated.

"Why do you torture our Partisan boys," repeated Zena. The German nazi replied haughtily, "Well, you are brigand dogs, are you not?" Fifteen minutes later they faced the firing squad and Zena and I walked slowly and silently back to our camp among the rocks.

CHAPTER 9

Surrounded by Germans

The continued diet of meat alone, without even salt, began to tell. I became constipated and had griping abdominal pains. The mirror showed a mild degree of scurvy setting in: swollen gums which bled without any stimulus. A general tiredness pervaded us all. I decided that we must have green food of some kind, so we gathered fresh blades of grass and the tips of spruce firs, the young green tender tips, and stewed them up together with our portion of old bull. It changed the whole outlook. Then one day Zena found an herb she knew of old. When she had been in Bosnia before, she ran a hospital for ten in a cowshed, and they never even saw a medical student. She had scurvy then and had used this herb to cure it. It was a leaf like that of spinach and when boiled, without salt, of course, tasted "dry" and acid, but it was good and filled the empty belly.

They brought a small boy to me one day with osteomyelitis following a mortar wound. Under a heavy dose of intravenous morphia alone I removed the sequestrum and pinch-grafted the large raw area. He followed our wanderings for days. To be near us, his mother led a pony, on which he sat, over the steepest and rockiest of mountains, and when we went over the tops, she went into the valleys and came through the German lines.

Supplies were practically nil by this time, as we had had no communication with Italy for a month. The brigade joined a division and by forced marches at night we crossed the Una and started making our way toward Bihac for an attack on the airdrome. Down over the hill of Martin Brod again we came,

and then I found that since we had passed through, scarcely
three months before in company with Terric from Croatia, the
Germans had been there and burnt down the entire village.
But we pushed on in the night and swam the horses across the
river and started along the bank toward the German-held town
of Bihac. Thousands of nightingales were chortling in the
bushes along the banks. I was walking automatically. I could
see Zena outlined against the night on her horse ahead of us.
An old song, "The Rose Enslaves the Nightingale," rang in
my ears.

Still retreating, we left the riverbank and climbed up to what
had been the main railway line, the Knin–Bihac, but now no
more. Not even a rail remained for the Germans to use. I
seemed to be walking in my sleep. We passed a group of
Partisans in a deserted village. They gave us some apples, the
first I'd had for four years. We rolled them around our mouths
and crunched them, core and all, keeping the apples in our
mouths until the flavor had completely disappeared.

That night we stopped just near Bihac, in the hills. I learnt
that we intended to attack Bihac airdrome in the early hours
of the morning. We were just getting ready to move when a
perfect barrage of 105-mm. German shells swept our hiding
place. Bill and I were in a little hollow. A shell landed on the
ridge above us not ten yards away. We heard it whining its
way toward us and crouched low. Luckily it ricocheted and
sped down the valley beyond. Then it exploded. We decided
that that spot was unhealthy and moved to better cover. But
the order for retreat had already come and we started back on
our own tracks.

Next night we reached Martin Brod again and swam the
horses across. Then we started climbing, climbing all night, it
seemed. The path led up the side of a cliff. Gradually the
rushing of water over the falls became fainter and fainter the

higher we climbed. It was bitterly cold. A British plane flew
over far above us—we could just hear it. In vain we tried to
pierce the darkness and see it. So safe up there, I thought. At
last, the top; no—only a little false saddle in the climb, still the
black rim far above us. We could hear the stones the ponies
dislodged rattling down the hill. Again "*Tišina*" (silence)
passed down the climbing line, for we were close to a Chetnik
stronghold. We reached to top ahead of Zena and Milica.
Sitting down on some stones, Bill produced a small flask of
rum to ward off the cold, but I suggested waiting until Zena
and Ivo came up with the horses. We waited, then we heard
them and they almost passed us by in the night.

"Zena," I called.

"*Majore*," she replied.

"Have a rum!" I said. She took the flask and drained the lot.
I handed it back to Bill empty.

"She left us the smell, anyway," he mumbled.

When daylight came we camped near a peasant house, and
we lay on the ground, which probably had fewer lice than the
house. At eleven we arose, refreshed by sleep. Zena was already
up and talking to the peasant, an old Bosnian who did not
want to have much to do with us. He was an old man with a
huge, obvious hydrocele hanging down like an udder between
his legs. He sat straddle-legged on a tree stump smoking a pipe
of tobacco he had grown himself. His son was away fighting
and he lived alone with a daughter-in-law. She came from
milking the cow and gave us fresh milk and a kindlier welcome
than the old man. It began to rain. Ivo seized our sleeping bags
and ran into the house with them. We followed. The fire
smoked the room out, for there are never chimneys in these
Bosnian houses. The daughter-in-law made sour cheese and
gave us each a portion. It tasted like heaven. The old man spat
continually on the floor but became more friendly as time

went on, when he found out that we were not Germans, as he had suspected. That night we left and arrived back quite near the Drvar–Petrovac road again, high above the Una. Water was scarce up in the mountains, for there were no creeks, the water all soaking away through the limestone rocks to the river beneath. Sterilizing tablets we had long since discarded, just taking potluck. I always kept a little sulfa guanidine in case of necessity, as I had had one experience of dysentery, or whatever it was.

Next day a courier arrived with a message. Would I go to a certain place and meet Velebit? We found him and he asked if I would be prepared to go back to Otocevas, where our old hospital was, to get some medical stores, for there was going to be a big attack soon and we had no stores whatsoever.

I returned to Bill and Ivo and asked them to accompany me. At sunset we returned to Major Velebit's camp and left with a group of twelve Partisans to cross through the German lines again and go to Otocevas. I was keen to go and see if any of the hospital remained.

It was midnight when we crossed the main German road and saw not a soul. In silence we climbed the other side of the valley, up over the crest, then dropped into the high mountain *polje* beyond. The first streak of dawn was just about to light up the snowy top of Kasekovac when we decided to hide and sleep. A group of tall pines stood apart from the main forest and in the middle was an abandoned cattle shed. I was hungry and tired, but I knew that hidden away, almost at hand, were chocolate, bully beef, and all kinds of good things. So I lay down under the pines, thinking of the good feed we would have in a few hours' time. I dropped to sleep, deep, tired sleep; I was under one tree, Bill and Ivo under another.

I heard Ivo shout, "Quick. Quick!" but turned over to sleep

again. Then he seized me by the shoulder and shook me
vigorously. "Quick. We are surrounded by Germans," he said.

I rose on my arm as the bullets began pitting the trees
around me. Already the Partisans were returning the fire. I got
up quickly, keeping behind the tree trunk. I could see the
Germans all around the *polje* on three sides of us. Machine-
gun fire was sweeping the area where we were. We got our
rifles and started firing, then made our way slowly and with
great difficulty toward the main forest. It took just about an
hour's hard fighting to reach the shelter of the forest. Hardly
were we there when heavy shells began crashing among us.
The Partisans seemed to disappear like magic. Bill said, "Someone told me to go up the wooded valley," so we ran over the
huge stones, crouching behind them every time a shell landed
nearby. Trees fell, crashing and echoing up and down the
valley as the shells cut them down.

We ran hard, but on empty stomachs, without any salt for
weeks, it was not easy. At last it was broad daylight and we
seemed to have left the shells behind us. But no! Down the
valley toward Potoci they continued crashing, and we continued stumbling and running. We passed a peasant with his
wife and two children crouching behind a rock. They had
three sheep with them, madly terrified at the noise. I suggested
a halt and a rest. We heard something stumbling through the
trees. We watched. It was a Partisan. He said that he was
going to Potoci and that there were a thousand Germans
where we had just left. He disappeared into the forest. We sat
for a time, then I decided that Potoci was almost certainly in
Partisan hands and that we should make for there. We set
out, and came across an old bush tramway and a little clearing. The sun was shining hot by this time, and I thought it
wise to have a proper rest, so we went a hundred yards from

the track and all three of us lay down under rocks and soon
went to sleep.

I awoke to hear a lot of voices around me. Cautiously I
raised my head and saw a German patrol not a hundred yards
away walking along the track from the direction of Potoci.
They were talking and laughing among themselves. I looked at
Bill. He was lying on his back, mouth wide open, and snoring
audibly. I waited in horror, but they didn't hear him and the
forest swallowed them up. As soon as it was safe, I woke Bill
and Ivo. We decided that Potoci must be in German hands,
and because of our thirst decided to make for the top of the
mountain, where the snow was still lying, to get a drink and
continue over the top down into Drenitz, where I already
knew the peasants.

We began climbing. The forest was open; hundreds of lilies
of the valley perfumed the air; orchids and aquilegias raised
their beautiful heads toward the sunshine. Shelling and
machine-gun fire were still breaking out sporadically away to
the west, and we went on climbing upward. Suddenly I heard
Ivo say in a muffled voice, "Quick! Hide!" and I ducked down
behind a fallen tree. I couldn't see Ivo or Bill, who were behind
me, but above me and walking along a track were ten Chetniks
and two Germans, one an officer. They hadn't seen us, so I lay
still, heart pounding, and sweat pouring from my brow; for
here it would be shoot first and ask afterward. They passed.
We waited, hidden behind the fallen tree, and had a conference. We couldn't go back to Otocevas; we couldn't go to
Potoci; we couldn't go to the top. Where could we go?

We decided to watch the track the Chetniks had come
along, to see if any Partisans also used it. We crept upward,
listening for the minutest sound, got to the track (a well-worn
one), and there found, just above it, three good trees, which
we climbed. All day we hid and waited. Chetniks and Germans

kept passing down the track just below us, within a few yards of where we hid above them. At about 4 P.M. the traffic lessened and then ceased. Just as I was about to descend, for the thirst was intolerable now and the belly empty as a burnt-out house, I heard voices. I looked and saw a group of Chetniks and two German officers coming. They passed underneath my tree and just as they passed Bill's tree I heard his gun. I looked and saw the whole six fall. One was still alive, but a further shot disposed of him.

"What the hell did you do that for?" I shouted to Bill, for we didn't know who was following.

"Couldn't help it, sir," he replied; then silence.

"Come on," I said. "Let's get busy."

We scrambled down the trees, looted the German officers' watches and underclothes, dragged the bodies behind a dead tree, kicked fresh earth over the blood, and set off into the forest. Hardly had we got going when we met a peasant girl hiding in a small hollow between some rocks. "Don't go up there," she said. "There are sixty Chetniks camped there." The forest was getting dark by this time. We stopped with the girl a few moments and waited to listen for anyone coming to investigate the shooting. No one came.

We then decided to wait until night and go back again to Otocevas, where we knew the tracks, and work our way across to the Una; then make a great sweep around, back again to Martin Brod, where I was sure I would find Partisans. We crept silently and slowly down through the gloom. In three hours we reached the outskirts of the forest near our hospital. It was still smoldering, burnt to the ground; the peasant houses in the *polje* were all burnt flat, and as we lay hidden, watching the open *polje*, we heard someone coming. All three of us covered him with our guns. Closer he came, alone, so we knew that he must be a Partisan. We called out, *"Stoj,"* and he stopped. *"Partizani,"* he replied, and he was. We joined him, then found another and another, and by midnight we had regained the patrol and made our way across the German road and back to our camp.

They had heard the heavy firing and Zena was sure that we had all been killed, for one Partisan had gotten through much earlier and he had thought we had been taken. We hadn't; we were all O.K. But we had no stores; just the memory of our burnt hospital.

CHAPTER 10

Air Lift from Yugoslavia

Some days later we crossed the Una to its south bank and climbed up into the hills beyond. During the intervening days I had heard from a Partisan who escaped from Drvar that some of the British Mission had been shot and some taken prisoner; but where he didn't know. He thought that Talbot, the Reuter's correspondent, had escaped and was in the hills to the south. I never heard whether this was so and didn't place much reliance on the report.

At nights we could still see the glow of burning houses in the Drvar area. The Germans were methodically pursuing their policy of complete destruction of the whole district. We met very few who escaped. Food was becoming a great problem. We would have two pieces of boiled beef for days on end, then we would get beans boiled without salt; never any salt or sugar, no tea or coffee, and no lights at night. We were always wet, for we had no means of drying blankets, and Zena was getting worse and worse with her bronchitis and more and more exacting in her demands. We did our best for her, but it was impossible to do very much.

We camped near one village the Germans had just bombed. Why they should bomb a defenseless mountain village I never could understand, unless they had bombs to waste. The villagers were all hiding in a bush-covered gully about a mile away. There I did a fair amount of operating with nothing, nothing, I mean, in the way of anesthetics, antiseptics, or sterile equipment. With the aid of *rakija* (about half a cup) followed in half an hour by three quarters of a grain of intravenous morphia we were able to remove pieces of bomb fragments, to drain deep abscess pockets, and to set unreduced fractures. The patients just lay on the grass in the gully floor while Ivo, Bill, and I got to work.

Shortly after this we began moving southward and arrived at Ticevo to find all the houses burnt to the ground and still smoldering. Food was getting very short indeed, so the divisional commander sent frantic messages to 8th Corps Headquarters to wireless the British in Italy for food. This had been asked for many times before, but the planes had not been able to get through. Now, fortunately, they made it, and along came the food.

As we moved forward, the planes followed us by night, guided by the glare of the fires and previously reported positions. Down from the skies came bags of dehydrated vegetables, bags of rice, of flour, of dehydrated meat. Our bellies were full again.

Glamoc seemed to be the final southerly point of the circuit. The Germans were in heavy concentrations at Livno, not very far away, in the north at Drvar, and also to west and east. There we stayed on the edge of the Glamoc *polje* just hiding and waiting. The rumor was that the Russians would soon began attacking in the east and the whole of 1st Corpus would join up and assist them. Until that happened there would be no further action.

Zena was now fairly bad with bronchitis and the constant traveling by night had worn her out, so I decided that she should go back to Ticevo and there wait for an airplane which was expected shortly to evacuate to Italy a few wounded I had hidden in the forest. When Zena left, things quietened down a bit to a humdrum existence with no work to do at all. Moreover, it became increasingly apparent that the Partisans intended to hold their forces and await the Russian Army's arrival. I decided that we should go out and re-equip and go into Slovenia, where there was constant fighting, and where I understood the hospitals were more static.

A long talk with the divisional commander and the commissar confirmed my view of the future, so I told the commissar my plans and he agreed that it was better to be working than enjoying the summer sun at Glamoc. So next day we got together a bit of food, our few remaining possessions (now very few), and set out, Voyasin, Ivo, Vic, Bill, and I, toward Ticevo, where a plane could land.

The rain was pouring down practically all the way, and when we arrived at 8th Corpus Headquarters, we found the American liaison officer sitting under a parachute looking damned uncomfortable, with the rain dripping in and no fire. It was no place for us to stay, so we got two parachutes from him and went back to a patch of forest about six miles away. There we built a good camp and settled down to await suitable weather for a plane to come in.

. Three planes arrived one afternoon, escorted by fighters, for some of Tito's staff had gathered themselves together after a month or two of hiding and wanted to rejoin Tito, whom we now heard was settled on Vis.

It appeared that British planes had been detailed to take

him and the British Mission staff back to Italy about three days after Drvar fell. A hasty landing strip was gotten ready and the planes duly arrived. But they were headed some minutes before by a Russian plane from Bari, a DC-3, which came for the Russian Mission. Before anyone realized what was happening Tito stepped into it and was gone. Meanwhile, at the airdrome at Bari the whole British staff stood awaiting his arrival, including General Wilson, commander in chief. Twenty minutes before the first British plane (which was supposed to be carrying Tito) was due back, he had landed on the opposite side of the field, where a Russian car met him and carried him away. That was the first inkling I had that relations could have been better.

CHAPTER 11

Italian Merry-Go-Round

Bill, Vic, and I, together with the Partisans, arrived in Italy. It was good to see green fields again, filled with vegetables, and a peaceful summer sun. We stepped from the plane and were met by the security people. Eventually I got it home to them that Voyasin, Ivo, and Milica were my responsibility, and were not to be whisked away to an alien concentration camp. We all tumbled into a mission truck, which arrived only after I had telephoned frantically to the office for it, and I delivered my three Yugoslavs to the care of General Nickolic and Colonel Krause, whom I found at the Yugoslav Medical Mission. I told the general that I wanted them back in a day or two. "*Sigurno, sigurno*—certainly, certainly," he replied. "You shall certainly have them back." Boravic from Croatia was also there, and

indeed I wondered just who of importance was left in Yugoslavia.

Bill, Vic, and I went down to the office and then out to a
small Italian village south of Bari called Castellani. Major
White, who was attached to our Medical Q depot, gave us
the usual base welcome and told me that they had a Canadian
there called Colin Dafoe waiting to go into Serbia. I soon
rooted him out and he told me his long story of base life in
Alexandria and Cairo and how he eventually got into our
"firm." The night passed quickly, punctuated by glasses of
vino, the first vino we had had for a long time. And the food!
tables full, vineyards full, fig trees full, chicken roosts full, and
finally stomachs full.

At Castellani were gathered all the "Operational Bodies" of
Southern Europe. Bound for Poland, for Germany, for Ruma-
nia, for Yugoslavia, Greece, Albania, and an increasing number
for Northern Italy. There they kept us all, out of the way, and
the camp was called "Convalescent Officers' Camp." It was
that, all right. After a day's rest we all went down to the medical store at Monopoli and started to get ready another kit.

At the base office I found that a new medical branch had
opened with an A.D.M.S., a full colonel, a D.A.D.M.S., a captain, and in the store another officer. It seemed an enormous
setup to supply routine stores to various dropping grounds
and to look after some two medical officers in Yugoslavia, one
in Albania and one in Greece. As time went on I learnt to my
sorrow how inefficient the whole setup was.

The A.D.M.S. had previously been engaged on the mythical
side of army attack, chemical warfare—gas. It had never been
used, but provided for certain officers a quiet home for many
months. The D.A.D.M.S., who had been a country practitioner
near London, had been employed as an M.O. in a P.O.W.
camp where all the work was done by the P.O.W. doctors

anyway, and the other two just hadn't a clue as to what was necessary for a surgeon's work. The more I saw of the office, the more appalled I became. The only redeeming feature was the "Fanny" who did all the work. She at least did try to get us what we needed.

Every day Dafoe and I were down to the store gathering up sufficient instruments and drugs to set up a reasonably well equipped hospital over there. With my previous experience I was able to cut out a lot of unnecessary stuff and concentrated, after the bare surgical essentials, on clothes, soap, candles, lamps, and things which make a wounded man comfortable. As the years crept on, it became more and more apparent how little equipment one really needed in war surgery. And as I hoped that my next location would be more stable, I took more hospital stores and less surgical.

I went up to Bari one day and talked to all the administrative officers. I noted a certain coldness in the reception, so I asked the reason why. "Oh, nothing," said the G.2. I then went to a brother colonial, a South African, and indeed the most co-operative chap in the whole outfit, and asked him. He told me that they had read my reports "with interest," but that I had expressed "a far too pro-Partisan outlook," and this apparently was not to be encouraged.

"But, Bill," I said. "Jesus Christ, wasn't I sent into the bloody country to *be* pro-Partisan?" He laughed and agreed. It was clear to me that in our own office there was still a considerable sympathy for the Mihailovich faction sustained by one group, while the other group was pro-Partisan. It was time some of them crossed the water and experienced the Chetniks and their German friends, I thought.

That night as Colin and I sat on the high seats in front of the bar at Castellani, sipping a good-quality vermouth and chewing nuts, I told him of my interview at the Bari office.

He laughed and told me that he had been warned by the
A.D.M.S. not to be as outspoken as Rogers, and not to be
pro-Partisan too enthusiastically. I thought of "the Fetus,"
with his torn back; of Borgo, my commissar, who had blown
up the German ammunition train going down to Salonika
from Serbia; I thought of Lavro Ribar, the great friend of
Tito, and his almost evangelical fire for the "New Order"; of
Nazor, the poet, who, though bowed and gray, yet worked on
toward the shining new morning star; of Anton, whose leg we
amputated while he lay groaning and singing, and a whole
host of men whose sacrifice towered above mine like a mighty
mountain.

Next evening I went and had dinner with General Nickolic,
now in Italy. He was living a few miles from Bari in a villa half
hidden by enormous vines, and as we climbed the stairs to the
room, we stopped and looked away to the east. Bari's steeples
raised themselves above the sordid mass of building I was beginning to know too well. The great oil refineries, where the
Albanian oil had flowed in the days of peace, took up the
horizon to the left of us, and to the right crowning the low hill
behind the city stood the Polyclinic, a fascist's conception of
modern medicine. Luckily for the Italians the British had
taken it over for their general-hospital area. I stayed on the
little balcony while Nickolic brought out some wine. Somewhere away to the east on the gray horizon was Yugoslavia,
on bended knee, yet with head high. I was anxious and eager
to get back again, for life at the base, with its petty intrigues
and its bored officers, too tired even to be civil sometimes, was
stifling me. Not only me, but the boys also were heartily sick
of "resting," and were eager to return.

We had dinner, a good plain Italian meal, with spaghetti
and tomato pasta and a good red wine. It did not take me long
to find out that the general had only a vague conception of

things in Slovenia and Carinthia, where I wanted to go. He had little idea of the number of casualties, of the type of hospital, or the names of the doctors. He appeared to be much too interested in the arrival of the Russians at Nish to worry over Slovenia, and he spoke almost continuously of what they would do when again Belgrade was in their hands.

He asked me the position of British stores for Yugoslavia, but quite truthfully I just had no idea. I told him so, but he didn't believe me. He gave me a list of his requirements for Belgrade and asked me to use what influence I had to get them immediately sent to Vis. I glanced at the list. It was the usual list, double the amount necessary to equip the whole country on a most lavish scale, and almost certainly beyond British-American means at that stage of the war. It always made me wonder why they needed tens of thousands of ampoules of the so-called cardiac drugs, camphor in oil, caffeina, and so on. In all the many many thousands we had operated upon in our casualty clearing station in the desert I had never had occasion to use such drugs. Perhaps it is a different conception we have. I put the list in my pocket and promised to go over it and take it to the A.D.M.S. in the morning.

Nickolic was a good general; he had a good manner, a fine carriage, but despite all that I knew that he was anti-British in feeling. One felt the subtle sneers ever ready, and one listened to the often-repeated question about the Second Front. He suggested that the British could do much more for them in Italy, yet in reality the British looked after almost the total casualties in Yugoslavia and thousands of evacuees. I knew that many thousands were treated by British surgeons in Italy alone. His constant implication that if the British couldn't supply such and such he would ask the Russians for it made me rather annoyed, as I knew full well that the Russians had supplied no medical stores for Yugoslavia at all. In all my

wanderings I saw only one set of Russian instruments, and
that was at the 8th Corpus hospital. I knew that from both
British and American sources thousands of tons of war matériel
were pouring into Russia, including surgical equipment. Then
he would say, "I shall ask the Americans for it." Looking at it
from his point of view, I could see his urgent desire to get as
much as possible from any source at all, but he was really
defeating his own ends in the matter, for it made people sick
of the same requests coming in from different sources.

Nickolic was a dermatologist in civil life, I understood, and
had with many others fought in Spain. He saw in the British
people directly opposed political aspirations and a decadent
but courteous source of his immediate requirements.

Talbot, the colonel in charge of the Yugoslav hospital, run
and equipped by the British at Grumo in Italy, had told me a
curious story of Nickolic, one which, as we sat on the veranda,
kept running through my mind.

It appeared that one night about midnight a car drew up in
front of the hospital at Grumo and out stepped Nickolic and
Pape, a Yugoslav doctor then undergoing tuition in British
hospitals. They asked to be shown to the operating theater,
and the orderly took them along the corridor to where the
theater stood in darkness. They asked that the theater be
gotten ready for an immediate operation. The orderly, dumfounded by these strange people, suggested that he should get
Colonel Talbot to come, but they replied, "No, it is not necessary." The orderly then asked whether he should call the
theater staff. "Yes, of course," Nickolic said.

The theater staff was dragged from bed, sterilizers put on
to boil, instruments put out, and all the time Nickolic and
Pape went around smelling bottles on the anesthetic table.
Then they turned on their heels and went, leaving the staff
standing there in amazement.

When Talbot told me the story, I immediately asked, "Was Nickolic drunk?" and he assured me that he wasn't. A few days later came an official complaint from the Yugoslav Medical Mission in Italy regarding the theater efficiency at Grumo.

This was the beginning of a whole series of regrettable incidents at Grumo, incidents and ill-feeling festered by commissars to such an extent that several Yugoslav doctors who appreciated British help left the hospital in disgust because of the extent to which political biases were leading them. Every British hospital in Italy which treated Yugoslavs found the patients to be the most grateful and the best patients they could possibly have; every British hospital in Italy found the political atmosphere nauseating and distasteful.

Nickolic and I talked of the dissemination of information on medical progress. Now that a medical school was out of the question, I suggested that I should start a medical journal and have it printed in Italy and dropped by parachute over Yugoslavia. He was not in favor of that at all. He, a dermatologist, wanted me to write the articles for him to publish in his own journal. But I felt that a purely British journal would be better from a propaganda point of view and would let the Yugoslavs throughout the country know that we were helping them, and working for them not only in their own country but, by this time, late 1944, very considerably also in Italy. I had always felt that the British and American achievements were almost entirely left out of the picture among the Yugoslav troops, who knew only of the great successes of the Red Army. I could see that Nickolic was not in favor, so I dropped the subject. But at the same time I was determined to carry it out, and we did.

Before I left, he gave me a most laudatory letter to the Slovene High Command and a faithful promise that my Yugoslav boys, Voyasin and Ivo, should be sent into Topusko by landing plane and should walk into Slovenia and join me there. Despite this promise and many many subsequent requests I never saw or heard of them again.

Next day I left by jeep for Naples to interview A.F.H.Q. (Allied Force Headquarters) and to tell them something of the medical position in Yugoslavia, and the need for a tuberculosis sanatorium in Italy. It was a pleasant run over. Once Foggia was passed and the Adriatic coast was left behind, I turned toward the hills, leaving behind the never-ending stream of lorries and trucks, staff cars and jeeps, Diesels and wagons, and saw ahead the long, straight, empty roads. It seemed like home again. Then the road climbed, climbed and twisted in great loops as only Italian roads can, up and down, over hill and valley. Here a village perched on the hilltop, here one sitting precariously on a cliff edge. Afar, in the blue on the skyline, Campobasso, the town of many memories, for it was there that I said farewell to the 15th Casualty Clearing Station and joined the Balkan Partisan force.

I stayed in Naples at the 98th General Hospital and there met two old desert pals, the radiographer Steve Maddox, and old Tom Armstrong, the physician, now a lieutenant colonel. We had a great talk about the old times and Maddox told me that the C.C.S. was only seventy miles away up at the front. So we left in the jeep to go and see them. Along the poplar-lined roads of Italy we went, and then turned away, up into the mountains again. It was just dusk when we saw the old familiar sign stuck up in the area, the tents still in the same general layout, and the ambulances waiting at the reception tent. What a home-coming we had, and how the smoke drifted across the room and the glasses clinked on the wooden tables. There was a new Old Man called MacIntosh, who had heard all the old stories of the early escapades of the C.C.S., so we were not really new to him at all. We met most of the boys we had known, but all the old ones had gone back to England on leave.

It was early morning when we left, for Steve Maddox had to be back on duty at 9 A.M. In the cold and under the stars we hurried back to Naples. Then a good bath and I left Steve, saying, "Good-by till we meet in London."

I stopped at Caserta and there in the palace found the Medical Directorate, and for the next two hours poured out a plea for Yugoslavia; more help, more medical men, more hospitals, more drugs. They listened stoically, knowing well their own commitments and the war to come. But I did get a tuberculosis hospital promised, a forsaken British hospital at San Fernando. So I left, and next night was back again at Castellani with stores almost packed and everything else ready to return.

It was decided that I should take in only a few essential stores to open a hospital, and I made a special trip to the D.A.D.M.S., asking that he arrange for certain parachute containers with stores to go on the plane which was to drop me in.

The war had shown me many countries since I left New Zealand five years before. Not only many countries, but many men. The vision had become wider and the underlying urge for better things had become more rationalized. I had matured, and also had learnt to appreciate more fully those I had left behind, whom hitherto I had regarded as reactionary and self-centered. No other country had the beauty and the possibilities of New Zealand. Colin Dafoe had preached Canada to me, South Africans had shown us their mountains and deserts, men from the islands had spoken of the tropics and the lure of the trade winds beating the surf against coral reefs, but everywhere I had been, and everything I had seen, everyone I had listened to had failed to convince me that my own country was eclipsed. How few of us New Zealanders really appreciate the home that bore us.

The war had made me appreciate more fully not only New Zealand, but the training I had received at our medical schools and hospitals. During these years I had seen a transition in war surgery. From the days almost before the sulfa drugs, then to the universal use of sulphonamide, associated with the open-wound technique of debridement or the total excision of all damaged tissue. Now penicillin had come, and with it another change, when wounds could be closed with safety, and compound fractures could be converted into simple fractures, thus shortening the long convalescence and the all too frequent onset of osteomyelitis. Not only in wounds of the limbs had we made advances and changes. In abdominal surgery the death rate had fallen because of the now universal use of continuous gastric suction on the Wagonstein principle. Why we did not use it at the beginning of the war I never knew, for it had been in vogue for years.

PART IV

Slovenia

Return by Parachute

The truck called for us at three o'clock, for that night we were to parachute into Slovenia, somewhere in the Crnomelj area. All morning we had been packing up the little things one takes, needles and thread, bootlaces, matches, razor blades, and so on. Our rucksacks were full to capacity, yet there always seemed to be more to find room for. Mine was finally full, and on the outside I strapped an anti-gas cape, a very valuable asset. I had changed my Sten gun for an American sub-machine gun, considerably lighter than a tommy gun and therefore easier to carry on long journeys. Bill and Vic were taking Stens, and an automatic pistol, a Llama. We understood that these Llamas had been made for the Spanish Civil War, and were being "sold off" to Yugoslav personnel. Actually they were not nearly so good as Colts, for just at the critical moment the spring would jam and you were left with an open breach and a useless pistol. I took a Colt. A box of hand grenades I insisted on taking, if not for protection, then for fishing, and finally the good Major White filled our rum flasks, and we said good-by.

Dafoe was going into Serbia and was waiting for suitable dropping weather, so we had lunch together and then sat down at the bar, open, as it was, until two o'clock, and sipped brandies, talking of his coming to see me in New Zealand and my going to see him in Canada. I told him all I knew of the

Yugoslavs, what great people the fighters were, and how grateful they were for what we had been able to do. I told him of
the good commissars I had been associated with in Bosnia,
but I also told him of the petty difficulties that seemed to be
forever cropping up with the administration of the Yugoslavs
in Italy. I found it hard to understand why sinister things
should be happening here, almost universally in every hospital,
when over in the country itself I had experienced the utmost
kindliness and consideration. Perhaps it was a reflection of our
own base troubles. It seemed to be a Montenegrin element at
the bottom of it all, but the whole Yugoslav attitude in Italy
was completely foreign to me and I couldn't understand it at
all. The bar closed, I shook Dafoe by the hand, and went and
collected Bill and Vic, who had had an enjoyable lunch too,
it seemed.

The conducting officer, whose job it was to see us off in the
plane, hurried us along. He had sent off a great number of men
into Occupied Europe and I wondered how he felt as planes
rushed into the night, leaving him standing alone on the field.
We clambered into the truck on that hot sunny afternoon and
started down the rough stony road toward Monopoli. Silence
fell. The sun was smudging the shadowed stone walls with
gold. Sleepy Italians were just rising from siesta. A bronzed
fisherman came up the road with a bundle of fish swinging
from a cord tied through their gills, and as the truck passed
he turned to watch us, cursing the trail of gritty dust that bit
his lips. We turned into the parachute store, swung past the
sentry, and pulled up at the door.

We climbed from the truck, jumped to the ground, feet and
knees together, for all my training was rapidly assuming importance now, and the few days I had once spent at the parachute
school came back with stark reality; in less than five hours I
too would be jumping into the night, I knew not where.

I remembered the school and its personnel, the three tough paratroop sergeant-instructors, the Polish captain in charge. It was said that he had made a descent in an unopened parachute and had been saved by a tree which caught the canopy in the race to death, held it, and saved him. Then there was that German girl, blond and sun-tanned as though she had just come from Honolulu. She wore shorts in the heat, blue shorts, and just before we assembled to jump, she would change into her green jumping suit, complete with rubber helmet. Some said she was jumping into Germany as an agent, some said Poland. She would stand at the plane door, terrified, with an instructor on each side of her. They would shout, "Go!" but not until she felt their strong arms around her buttocks and felt the shove would she spring out. Then there was that small Rumanian boy. He couldn't have been more than fifteen. He used to land miles beyond the dropping ground, for no chute was small enough for him and the slightest wind blew him far away. Every time we would have to wait for him to come up from where he landed. I used to watch him going to the door. His small arms hardly enabled him to grip the wide door of a DC-3, but he didn't need to, for he would just walk out as easily and as unperturbedly as though he were going from the kitchen door to school. I wondered where he was now. And the old man with the gray hair, his spine already kyphotic and fixed, and his sight myopic. He would slowly take off his glasses just before he jumped and methodically fold them into their case. He would ease his leg straps, as though he had a rupture which was apt to get caught when the strain came, then he would walk toward the door with fixed white features, take up his place, and, when the moment came, fall awkwardly into the open. They were courageous people, those, all jumping with death and into pretty certain death.

Bill was saying to me, "Come on—take your chute." And I

turned and saw the R.A.F. officer in charge of the packing station holding a chute out for me. I took it and turned to find a spare space to fit the harness on. A very drunk sergeant came through the door. He was going home to England, while we three were fitting on our chutes to go into Slovenia. The officer pushed him away, saying, "I'll deal with you later." The shoulder straps were too tight, so we loosened them until they just gripped. We released the harness, took off the chutes, and carried them into the truck, laying them gently on the floor. Then away again down the long white straight road gleaming in the evening sun.

At Brindisi we halted and went to a flat for food. It was a hurried meal, with the conducting officer glancing every few minutes at his watch and the boys wolfing down the last decent food they would get for some time. At 7:30 P.M. we left again in the truck, and in less than quarter of an hour arrived at the airfield. Straight across in the gathering night we went to where about a dozen DC-3 planes lay grouped, all with doors open, and already the air crews standing alongside, smoking and waiting their turns to take off. I was getting a bit silent now, already thinking of the moment, standing there by the open door with only the night beneath. We put on our chutes with rubber pads down the back to protect the spine. We asked the number of the plane, were duly inspected by the ground officer, and then again climbed into the truck, which took us to the plane door. Here we shook hands with Davis, the conducting officer, and as we stood there, the pilot and navigator came along and stood talking to us for a few moments.

"Time to get up and in," the pilot said, and up and in we clambered. The lights were on in the plane and we found the whole of the space taken up with bales of boots, bales of uniforms, boxes of ammunition, crates of mines, and a few boxes with Red Cross labels. Indeed there was nowhere to sit, let alone lie down, during the journey. But just before we left, we pushed some bales together to make a more or less uncomfortable bed, or a place to rest our bodies on, anyhow. While so doing the lights went out and with a choke and a gasp the port engine started. The dispatcher came from the cabin and closed the door, bolting it fast, and then the starboard engine sprang into life. The plane quivered and shook, then slowly moved down toward the runway.

Just before turning into the straight the plane stopped. First one engine roared and died away to a gentle purring, then the other engine roared, and as I looked through the window I could see the glow of the red-hot exhaust. We moved into the straight and started on our journey. Such a roaring, a quivering, and trembling; we rushed down the straight, up went the tail, then into the air and we were air-borne. The engines died slowly to a steady hum, we circled the drome, and far below I saw the lights of Brindisi. Then only darkness as we headed out to sea and to the north.

I could hear Vic turning and trying to get himself comfortable somewhere behind me. Then he got up and started twisting a bale of boots around so that he could rest his chute on it. Bill had already turned over and was trying to get some sleep and the plane was soaring through the night, which sang shrill beyond the aluminum wall. We settled down to the monotonous hum of the soaring. I tried to sleep. Even to doze would be a relief, but the coming fear kept ever before me, and I envied the boys, who had lapsed at least into forgetfulness. I leant forward and looked out the window. Nothing but darkness, and a singing of the wind through the taut wires. Occasionally red sparks would shoot from the exhaust to disappear into the blackness. I turned back and buried my head on my arm and tried to sleep. A while stream of visions flashed across the stage. Ivo and Voyasin, mixed up with the roaring of the surf at Piha and the warm summer New Zealand nights. Faces passed before me in never-ending sequence. Faces of yesteryear. Where was Linturi now, the child of the sea and the moon from the South Sea Islands? Where was Marjorie? Perhaps racing down the Tapanui road on her roan horse, hair to the wind, dress high on her thighs, and the horse with dilated, steaming nostrils and a wild look in his eye as he flashed by. And Gladys? The mother of two children now, she would be sitting by the pine-log fire with needle and thread in her hand, and the fire burning on, she heeding it not. And Goyko, who was shot. Slowly sleep came.

It was Bill who woke me. I heard him turning over, pulling on a rope which passed under my legs. He sat up and said, "Have a rum, sir?" Then I felt his hand waving around in the dark and in it the flask of rum. It tasted sweet and warm and as I handed it back I felt the flames deep down in my belly. We had been going about two hours now, so we should be well up the Adriatic, I thought. My head rested on the bale again and the next conscious moment was the door opening in front of us. A figure clambered down over the cargo to where I lay.

"We are getting close to the target area, sir. Will you get ready? It looks all right below."

My mouth began to go dry, and physical fear swelled up within me. I stood up and tightened my leg straps again. The lights of the plane were on now, and already the dispatcher was at the door, swinging it in. Bill looked as white as a sheet, his thinning curly hair awry, almost standing on end. Physical sickness began to creep into my belly. Science said, "Just a vasomoter change, old chap; it will be all right in a few minutes." I stood at the open door; far below I saw a few red dots, the fires gleaming in the night. The plane was circling before running in; how the night screamed and raced by outside. Why was I jumping into this bloody country? I seized hold of both sides of the open door, and could feel Vic behind me. A last look at the static line—had I fixed it securely? Then the tiny red light beside the door came on; the plane was righting itself. Someone shouted, "Action stations!" I crouched low, threw my head back, and waited. Eternity seemed sweeping by. I tried to get a better purchase with my legs, to spring well out. I thought that fear was going to paralyze me. The engines slowed, the green lamp flashed on, and in my ear I heard "Go!" Just a second I stayed—or was it a second? Then I leapt into the night below.

The cold air cracked me and swept me backward in a terrific rushing. For a moment I was nowhere, conscious appreciation had gone. Then quite suddenly profound peace. The plane was far away, just a red taillight and a low droning in the distance. Above me I saw the great white dome of the chute billowing tight, and on the horizon below the stars ending in a vast blackness. Somewhere were seven red dots. There was no sensation at all of falling, just a great peace, and I wondered why I had been so frightened. I seized the front shroud lines and pulled, for I appeared to be swinging slowly backward and forward. A gentle wind cooled my face. "Feet and knees together, you bloody fool," I remembered an instructor shouting at me once, and I got into position for landing. Where was the beautiful German blonde? Did she land all right, I wondered? And the little boy and the old man? Could he draw his rheumy feet and knees together to stand the shock? In a flash I saw, appearing from the blackness, hills and valleys, cliffs and trees. The coolness seemed to be on my face and I wondered if I would land backward. I changed my hands to the rear shroud lines and pulled hard. I drew up my knees and held them hard together, a tree swished by, and then, suddenly, crash! and I rolled over and over down a steep little

hill. The chute billowed in the wind and then collapsed; it
caught on a stone and pulled me up with a jerk. I punched the
quick release on my breast and the harness loosened; I dragged
the leg straps through and then rolled a little farther, free;
bruised and sore but free. It was pitch dark. Would they be
Partisans or Germans who met me? I made my way toward a
clump of trees and hid, waiting. Where had Bill and Vic
landed? I hadn't seen them since I left the plane. I heard voices
approaching and kept in the shadow, still, listening. In the
gloom I saw someone silhouetted against the top of a little
hill. My pistol was ready; then I heard, "Say, I thought the
first guy landed near here!" Americans. I shouted, and then
heard a Cockney voice say, "One of them landed near here,
I saw his chute fold up." I shouted again and the next moment
I was shaking Captain Jack Wick by the hand and together
we walked over to where the fires were.

Bill and Vic had already been gathered in and were sitting
down in a well-made shelter, each with his rum flask on his
knees, half empty. Soon they were empty and soon too we were
in bed, in a peasant's house, asleep, while the plane was still
roaring through the night home again to Italy. Three more
"Joes" had been dropped into Slovenia.

CHAPTER 2

Forest Hospitals

Next morning began with eggs and coffee. I marveled but said
nothing. We went outside and found a green countryside with
fields half cut for hay, and peasants working in the warm summer sun. Forests topped the hills around us, long plots of
cultivated land spanned the narrow valleys, and here and

there were dotted whitewashed houses, each with its trees around it and children playing on the veranda steps. Everything looked so civilized, so contented and prosperous after the pervading barrenness of Lika and Bosnia. We left Packa about 10 A.M. bound for the British, or rather the American, Mission, which at that time was in a schoolhouse in the village called Petrovas. A truck took us along the roads and soon we arrived at the town of Crnomelj, the largest town we had yet been in during our sixteen months in Yugoslavia. There were great numbers of Partisans walking about the streets, fair-haired, tall boys, thin, and quite unlike the dark, stocky Bosnians. *Kola,* or wagons, passed along the streets, and here and there trucks were drawn up, with loads of stores, wood, and sacks of corn. We stopped for a moment, then continued our journey toward Petrovas.

The welcome we received from the American officer in charge of the mission was cool, to say the least. Firstly, he had been expecting an American increment and had received a British one, and, secondly, General Nickolic had failed to let the Slovene High Command know that we were coming, and no permission had been granted for us to enter the country. (This made me extremely angry, because even before we left Bari, Nickolic assured me that he had already done so.) The American officer had therefore to explain our presence to a fairly difficult Slovene Command. Thirdly, and perhaps of major importance, the barrier was a temperamental one. We just didn't suit one another.

However, that day I met the remaining members of the mission, both American and British, and found that they completely made up for what their chief lacked in hospitality. There was Jack Wick, a sterling English officer, from Devon, I think. A regular soldier, slow, methodical, reliable, he always had the unpleasant jobs to do but never grumbled or growled, and to us in the months that followed proved a good friend. An American intelligence officer of Slovene extraction, with whom we lived for the next day or so, was a humorist, a happy-go-lucky type, who in civil life had done every job imaginable from being a hobo in the depression to a salesman of railway engines. Then another Slovene, a Canadian, I think, working for the British side. He seemed wrapt in perpetual gloom, gloom for his country and gloom in his private life. The wireless operators were headed by a sergeant called, for want of something better, Raffles. He looked after our interests for many months. He was the oldest member of the mission and had been there in the days of the notorious Major Jones. Major Jones, a rough Canadian type, had incurred displeasure and was at that moment writing a book in Bari at the Imperiale Hotel; probably a rather outspoken book, on the political maneuverings of the British in Yugoslavia. I heard a year afterward that he was still trying to get his book published and still trying to get home to Canada, but unfortunately a passage at that time "could not be given." He must have been a grand chap in his own way, Major Jones, and echoes of his exploits will be heard for years down the valley of the Kupa.

In Slovenia we found a proper liaison staff appointed to deal with the mission, and through them all approaches to the Slovene Command were made. I quickly got in touch with the chief of that staff, a lieutenant at that time called Jiggar. In civil life he had been a lawyer in Ljubljana. I pointed out to him that I couldn't understand Nickolic's failure to let them know that we were coming and that I was sorry if any misunderstanding had arisen. All we wanted to do was to help them, and if we could not help, then we would go back to Italy.

On the contrary, he said, he was sure that we would be of great help to their wounded, and already he had let the chief of the Medical Service, one Luka, know that we had arrived. He said that all the Slovene hospitals were hidden away in the forests, and were so secret that the staff itself had no idea where they were. It would therefore be some time before a doctor would come to see us, but would we wait at the mission until that was possible? We said we would, and prepared to settle down for a week.

Owen Reed of Croatia once said to me, "It's always a month before you can start to do anything in this country." And by now I realized that he was right.

That very afternoon word came through that we must move, because the enemy was coming up through the valley of the Kupa and would threaten Crnomelj. So we packed up again and got ready to hike. To my amazement, at 4 P.M. a truck drew up and we all piled in, complete with belongings, and started away from Petrovas toward the forest-covered mountains. The roadside was so different from the Bosnian. Beautiful farms were scattered over the valley floor, and as we drew near Semic, we passed through the center of the vineyards. All the vines were in full leaf, but the grapes were still small and green. Plenty of vino seemed to us to be assured.

Up over the saddle and down to Crnosnitza, where we halted. A terrific outpouring of people and matériel onto the road, and then we started up the low hills on our left, carrying what we could with us to the darkening forest. In the middle of this tree-clad slope we found a camp already prepared. Log cabins made from freshly cut timber, still oozing its resinous gum in little blobs all over the place. The American officer in charge of the mission assigned to us a small hut in which Wychenich, the U.S. intelligence officer, was already installed. This meant seven of us in a small hut about ten feet by ten. The senior officer took commodious quarters higher up in the forest.

Luckily the Slovene liaison staff was close at hand and I immediately became more friendly with them. Jiggar, a well-set man of thirty, was in charge. He spoke excellent English. Florian, tall and dark, was of no rank then. His mother had been in New Zealand and indeed was born in New Zealand, I think, I often tried to persuade him to come back to New Zealand after the war. But no, here was Slovenia, a young country, liberated for the first time from foreign domination, and he was needed to help build up the great and new ideal. Next came Nada Pirnat. She had divorced old Pirnat the sculptor after years of trial and error. Nada proved a great friend to us and it was she who accompanied me on many long tramps through the forest, visiting hospitals she had never seen before. Unfortunately Nada had a tubercular lesion of both lungs and finally broke down, owing to excessive exercise and bad food. She went to Italy and became secretary to Naubauer, the great Slovene tuberculosis doctor. Boris Kraeger, the chief commissar to the Slovene High Command, was Nada's cousin. So days passed in waiting and in wondering when we were going to start work and where.

One morning Jiggar came to our hut and said that their best surgeon, Dr. Bogdan, was coming down from the forest to meet me and would arrive that morning. He had hardly gone when I saw coming toward our hut a middle-aged man in riding breeches, clean-shaven, Red Star in his hat, and the look of a surgeon written all over him. I said, "Are you Bogdan?" "Yes," he said. "I'm Bogdan."

We sat under the trees and talked. I told him about the work we had done in Lika, in Kordun, in Bosnia, and on the island of Vis, and said that here we would like to help also. He told me about conditions in Slovenia. The hospitals were more stable because they were better hidden, but the same German atrocities took place whenever one was found. And they had

found several, during the years, and after knifing the wounded
to death and shooting the doctors, they burnt the hospitals to
the ground. So elaborate precautions were now taken, and
great secrecy surrounded the positions of all their hospitals. If
I stayed here, he said, I must take the same precautions.

I told him that already two of my hospitals had been found
by the Germans and destroyed. The first was that well-hidden
peasant's house deep in the *jama* near Turnavic. There the
old Jewish gynecologist from Zagreb had been killed, after
seeing his wounded burnt to death in the flames. Then there
was Otocevas, high up in the deeply wooded col on Mount
Yasekovac. The pilots of the Heinkels and Dorniers who
searched for it every day had finally located it by the brightly
colored dresses of the Bosnian girls who carried the wounded
on stretchers through the forest to the hospital. I told him
how I had returned there for stores after we had evacuated the
wounded, only to find it smoldering. And I told him how,
much later, I had learnt the fate of the parties of wounded,
whom I had tried unsuccessfully to trace in the forest. For the
Germans had not been content with burning the hospital to
the ground, but had sought the wounded with Alsatian dogs.
Two groups they never found, and for two months the
wounded lived and starved in the forest. The third group
found their way to Kerenitsa, and there, with Dr. Kayfesh,
they were caught, their throats cut, and their misery ended.

"Yes, I remember," said Bogdan. He turned his face away,
and bitterness overcame us both.

He told me of the 9th Corpus, working near the coast, and
of the 4th Zone, north of the Sava, where conditions were so
bad they rarely heard of their wounded, except when some
doctor was killed and a request came for another. We spoke
about the question of medical stores and he pleaded with me
to get in more and more stores, for they were so terribly short.

Short of all kinds of dressings, of cardiacs, of anesthetics, and
of food. I promised what help I could give. He then said that
he had to go to the headquarters, and that tomorrow I would
meet Dr. Luka, who was really in charge of all the hospitals.

The next day Luka came, dark and tall, thin and serious-
looking. In civil life he was a gynecologist, and his smooth
voice recalled many of his kind I had known elsewhere. He
asked what we wanted to do and briefly I told him we would
appreciate a hospital of our own, to run ourselves as a British
hospital. We would undertake to supply all the medical equipment if he would supply the nurses and the food. That was
agreed upon, and he suggested that I start seeing their hospitals, so that I would understand the "Partisan life."

I felt that I already understood the Partisan life well enough,
having lived with them, eaten with them, fought with them,
and worked with them for over a year now. But still, it seemed
to be an old-established Yugoslav custom, this learning about
the "Partisan life," so I agreed. Besides, I had already seen
that Slovenes were very different in their relations with the
British than were the Bosnians and the Croats. They seemed
to have an unconscious reserve and suspicion toward us.

Next day, in company with Nada, we climbed to the top
of the hill above the forest, leaving camp at six in the morning.
Even at that early hour it was a long and hot climb and when
I arrived at the little burnt-out village at the top where the
medical *glavni stab* (headquarters) was, I was ready to sit
down. We were welcomed into the house, which was the main
distributing center for all the hospitals in the forest, by Colonel
Igor. He too was an obstetrician, from Ljubljana, and with
him was Cedric, a doctor who later became attached to
S.N.O.S., the Slovene Parliament. Cedric liked his *rakija* and
he filled our glasses. Nada and I drank down the glass and
followed it rapidly with another. Valerian gathered from the

hillside had been steeped in the *rakija*, giving it a bitter taste, something resembling vodka. Then followed coffee, and while Nada and I drank and ate our bread—maize bread and very good—I could see Cedric and Igor taking me in from the tips of my hobnailed boots to the top of my black beret. Igor spoke good French, while Cedric spoke only German and Slovenian, and I spoke neither. Indeed I realized that all my Serbo-Croat had gone for nothing, for Slovenian was almost a different language. But I quickly learnt it under Nada's guidance.

We started out for the hospitals, Bogdan having joined us, and within ten minutes were in the shade of great pine trees, the tallest pines I had ever seen. The track seemed to be an old unused road, and along the sides the moss grew green and thick, like a silent carpet, covering the huge stones which lined the road and formed the forest floor. After we had been walking the forest road for almost an hour, Igor stopped, as though searching for something among the small trees on the roadside. We pushed our way through the low undergrowth, covering our tracks with dead branches, and then found, leading off at right angles on the stony forest floor, a series of mossy "steppingstones." Igor carefully turned each stone over, exposing its bare side for us to step on, and so we crossed from one to the next. Then, as we passed, the mossy surface would be turned back again so that no sign was left. Thus we went for fifty yards until we were well screened from the main route, and our track started again. This method of conspiration was repeated several times, and then another method adopted. After a moment's searching we stepped into a clump of weed and found two parallel tree trunks, long and thin, leading through the hidden greenery. We walked along these and then stepped up onto an above-ground ladder. This was a series of tree trunks, either suspended from the lower branches of trees, or else supported on built-up rocks. My eyes were now well opened to the absolute secrecy which surrounded their hospitals. For over a hundred yards we crossed this overhead bridge and then came down to terra firma again. Here we met a lonely tovarisch standing, rifle at his shoulder. When we had crossed, he greeted us, then set to work to take down the bridge. When he had finished, the tree trunks were completely hidden by moss and leaves; no sign, noise, or track would lead the way to where the wounded lay hidden. It was all very elaborate, and Luka told me that since they had adopted this system of "conspiration," not one hospital in this forest had been found.

At last, down in a hollow, we saw our destination, three log cabins, built half below the surface of the ground, and well camouflaged by a screen of pines. We were met by the doctor, a medical student in about his third year, from Ljubljana. The wounded were lying in decent beds. They had sheets, a thing unheard of in Bosnia. None of them had that creamy, toxic look I was accustomed to see so often, none of them was thin, or famished, or had scurvy, with great swollen purple gums which bled without provocation. As I looked around, I saw that all the fractures were extended on homemade Böhler frames, a real tribute to Bogdan, who had been in charge of them. I saw at once that here the standard of surgery was much higher. Moreover, as we left the hut door, I saw pasted on to a board called the *Sten Cas*, little drawings and paintings, poems and prose, the work of the patients. Why, in Bosnia there were many who could not write their names, let alone poems.

We left that hospital and soon were on the open road again, getting deeper into the forest. Sweat was pouring off me. Nada and I were ahead of the group, when Bogdan called out, "Here we are!" And he lifted an overhanging branch on the track to disclose a fallen log lying at right angles to our previous direction. We walked along the fallen log, thus camouflaging our tracks, and then down into a hollow between rocks, where a fresh track was visible. In half an hour we were at Peter's hospital. Peter was a pathologist whom Bogdan had trained as a surgeon and his hospital high on the top of that mountain was a great eye opener to me. There he had a perfect little laboratory and showed me slides of a new type of gas-forming organism he had isolated from a group of seven cases. He showed me his instruments, a good collection, though he did not think so. He had septic and aseptic wards, and in his main ward the windows were curtained with bright silk curtains made from parachute cloth. To his wife, Maria, who was also his chief nurse, went the credit for turning this forest hut into a modern hospital, complete even to curtains on the windows. Among his patients was a young American airman who had crashed in Slovenia. Bogdan had had to amputate one of his legs and now he had a perfect stump for an artificial limb. How different from the guillotine amputations elsewhere. Nada asked me what I thought of it all, and I replied that here I saw little need for a new surgeon. "Ah no," said Luka. "The need is great. We have only one surgeon, and that is Bogdan." I thought to myself that Bogdan must have spread his influence widely.

Next day we visited what proved to be the greatest eye opener of the lot, for there, surrounded by German divisions (and there were at that time enough of them in Slovenia), was a perfect maternity hospital. There, lying in little forest-made cots in the sun, were seven babies, each covered by an ornamental blanket as though straight from Bond Street. In charge was a woman doctor from Ljubljana who had studied pediatrics at Vienna. Beside each cot was the baby's weight chart, showing the amount of milk at each feeding and the gain, the condition of the mother, and various other medical

refinements. Some babies were on artificial food, their Partizanka mothers having been killed. In other cases fighting and
starvation had been so severe that the milk flow was impover-
ished. Every such baby had a perfect chart, and my appreciation for the work knew no bounds. The doctor had prepared
a meal for us, and we had beautiful tender venison with a glass
of *rakija*. Even the little room where she lived was as though
in the midst of a great city. The rug on the floor, the pictures
of the mountain Triglav on the walls, and the delicately
stitched curtains and tablecloth made one feel a Partisan no
longer.

The commissar at that hospital had a tame fawn, and after
lunch we went out in the sun to see the babies again, and to
watch the fawn feed from his hands and then gallop off into
the forest, only to return in a few moments for some more
maize bread. Nada was thrilled with the hospital, and on our
way expressed my appreciation for the determination and
the organization of the doctor who gave to all those Slovene
mothers such a peaceful haven of rest wherein to bear new
leaders for the new nation.

Next day again into the forest. This time Bogdan did not
come, for he was busy in his own hospital, but Igor slowly
padded along, and we had with us Boris, the engineer, who
was responsible for the building of all these hideouts. All
morning we walked and that night we stayed at another hospital in charge of Dr. Meta, another woman doctor. Her hospital
was quite near the main road, and Luka told me that for three
weeks the Germans had camped within two hundred yards of
the hospital and searched for it every day, but never found it.
Meta did not run away, and all during that time she fortified
her patients by her own heroism and stoicism. She was re-
warded by thirty grateful patients and by the High Command,
who presented her with the Medal for Bravery. Everywhere

I went I was struck by the high standard of surgery and the perfect organization which seemed to be in existence. Next morning we rose early and started for Ajdovec, an almost-completed hospital, but not yet with any patients or staff. It had water near at hand, and though high up the mountain, was well hidden. From lookouts we saw Novo Mesto on one side and Kocevje on the other. It lay in the bottom of a deep *jama,* and was invisible to those above it, even when within a few yards.

These *jame* were a common configuration of the forest country, owing to the limestone formations in the area, and when one walked through the forest, every *jama* resembled every other one. The huge depression, shaped almost like a gigantic funnel leading into the ground, would have a circumferential area of up to two or three acres, and a depth of two hundred feet, with rocky steep sides, while from the bottom grew the thickest and tallest pines I have ever seen, struggling and soaring to reach the light above.

Deep in the everlasting shelter and gloom of these trees we made our hospitals and kept our wounded secure.

CHAPTER 3

Underground Hospital

It was to Ajdovec that we eventually came. We were glad to leave the mission with its little discontents, its American-British make-up, where Wychenich rated all day at his superiors and filled in the intervening time by telling us his own long string of troubles. Indeed so often did I hear of them that in the end I examined him, and decided, as I had decided many times before with "browned-off" officers, that he should return to Italy for treatment and operation. Within a few moments of my telling him he was encoding a message: "Coming out by the first opportunity on doctor's advice." I smiled at the relief which spread all over his face, but I thought it a little hard when the night before he left he gave all his belongings to the Slovenes. I dearly coveted his Leica.

So we left the mission and decided that nothing would drag us back except necessity. Nada came with us as far as the hilltop, and then, with rumbling *kola* in front of us and rucksacks on our backs, we swung off through the forest, cool in the hot summer's day, along the mossy paths, over the hills, down the valleys, past all the hidden paths until we arrived at the end of the road where we unloaded the *kola* and sat down to wait for it to go, lest the driver should see where we entered the forest to reach the "conspirated" track to the hospital.

Arriving there, we saw that already another hut had been built to accommodate the three of us, a good hut halfway up the *jama*, so we could look down on the hospital and look up toward the treetops which hid the sky. The workmen, Janus, France, Jose, Bicele, and Vinco, welcomed us and that night we sat out under the huge trees eating a delicious meal of wild pig, fawn, mushrooms, and potatoes.

Next day we worked. Bill got the operating theater ready with what little we had brought, and Vic started on the wards. The men were all skilled woodsmen and very soon bunks were made, shelves were put up, windows cut, and in about three days, with the arrival of more stores, we were ready to open.

For the opening the medical *glavni stab* provided a great barrel of wine, and a keg of *rakija*. Bicele provided another young deer and France spent the whole day cooking and tasting, tasting and cooking, until I wondered whether, when the guests arrived, any food would be forthcoming at all.

I saw them coming down through the trees on the far side

of the *jama* and went to meet them. Bogdan, Boris (the hospital architect and engineer), Nada, my beautiful Nada with her fair hair and a constant desire for what she mechanically called "petrol," in other words *rakija*, and two couriers. It was a warm summer Slovene night and before long song echoed up through the trees. The Germans, had they been near, would have heard until the wee small hours Partisan songs of themes and melodies quite different from those farther south. The Slovenes were not as gloomy as the Bosnians; they hadn't forgotten *"Triglav Moj Dom"*; they hadn't forgotten love and all its tender associations. Often and often I heard *"Počiva Jezero v Tihoti"* ringing through the trees to the blue sky beyond. I don't know what time the opening finished, for the heavy labors of the previous three days and the strong red wine soon made me sleepy, so I climbed up to our hut and fell asleep.

All the guests had gone and left a message that we must expect patients any day now. All day long there was firing in the valley below us, and that night our first patients were brought in from the *javka*, or secret hiding place, some miles away down the forest road. These *javke* were our only contact with the outside world. The wounded coming from battle were taken to them, often in bullock wagons, and left under branches, or in caves, for the situation of the *javke* was frequently changed. There they would be left and when their bearers had disappeared back again to the battle, we would go by night and carry them over the hidden tracks to the top of the mountain and there to our *jama*, where the Hospital Ajdovec received them. Sometimes the long journey would freeze their broken legs and gangrene would supervene. Often shock was so severe that life hardly remained when we reached them, but for the sake of those who lived we had to adopt this method of concealment.

There were twelve patients carried in that first night. Most of them were limb wounds, and after the delousing process we quickly operated and got them safely into bed. There was a penetrating wound of the brain and a large haemothorax, which we let settle down before aspirating.

The wound of the brain was an interesting one. The boy was completely blind when we admitted him, with a penetrating wound just above the occiput, in the mid-line. We shaved his skull completely and prepared it with some petrol, which we reserved for important cases. Then, under local anesthesia, supplemented by a small dose of nembutal, I made a large crossbow incision after the technique of Cushing, and dissected the flaps back to the bone. All the time I was operating the boy kept saying, "I cannot see. I cannot see. How can I live? Why was I not killed?" Then Ivitsa, the operating-theater nurse, would speak gently to him and he would settle down for a bit longer. The bone was well splintered. Hair and part of his cap had been driven through the oozing hole into the brain. We gently washed the debris out with snow water—we had no sterile water at that time. We lifted out bone chips and then enlarged the hole and at the bottom saw the end of a moderately large piece of mortar shell. Carefully we nibbled away the bone edges until we had a fairly large hole the size of a matchbox. Then we continued washing the debris from the dura, which was now exposed, torn, ragged, and bleeding. We carefully trimmed the loose, straggling bits and then saw the metal clearly. It was wedged exactly in the middle, and as we moved it, blood oozed up all around. It had perforated the large venous sinuses, so we underran them with fine silk taken from parachute cords, and then, in a dry and unobscured field, removed the piece of metal. It had buried its way right between the two lobes of the occipital region and, as far as we could tell, had not produced any permanent damage to the brain cells beyond shock and bruising. The surface of each lobe in the great longitudinal fissure where sight is appreciated was not irreparably damaged. We washed it out carefully and dislodged another piece of his cap and then, for the first time in Slovenia, used penicillin. We dusted it in between the lobes and around the torn dura mater, then replaced the large flaps, dusting sulphonamide powder over the muscle surfaces, and finally closed the skin completely except for a small dependent drain.

We were so anxious about this case that we continued giving him our precious penicillin for three days. His whole head and eyes had been bandaged up in the meantime, and on the fifth day we took off the bandage, removed the drain from a clean healed wound, took out the stitches, and looked at his eyes. From one eye he could see what he described as flashes of light, but from the other, nothing. We covered them over again, disappointed but not yet without hope. In ten days' time we again took the bandage off and the boy said immediately, "I can see. I can see!" And he could. With one eye he could distinguish my fingers when two yards away. In a month he had almost complete return of vision and great was his joy.

It was about this time that Luka came to Ajdovec. He was a funny chap, Luka, and I always felt with him that his communist principles made him antagonistic to us because we were British, but with his professional eye he regarded us as staunch colleagues. He had a habit of disappearing from my hut after our evening meal, and going down to the men's quarters to get a report from the kitchen, confidential, of course, on what the British capitalists were doing and where they went. If he had asked us, he would have been told. Indeed I said to him that it wasn't necessary to go to the kitchen to find out our technique, he could come and watch and see. He belonged, I'm afraid, to the suspicious communist group which saw little good in anything the British achieved. Luckily neither Bogdan nor Igor, the other two medical colonels, was like him. They were older and more concerned in helping the wounded than in worrying over political aspirations.

CHAPTER 4

An Evening of Music

Luka came to ask me if I would go to Italy to plead with the British to land planes to take out the Slovene wounded, about three thousand. He said that the German troops would undoubtedly concentrate in Slovenia as they came north from Greece and the general situation would deteriorate.

I was not keen on going back to Italy at all just as we were starting, but nevertheless it was a reasonable plea and if anyone could tell them about the wounded it was I. At the same time I knew that in Slovenia the wounded were treated better than anywhere else in Yugoslavia, and that their stores situation was also better, for they drew by means of Partisan agents on Trieste and Milan and also from Germany itself through Zagreb and Ljubljana.

Next day I left Ajdovec and joined Luka at Crnosnitza and together, in a captured German wood-burning truck, we started for Naslek, where a temporary landing strip was being used. Just as we were leaving, who should come but Nada. I helped her into the truck and we settled down for a long and rough ride. It was evening when we arrived and at the *komanda mesta's* I found about twenty American pilots and four British P.O.W.s.

The R.A.F. was running the air strip and presumably, being

a British unit stationed at Naslek, it was responsible for the well-being of the P.O.W.s. But unfortunately when I arrived I found great discontent and ill-feeling. It was all over the food. The Partisans had nothing for the P.O.W.s except beans, occasional maize bread, and coffee. The British P.O.W.s all ate with the Partisans, had their beans and coffee, and then went into the R.A.F. mess with its Spam, jam, bully beef, and so on. It was galling to sit and watch them eat the bloody stuff in front of your very eyes and never be offered even a crumb. The mere fact that I sat down with the Americans to beans alone helped the situation a little. Added to this stupid differentiation there was the feeling of "To hell with the Americans anyhow. They'll be back in Italy soon." And that was the argument put up by the R.A.F. squadron leader when I went and spoke to him about it.

"Yes," I replied, "that is so, they will be back in Italy soon. But you too can get your own stores replenished by the plane that comes to take them out."

It made no difference. Those Americans would leave the country feeling justifiably sore, and I felt rather ashamed, in fact very ashamed, of the position. Not only that, but the R.A.F.'s attitude to the local Partisans was deplorable. They treated them not as allies at all but as nonentities and inferiors. Fortunately the officer concerned made such a bad break later with General Stane and Commissar Kidrich that his removal was instantly asked for, and took place. He was a real Colonel Blimp, walking about Naslek with a lovely uniform and a large stick and ringing his bell for his port at night. He was an isolated case in the country and thank God for it. That sort of thing didn't go down too well with the communists.

The night I arrived, one of the pilots asked me to see an American airman who was ill in a hayloft. It was seven miles from the village: I took Nada and together we climbed the ladder into the loft. It was just light enough to see, and there, lying on the hay, an Italian ground sheet under him and practically nothing over him, was a boy, thin, toxic-looking, hardly noticing our arrival, and covered with the most indescribable filth imaginable. He hadn't been washed for days, he was too weak even to move, and the dysentery was just a slow, continual dribble of blood and mucus.

I saw at once that he was going to die if we didn't do something quickly. Nada got a peasant woman to give us a room, we washed the boy as best we could in that light, and carried him to the new room in a *kola*. I took some rubber tubing from my stethoscope and gave him a bowel washout immediately. Then with a 10cc. syringe and some boiled water and sugar gave him a pint of intravenous fluid and repeated it later during the night. Luckily I had plenty of morphia. We settled him down and in the morning found a little improvement, psychologically if nothing else.

I went to the R.A.F. and sent an immediate urgent message to U. S. Army Air Force Headquarters for a Lysander plane to come and pick him up. Later I found out that the message arrived at the 15th Air Force Group (U.S.) ten days later and they decided he was either dead or better by that time. Nada found eggs and milk from somewhere, and we fed him with this mixture every hour in spite of the vomiting. Luckily I met Andrianich, the Partisan chemist who did all the secret trading with Trieste, and he was able to send a fast courier to Trieste, and get some sulfaguanidine. The boy slowly improved, then rapidly, and when the plane eventually came and he was carried into it, I was quite sure that he was well on the way to recovery. He was a grateful lad. Months later I got a letter from him from America telling me of his safe arrival and his long leave home.

The Germans kept pushing all the time in and around

Naslek, for they knew that we had made a landing strip and they intended to take it. As a precautionary measure the Partisans moved us all away from the village and Nada and I went to a tiny village near the forest. At nights we used to go to the place where Andrianich lived, a great deserted old German castle. It was beautiful, full summer; the yellow strips of corn straddling the narrow valley, the golden oaks and beeches, and the great green sweeping forest that threatened to engulf us all.

One day, walking down a forest track, I heard sounds of someone approaching. I stepped behind two big pine trees, pulled out my pistol, got a hand grenade ready, and waited. As I watched, I saw coming up the track a tall, thin man in a blue suit. He was carrying no gun, no grenades, but a violin case! Surely this was no Partisan! I baled him up, and with pistol in his belly, asked him who he was.

"Ruppel," he replied, "from Ljubljana. I'm going to S.N.O.S."

The name meant nothing to me. I was going to stay that night with a group whose job it was to gather up jettisoned American bombs, and extract the explosive to make our road mines. Night was fast approaching, so I decided to take him with me. I blindfolded him and led him through the forest, until at last it was safe to take the bandage from his eyes. Then, almost in the dark, we scrambled over stones and stumps and logs, and finally came upon the half-sunken log cabin where the group lived.

There was Kostia, the commissar, two Partizanka, and one Partisan. The room was filled with unexploded American bombs, which I didn't find the most reassuring company for the night, and there was no food. But, warmed by the fire and many a *rakija*, I felt the glow of hospitality, though Ruppel still shivered in his city clothes. Kostia took out his piano

accordion, and before long the whole forest was alive with
singing. Ruppel looked and listened, and then took his violin
from its case and played and played, while Kostia improvised
a soft accompaniment. All night long, till four in the morning,
we had a feast, though the belly was empty. When the first
gray dawn came over the forest, we set out on our separate
ways—Ruppel and I in one direction and Kostia, hunting for
bombs, in another. Two days later Kostia was killed, but Ruppel and I arrived safely at Andrianich's depot, our center for
contraband trade with Trieste.

When Andrianich saw who was with me, he was delighted,
and welcomed Ruppel, saying, "Now we'll have music. We
must get some wine, and we'll have music." How he got the
wine I don't know, but that night, as Nada and I walked up
to his house, we heard voices and laughter and Andrianich
singing. We climbed the stairs and sat down. The old castle
was homely, but so like a museum. Stuffed birds looked down
from the walls, great deer with glass eyes stared mutely from
hanging wooden shields, little knickknacks had been placed on
every available ledge, and here and there a stuffed squirrel or
fox. I couldn't help thinking of the huge hedge surrounding
the sleeping beauty in her frozen castle, waiting for the prince
to come.

Andrianich was busy filling glasses with deep red wine, and
asking Ruppel to play. "Play for us, maestro," he said, "play!"
And Ruppel, the long, thin virtuoso, rose and, taking the old
violin in his pencilly-white hands he began. It was a violin
concerto. The glasses sank to the chair arms; we could hear
the odd tovarisch stop and listen outside the window. The
old lady of the castle and her onetime-hunter husband crept
rheumatically to the door and stood, watching and listening.
The whole place echoed and resounded to his music. Nada had
closed her eyes, her hand resting on her knees, her thoughts

years back before the days of the struggle. Andrianich had tears in his eyes, for the hypnotic music brought back to him memories of his wife and children. Where were they now? Once he had been a thriving chemist in Novo Mesto, his home with scarlet geraniums by the window ledge. Now he lived a hunted existence, now here, now there, his wife carried off by the Germans, he knew not where or how; darkest thoughts and saddest scenes fogged his eyes.

Ruppel's clear blue eyes never looked at us. I was lying on the sofa, sometimes watching him, sometimes far away, listening to the splash of the tide on the rocks of Ohope beach, and the wind sighing among the pohutukawa by Kawhia's shining waters. Ruppel's playing was the first instrumental music I had heard in five years. Somehow, in all the tragedy and suffering, beauty could still live. It didn't seem possible that among the Partisans was a man who carried a violin in place of hand grenades and Sten guns. Suddenly he stopped, whisked the bow in his hands, and placed the violin on the table. None of us spoke, and not until we heard the pouring of the wine in his empty glass did we come to life.

As we went home under the stars that night, Nada told me about him. He was the best violinist of the Balkans, professor at the Conservatorium in Ljubljana. For years he had been gambling with life. He had been a Partisan agent in the nazi stronghold, and at last the Germans had found him out and he escaped in the dead of night by train. When far from the town he had jumped into the dark, hoping to find friendly Partisans who would take him to S.N.O.S., the Slovene Parliament, where at least he could rest for a while. For years, not only had he fought the nazis, but he had had his own fight against ill-health, the fight against chronic fibrous tuberculosis. To join the Partisans was perhaps better than to die in a concentration camp, and Ruppel became a fighting Partisan.

CHAPTER 5

Troubles with Commissars

One night the planes came! such excitement for the wounded, the German guns had been barking all day just over the hills; wounded Partisans had been lying in hiding, waiting for freedom in the nearby forest. Luka had reappeared, General Jaka was there, and a host of peasants had been getting the field ready all the day before, clearing away stones, leveling the ground, filling in holes so that the planes could land in safety.

We heard them; away over to the south, they seemed to be. We piled wood high on the fires so that they would see our signals. They swept away into the night and our hopes fell. Then once again they came nearer, in less than a moment it seemed that they were right over us, then down they swept, their lights turned on like great fireflies; down, down, and in a flash they were on the ground. Hundreds of Partisans rushed to them and in five minutes the precious stores were lying in heaps on the grass. After the wounded were embarked, we climbed in. I said good-by to Nada and Luka, and in less than five hours I was back again in Italy.

Next day I got my bearings again and was in the office at an early hour. Bill Wilson, the South African lawyer from Johannesburg, was G.1. He still seemed to be the only person who knew much about things, and still the only one who seemed to care a damn whether the operational individuals lived or died. I poured forth the story to him and he promised immediate assistance, which, I may say, came. Apart from Wilson, it was obvious that the firm was growing stale.

I went to see the medical people. They still spent their time playing with pencils as they talked. It always annoyed me.

There were two medical officers in Yugoslavia, Dafoe and myself. There were four officers in Italy to look after us and a staff of about eight other ranks. What to hell they did I just didn't know. True, they supplied a monthly routine medical pack to each corps, but I shouldn't have thought that that took up too much of their time. The colonel was a charming chap to meet, but just didn't have a clue as to where we were, what we were doing, or what we needed. They had their swim every night, their clothes laid out for them when they reached home, and a pleasant mess besides the sea. Our personal worries about stores and little things for the fight just didn't worry them. It was: "Oh, that is not my department, go to see Q-Ops." You went to Q-Ops and someone said, "Oh, we don't supply that; go to the Quartermaster." You tramped along again and he said, "You will have to get that from D.A.D.O.S." So the Base Merry-Go-Round swung us around until the day came when we returned to the war to get some peace.

Ajdovec again, and I found the hospital full. Bill had done very well indeed, but the constant tension was getting Vic down. The Germans were very close to us and fighting was going on practically every day in the valley about twenty minutes below; the constant gloom of the tall trees, trees so tall that the sun never shone through; the continual watching along our tracks, covering up our marks, lest enemy patrols would find us; the constant lack of amusements after London life. Vic just could not take it; the uncertainty of it all wore him down. He would stand at the window of our hut looking through the great silent trees, just looking. Then he would turn and say, "How much longer will we be here, sir?" "Don't know, Vic," I would reply. He would continue looking, then finally sit down beside the fireplace, pull an old letter from his pocket, and start reading. I knew he would break soon, but

I didn't want to send him back yet, firstly because of the extreme difficulty of getting him out and secondly because we were so busy and he was an excellent worker. Somehow Vic didn't hit it off with the Partisans in the same way that Bill did. He was always too superior, without much to back it with, whereas Bill went about things quietly showing people but never letting them see he was showing them. Then Bill spoke the language much better than Vic. Vic just never tried.

Finally Vic broke. He came to me after a long journey, and told me that he had tuberculosis, that he was breathless and tired. I examined his great chest and told him that I could find nothing wrong but decided that he had better go out to Italy and have it X-rayed anyhow. He left us, and presumably in a few months would reach the lights and pictures of Italy.

Just below us in the valley lay the Kerka River and near it was the little village of Toplice. Toplice in the balmy days of peace had been a health spa. There were hot springs, about three of them, over which a bathhouse and hotel had been built. It was not very long before we found our way to the springs. It was a warm Sunday, I remember. We had run down the mountain slopes above Podhusta and crossed the valley to Toplice, through the little pine forest at the bottom, then across the log bridge at the sawmill, and finally had spent the rest of the afternoon with other Partisans in the hot clear water. Or was it clear? It was good, anyhow. Sometimes the Germans would use the spa and sometimes the Partisans, for the village itself changed hands at least once a week in those days. Always fighting, always tragedy, always tears, always stories of the Domobranci, or White Guard (Slovene Quislings), whom the villagers called "Our Ones."

It wasn't very long before we made friends in the village. Another summer Sunday afternoon we were just leaving to climb the mountain again when a woman came running out of a house and said to us in a very American voice, "Are you English?"

"Not English," Bill said patiently. "British."

"Well, I'm Slovene but speak American," she replied. "Will you come in? It is my birthday party and though we haven't got anything, yet we would like you to come, because the people here don't believe any British are in this country at all."

So in we went and met them all. There was Papa, aged about eighty-three and still able to toddle up to his vineyard and bring home the grapes. There was Anitsa, his unmarried daughter who had been in America many years. Her sister, who was married to the local doctor; she was a real go-getter and possessed more feminine attire, I am sure, than any other woman in Slovenia. There was Anitsa's cousin, and two Partisans, one a Partisan doctor and the other a schoolteacher. And Gruno, the Alsatian dog, who just couldn't figure what it was all about.

What a meal! Cold pork, pickled mushrooms and potatoes, and a sweet made of pastry with something inside it. Then coffee, and the whole lot washed down with flagons of wine. It was late summer, and, just as the long evening closed, without warning down fell German shells into the village. The guests fled. Bill and I were not so keen on fleeing because our way home led across some open country well in sight of the German mortars. Then the rattle of the Partisan machine guns raced up and down the valley. More mortar shells; one hit a tree and down it came with a hell of a crash. Anitsa showed us a secret place where she would hide us if they came into the village. Everyone had such secret places where they hid their personal possessions from the Germans. More shells. It seemed so stupid on a glorious summer evening. We watched and waited. The village, which before had been quite full of people, was now as quiet as a grave. Then it stopped. The Germans rattled their guns back to Novo Mesto, and we said good-by and thank you, and went up the mountain and through the forest home.

Next morning we started transferring all our fractured-femur cases over the mountains to a better-hidden hospital. It held thirty patients and was so well hidden that it was safe, or so we thought, from German or White Guard attack, despite the fact that often the Germans' camps were only five kilometers away. It took a whole day to carry four men over, for, though not far as the crow flies, the way was very steep and rough. Each had a good dose of morphia before starting, and Bill and I were there to receive them. Alas, we had only one blanket each for them and autumn was nearly upon us. Moreover we could use only charcoal for our fires for fear of the smoke giving our position away. Still we managed. The Partizanka Leanna and her mother came over. Leanna, an ardent Jewish communist, was a nurse. Her mother, Maria, an excellent, genteel woman, for whom the discomforts of the life must have been appalling, was the cook.

In all our fractures we used mechanical extension and when the Steinman pins gave out, once more we found that four-inch nails served just as well. Parachute cord was used for all extensions and the weights were bags full of stones. I could get over to this hospital only once a week, for I had four other hidden hospitals to get to, some of them a good eight hours' hard walking away. We would set off in the early morning, carrying all our stores with us to these outlying hospitals, work all day, then leave in the dusk and find our way home, sometimes. Often it was impossible to go straight home; a German patrol, heavy shelling, Domobranci in the forest, and so on. We often lost the way, and indeed even the most experienced woodsmen would get lost at night, for the tracks were so hidden and the forest so dense it needed only one slip and one was lost for hours.

The commissar we had at this time was a grand fellow called Tony. He came from Novo Mesto and many a night we sat around the log fire talking about our countries and their philosophies. We learnt much from our talks and it was through him we first learnt of the suspicion and the active antagonism the communists had for the British.

Alas, as we had already experienced before, one day a new fellow arrived and said, "I am the new commissar."

"But," I replied, "I already have a perfectly good one."

"Oh no, you haven't," he said. "He's gone." And gone he had, where we knew not and why we knew not. It was something we had to put up with. The first thing the new commissar did next morning was to come to me and say that he was going to take an inventory of our medical stores with a view to sending some of them away. "Oh no, you won't," I said. "These are British stores, and my arrangement with the Partisans is that the British provide their own stores and run the hospitals and the Partisans provide the hospitals and the food. I intend to stick to my agreement." He departed, knowing I meant business.

A few days later I set off for the British Mission to talk to Colonel Moore, who had replaced the American. I found him perturbed about the whole situation. The Partisans had stopped all movement by British personnel, and, owing to constant pinpricking and spying, life at the mission was becoming increasingly difficult. I couldn't understand the Partisans' attitude, for they had everything to gain from our being there and everything to lose if we left.

However, I enjoyed the visit to the mission and while there I heard that Owen Reed had left Croatia and was coming to do the intelligence work in Slovenia, and indeed would be there in less than a week. So I decided I would come down again in a fortnight's time, and we would have a party. It seemed to me a pity, all this anti-British feeling, inspired by whom I knew not. As far as we were concerned, we had done our utmost for the Yugoslavs, for almost two years now.

My new commissar was a proper anti-British communist. I met an old Partisan who didn't agree with the communist regime, and during walks in the forest or talks by the fireside he told me much of the activities of the V.D.V., an old communist brigade whose job, he told me, was the graceful elimination of people opposed to the regime. Every day in the hospital we had communist propaganda talk for at least an hour in the morning and again in the afternoon. It did not matter how ill the patients were. Even if they were dying, it made no difference, and I got so used to hearing the same old stuff over and over again that I, like the patients, could listen with eyes open but brains shut. Most of them loathed the communist principles, and though few would have the courage openly to show their disapproval, many were completely indifferent to the new faith. They adopted an attitude of "Well, it couldn't be any worse than the old one," and there it was left.

Just about this time I admitted a whole batch of Russian patients, mainly boys who had been at high school when the Germans overran Western Russia. They had been put into German concentration camps and at a later date had escaped and made their way to the Yugoslav Partisans. Here they fought and were wounded. I had long talks with them about their own country and about the fighting in Slovenia. They were adamant in assuring me that the type of communism then practiced in Yugoslavia was nothing like that in Russia. "For God's sake, no!" they would exclaim. "And as for the commissars, we wouldn't tolerate the ones they have here."

I didn't wonder at that, for I couldn't tolerate the one I had.

He was tall, dark, and always unshaven. He washed only occasionally, his clothes were dirty, his fingernails dirty, his teeth dirty, and his feet dirty. He always came to me smiling and as friendly as a Pekingese, then he would leave me. The moment I was away or busy operating, he would go through our hut, opening letters and so on. There was always a constant stream of reports on everything we said or did going to the Secret Police, and when on numerous occasions we caught him or them out, he would just smile through his decaying teeth and admit it. The climax came during the Greek debacle, when, in his morning "pep talks" to the sick and dying, he became violently anti-British and suggested that anyone who was friendly with Bill or me was not a Partisan but a collaborator with the British capitalist, and would be dealt with. They *were* dealt with, too, for everyone who was friendly with us was suddenly removed, usually when I was away at other hospitals. Finally I called him up to my room and read the riot act. I told him that I had written to Chief Commissar Kidrich and asked for his removal. I read him the letter, which was none too complimentary to either the Party policy or him, its exponent, in particular, and, having said that, I dismissed him. In a few days he too disappeared and a new one came.

This one was a very decent chap, a schoolteacher from Styria, a man who had been a fighter, knew all the difficulties of the soldiers, and was sufficiently observant to know that although the people were clamoring for a change in their political regime, yet at the same time they accepted the principles of communism only because the party was taking very good care that no other group arose. He had a good knowledge of contemporary English literature, could read English, and above all realized that the pro-Russian propaganda which was being used was futile and harmful to the party. It was so stupid that even the peasants would not believe it.

I recall one instance of this among many. It was a dull, cloudy Saturday afternoon. Even the low hills round Crnomelj were hidden, and from every bush and every dead vine fell little drops of mist that had come from nowhere. We were expecting a hundred and eighty Halifax planes in that afternoon to drop essential army stores, for the Germans were at this time packing into Slovenia and threatening even Crnomelj. Boots were again short, ammunition was short, petrol was nonexistent except for the general and commissars. Food was getting short, for winter was coming, and frantic calls had been going to our base in Italy for these much-needed supplies.

I had started out from Ajdovec, our central hospital and base, before daylight, and, at 1 P.M., was getting near Semic when I heard the first planes arrive over the valley. Far above the mist and rain I could hear them circling, circling, over the Ereka wireless direction finder, which the British were using from the dropping ground below. The mists thickened and thinned like smoke. Now we thought they would get through; now it was so thick the drops were falling from the boughs around us and the leafy tops above seemed lost in the veil of rain. For over a full hour they circled. More and more circling around in the clear blue sky above while we below could only watch the clouds and wonder, will they do it?

They did. One brave pilot found his way down through a crack in the clouds, down between the craggy mountain peaks, down into the narrow valley he swooped and then, suddenly, out fluttered the hundreds of parachutes, down whistled the free drops and the air was full. Almost on his tail followed another and another until the whole hundred and eighty planes had dropped. For two whole hours they came down through the clouds, and for two whole hours everyone stood and watched the drifting parachutes, drifting blue stars, red stars, green stars, black stars, drifting down the valley, taking their precious stores with them. Every now and then a chute wouldn't open and the heavy container would come whistling down to earth like a Roman candle, then crash! and the strong iron container would bury itself deep in the soft earth. My courier and I stood and watched all this from far off, up in the mountains near Semic. I felt a glowing sense of pride in the achievement. The courage of the pilots who risked so much to bring those precious stores down, the people in Italy who organized the whole operation, the aircraft factory workers in England who built the planes, and the many many people who had toiled over the uniforms, the boots, the mines, the barbed wire and all the thousands of stores which fell that afternoon.

Going home that evening along the valley, we called into a *gostiona*, or pub, at Poturin to shelter while the rain fell, and incidentally to have a *rakija* before starting on the mountain climb. The *gostiona* was full of Partisans, for the headquarters of the 9th Division had been beaten back to the so-called Free Territory. The air was full of smoke, from V's and Players I noted, and the Partisans were all in battle dress, or uniforms made from British blankets cut and tailored by their own tailors. No wonder we couldn't get blankets for the hospitals. Recently, too, they had all received masses of gold tape, and stripes and squares and triangles of rank were well to the fore. I knew many of them, and immediately the glasses were produced and we sat down and passed the time of the day with them. Inevitably the conversation turned to the drop of that afternoon, for it had been visible and audible for many miles. I said that I thought it was a great drop, and we should be extremely thankful that British pilots would take the risk in coming through the bad weather to drop stores for us there in Yugoslavia.

"Yes," they said. "It was a bad afternoon." Then someone asked what kinds of stores were dropped.

"I don't know," I replied, "but I expect it will be ammunition, boots and guns, pistols and food, blankets and uniforms, and so on."

A young commissar about eighteen or nineteen said then, "*Zivio Russia*," and then he explained to the assembly that the stores dropped were Russian stores and the planes were hired by the Russians from the English, and had Russian pilots.

I said in a quiet but inwardly boiling voice, "I don't think so." I had been at Packa one day, where the Slovene High Command was situated, when General Keder gave the list of stores they wanted to Colonel Moore, and pleaded with him to supply them as quickly as possible, and I knew that the drop this afternoon was the reply to that request.

"Yes," said the commissar. "The stores may be English ["Like the cigarette you are smoking," I interjected.], but the Russians buy them for us."

It was useless trying to convince him, yet even the simplest peasant saw what a stupid line of propaganda it was. Nevertheless it was a very common one at that time.

I remember a story I heard at the mission apropos of this. It was about a naval commander of an L.C.I. which brought to the coast some hundreds of tons of stores and equipment. He drew up alongside the battered jetty at Dubrovnik and down from the village came the captain of the town and the commissar.

"Good day," said the naval commander. "I've brought you a load of stores from Italy."

"Oh, Russian stores," said the commissar.

"No, these are British stores," replied the commander.

"But they must be the Russian stores we were told to expect," said the commissar.

"Well, I've come to the wrong bloody port. Cast off for'ard." The engine-room bell rang and the L.C.I. put back to Italy.

Every movement of the Red Army was followed with tremendous interest. Every week little papers about Russian advances came to my hospitals from the underground press. Every meeting place had its posters, good and bad, of the great Russian achievements. But information on our exploits, Norway, the Atlantic, the submarine fight, the daily bombings of Germany, the battles in Eritrea, Libya, Tunisia, Sicily, Italy, was hardly available to the average soldier.

Perhaps it was natural, for after all they are Slavs. Nevertheless one thinks of the enormous help we gave them: thousands of Yugoslav refugees at El Shat and in Italy, thousands of Yugoslav wounded flown out by night and treated by us in Italy, thousands of tons of matériel dropped by our aircraft throughout the country, help given almost every hour of the day by our Marauders, our Beaufighters and American heavies, to their exhausted troops. It appeared slightly discreditable for the people in authority to give all the credit of the war to the Rdeča Armada while accepting the help of the British and Americans to the extent they did. It was illuminating, however, to know that the peasants and villagers, though they didn't dare talk about such things publicly, privately felt ashamed of the communist propaganda about the Russians. Everywhere we went and everyone we got to know and trust told us the same story. "But after the war," they said, "it will be different."

CHAPTER 6

Talk with the President

President Vidmar invited me to visit S.N.O.S., the official Liberation Parliament, which at that time was, like everything else, hidden away in the depths of the forest. It was a long way from Ajdovec and I started early in the morning to walk there. It was summer, late summer, and the forest tracks were delightful to walk along, so cool and refreshing, so silent, and at that time fairly safe. I stopped at one of my hospitals, Yelen Dol, en route. There were about thirty patients there, and the hospital was so well hidden that although it was not more than eight hundred yards from the main forest track, the Germans had never found it. It had a new operating theater, and during the day I did a whole series of small operations. There was also the removal of plaster-of-Paris casts and re-application, skin-grafting of large wounds, and I remember seeing for the first time a knee which had been operated upon by an Italian surgeon. It was a penetrating mortar wound of the joint. When the patient arrived at Yelen Dol, he was in a fairly bad condition. He had been hit while trying to cross the Sava River, and had had a long journey down by night. About a week had passed since he was wounded. The knee, I was told, was extremely painful and swollen from infection, and the boy's general condition was so bad that he had stopped at another hospital where the Italian surgeon immediately operated. He had done a classical excision of the joint, put the leg in plaster of Paris, and had drained the wound. Then the Germans came and the boy had to be evacuated in the night, and eventually reached Yelen Dol. He was ill when I saw him. The plaster was broken and movement caused extreme pain, temperature was high, but pulse higher, and again came the problem of what to do. Should we reapply the plaster, drain the joint, and treat conservatively, knowing full well that we couldn't see him more than once in ten days, or should we amputate the limb? We gave him some pentothal in his bed and then carried him to the little theater hut and took off the plaster. Pus poured from everywhere. The infection had spread up into his thigh, as it usually does, the raw bone ends were heavily infected, and so we amputated the leg and left it all open, and the flaps turned back, so that when I returned from S.N.O.S. I could, if it were possible, put a stitch in the flaps to keep them over the bone ends.

In Yugoslavia the amputation rate was extremely high and the type of amputation different from the English-American technique. It followed the Russian school, which favored guillotine amputation. I read that the reamputation rate in the Soviet Union (quoting Dr. G. J. Kalmykov in B.M.J., July 1945) was 80 per cent, whereas in British hospitals it was only 25 per cent. Nevertheless I couldn't get the surgeons in the divisional surgical teams to amputate with flaps. I never forgot the first amputation I watched in Yugoslavia, when we first went to Vis. It was done by Dr. Novosell, and I should think it was finished in less than ten minutes. These operations were dramatic and lifesaving, but a little less drama and a little more thought for the future would have saved many a reamputation.

I had another interesting case that morning. I had already operated upon him once before. He had an almost complete loss of the forehead bone, with exposure of the whole of the frontal lobes of the brain. How he survived the original injury I just do not know, but when I first saw him the whole of the frontal lobe of the brain was a sheet of velvet granulating tissue, with a little purulent discharge from what had been the frontal sinus. First we curetted the small amount of sinus mucosa of lining away, and then treated the whole area with sulphonamide powder for three days. The next thing was to cover the exposed area as quickly as possible with skin to prevent deeper fibrosis and more sepsis. This I had done and it had all taken except one corner. That day I again did the corner and so covered the whole area with skin. That was the last I saw of him, for the enemy came and camped close by, we evacuated the hospital by night, and I could never trace him. But later on it would be a very difficult task to cover the area with bone or vitallium plate to protect the brain from injury. That was an example of the disappointments of Partisan surgery. Owing to the constant moving of hospitals when threatened by attack, I lost sight of cases and never knew what eventually happened to them.

At about four in the afternoon I left Yelen Dol and continued along the forest path to S.N.O.S. I had a courier with me to show me the way, for it was conspirated, as were our hospitals. Toward 6 P.M., just as the sun was sinking over the hills and streaming through the treetops, making golden roads ahead of us, we left the main track and turned abruptly over a secret path. Just out of sight stood a Partisan sentry. He interrogated my courier and we passed on. For about another twenty minutes we wound our way among the great rocks and the tall pines. Then quite unexpectedly I heard voices, and ahead stood a scattered collection of huts and log cabins, each one hidden or partly hidden behind the large rocks.

I was taken right through the collection of cabins and handed over to a comrade called Jeras. Jeras in his early life had been a soldier in the regular Yugoslav Army and during the First World War had found himself in France. There he met and married Simondia, a witty, intellectual Frenchwoman. They came back to Ljubljana and set up a school for teaching foreign languages. He was an old man who had dabbled in leftist politics, and now he found himself in S.N.O.S., with Madame attached to the Propaganda Department, editing a journal called *Nasa Zena* (*Our Women*).

I had met Madame before. Indeed she had acted as interpreter for us at Ajdovec, but as we could manage without an interpreter, and as the life was hard, food bad, and sleeping accommodation not suitable for an elderly woman, I had her transferred back to *Nasa Zena*. Jeras was a grand, kindly man who told me much of the inner side of political life in Slovenia.

We had a *rakija* and I had a good wash and at 7:30 P.M. he took me down to meet Vidmar, the President. Commissar Kidrich was there too. The dining cabin where the whole of S.N.O.S. met was built down at the bottom of a small *jama*, and as I walked down the steps, and saw in front of me a crowd of people laughing and talking, saw the tallow soaks and acetylene lamps flaring from the ceiling and the open fire of the cookhouse throwing its reddened shadows over the whole assembly, I was sure that here I was witnessing the most fantastic parliament in the world. I saw Bogdan talking to Luka in the distance; there were Nada and Florian, and speaking to Boris Kraeger was Stane, the great Partisan general whose name, famous in song and story, was a symbol of heroism throughout the country. There was Maria, the editor of the daily Partisan paper, and standing over in the gloom was the great artist Jakats. And many others I did not know.

Jakats had done a drawing of my head and shoulders some time before, in a hayloft near Crnosnitza.* He was a superlative artist and had sprung to fame in the old days, when he first did a drawing of King Peter. From his native town of Novo Mesto his fame spread all over Europe as a portrait artist. Then, at the height of his career, he went to America and did a series of portraits, and wrote and illustrated a book of

* See frontispiece.

his tour. He gave me the book to read—it was a delightful saga of an artist's life, and the water colors showed a blending of color and a softness of sky, a richness of detail and a clearness of atmosphere which can be seen only in the pure airs of the great American continent. He had captured it all, and there also in this book was Jakats himself: the cultured Slovene, with his soft voice, his delicate touch, his little pointed beard and his already thinning hair, his long fingers, and his curious way of drawing, at the same time carrying on a conversation with someone else in the room.

How different from Pirnat, the sculptor. Pirnat too was a Partisan and was the ex-husband of Nada, my first Slovene interpreter. He spent his time drawing propaganda posters or doing woodcuts or caricatures of prominent Partisans. His woodcuts and line cuts were reproduced in *Nasa Borba* (*Our War*). They recall so much of those difficult days. They bring back to me stockily built Pirnat, working, or, if it pleased him, sitting under the linden tree with his glass of wine. If he was modeling someone who was ugly, he made him ugly. Not so Jakats; he was too successful. If Pirnat didn't like you, he wouldn't model you. Jakats could reproduce the face with an unsurpassable technique and perfectness, but Pirnat in a few lines would unveil the soul in all its stark nakedness.

I asked Jakats if he was doing the members of S.N.O.S. for the forthcoming Partisan exhibition, and he told me that he was drawing every member, "Or all the important ones, anyhow," he added with a smile.

But here were President Vidmar and his wife coming down the steps, followed by Boris Kidrich. Jeras took me forward and without anything further Vidmar suggested that as all these people were hungry we would start. Throughout the whole evening, for dinner took two and a half hours, I compared the two leaders of Slovene thought and action—Vidmar and Kidrich. Vidmar, a stocky, thick-set man with rugged face, firm, clear eyes, and lined brow. His hair was already receding from his forehead, leaving a highly intellectual head shining in the lamplight. His English was correct, brusque, and quick, and he had a delightful method of expression in always ending with a question "Do you agree?" and expecting agreement. The first question he asked me was: "How do you like the Slovene people? They are different from the British people in thought and outlook—do you agree?" I replied that most people I had met had been the peasant boys and villagers. They had the same love of country and the land as did the New Zealand boys. They were honest and brave, simple in desire, hospitable, and Bill and I enjoyed doing what little we could to help them in their fight. They were excellent patients, never grumbling at the lack of comfort. Indeed, except for the language, there was little difference in their outlook and their desires from the Allied boys fighting across the Adriatic.

He looked surprised at that and asked whether we had the same political consciousness in our army as they had in Slovenia.

"No," I replied. "Perhaps we don't. Politics and soldiering haven't mixed in the past. But nowadays I think soldiers take a more active part in the political life of their country than ever before."

Did I think the Partisans were extremely politically conscious? "No," I replied. "From my observations, the vast majority of Partisans are tired of war, very tired of the daily Russian political propaganda, frightened of the future, and all they want is to finish the war, and get back to the narrow strips of land they left years ago."

"Very interesting," said Vidmar. "Do you hear that, Kidrich?" But Kidrich was talking seriously to Mathews, the B.B.C. reporter on his other side, about Trieste, an old sore.

"Are you interested in politics in New Zealand?" asked Vidmar.

"I was once, but my interest had waned now. I have seen that human good is more often done by the individual than by the politician. Our government, no matter under what label it holds office, has followed the same progressive path for many years, so far without bloodshed."

"Yes," replied Vidmar. "I admire your country and have read much of it. To me it is approaching the ideal of the democratic philosophy and has been lucky in starting the race unencumbered by the heavy shoes of corruption."

"Well, almost," I added.

Then I asked him if he thought that, after the war, the ideals which were so powerful and so cohesive now would remain, the ideal of the federated democracy of Yugoslavia. Or whether he thought that nationalism would assert itself and finally break down the bonds that had been forged in the crucifixion of his country.

"Yes," he said. "Nationalism will assert itself more and more in our freedom, but with it will come education, honesty, and the means of fruitful collaboration among the states. Look at the states of Soviet Russia," he said, "extending from the Japanese Sea to the Baltic, as diverse in tongue as the Western European states, as backward in culture as any part of the world. Read and see what has been achieved there."

An excellent dinner was progressing slowly, and I noticed that those in the shadows had long since finished while we had hardly started. So I settled down to eat and while eating I recalled what Bogdan had told me of Josip Vidmar's early life.

He was the son of wealthy parents who belonged to the best-known families in Slovenia. His father was an industrialist, his brother an engineering professor in Ljubljana, and he himself was a brilliant *littérateur* who had edited a number of journals in Ljubljana. He had been in Russia for a number of years, and though not a communist as far as I could gather, he was undoubtedly not anti-communist. He had studied Slovene cultural history and believed that national characteristics and national culture should be respected and developed alongside the wider conception of Balkan democracy. Bogdan told me that before the war he never spared himself in developing, fostering, and inspiring the national tradition. He wrote with a lyrical phraseology, and he spoke certainly with poetic forcefulness. When he rose from his seat and proposed a toast to me as his guest, I have rarely listened to such a eulogy, undeserved as it was, in language so simple yet so lyrical, so British and yet so Slovene, in praise of those who healed the wounds of war.

After I had replied, Boris Kidrich proposed the toast of Kenneth Mathews. This was the first real opportunity I had had to observe Kidrich in public, and I was struck forcibly by the apparent diametical opposition of the two great characters who had led Slovenia through her days of turmoil and who were entrusted with the uncertain future. Vidmar's rough countenance, firm, set lines to a fine brow, his brusque, flowing speech, like a stream rushing over rapids to fall into pools of serenity and beauty. Kidrich, smooth of face, smiling countenance, brow unfurrowed. He was ill that night. Sweat stood over his red forehead in beads. I puzzled about it. Did he have malaria or was it the fever of revolution which burned him up so? His voice was soft, his mouth small and almost cruel in its mouthing of words, words hard, concise, and dogmatically spoken. His eyes were small, almost ferrety, the eyes of a religious zealot, and the religion was communism. His uniform, made from British battle dress, was unadorned. It did not need to be; everybody knew and feared Boris Kidrich. His hands, small, red, puffy hands, seemed as alert as his face. He looked continually at everybody and I felt that he was addressing me, and me alone, all the time. His smile, ever present while he spoke, was the forced smile of the diplomat, and at the end of a quarter of an hour's address he had cleverly said nothing.

He excused himself on account of his sickness and left the room. Then there was dancing, and as they danced I met the wife of Vidmar, a kindly woman dressed plainly in gray, who spoke little. Yet I felt that in her rested something of the destiny of the two million Slovenes.

The dancing was spirited and hot, and after the grand meal and the copious flagons of wine that had been consumed I felt tired. I remembered that I had already had a full day's operating, and that I had come to observe and enjoy, not to have a further bout of violent exercise dancing the *kola*.

Kidrich came in again and within a minute had flung himself into an old folk dance, where one girl was inevitably left on the floor and the odd man went up to her and kissed her three times. I joined in this game, for it seemed a long time since I had been kissed. My first partner was a Lithuanian girl whose dark eyes and merry face flashed at me in wild Slav abandon. Seizing the opportunity, I drew her to me, and in the middle of the ring I kissed her lips full and deeply. Then she laughed and we all laughed, and I saw Kidrich watching and laughing too. It was hard to realize that here was the man who had eliminated the collaborator Dr. Ehrlich of Ljubljana. Kidrich had shot him, outside the church of St. Cyril just after Mass, and had pinned on his cassock a card: "With the compliments of Comrade Kidrich." Again it was Kidrich who organized the assassination of Dr. Natlachen, the last governor of Slovenia. His revolutionary path knew no road block, his ends justified every means, and his power was fearful in the land.

During the night I was again speaking to Vidmar and he asked me if I would like to come and live in Slovenia after the war. "There will be plenty of work for you to do," he said, "and Bogdan tells me that the patients in your hospitals are very happy and get better very quickly."

I hesitated for a moment and then said, "Truthfully, Comrade President, I prefer my own land. I care not for the political fears and troubles here. I hate the constant surveillance of the Secret Police over us all the time. It creates a tension and to my mind prevents the freedom for which we are fighting from ever becoming a fact."

Vidmar laughed and said, "Oh, don't worry about the Secret Police; they are just an evolution of the time. I have them following me. Indeed only the other day in Crnomelj I was being followed, so I turned on the man and said, 'There is no need to follow me. I am President Vidmar,' and he turned and went away. Oh, don't mind that. Come and have a drink of wine before we go to bed."

But I did mind it. Not because of the Secret Police, for I expect we have them in a war, and in peacetime, too. It was the universal fear and distrust, the apprehension of simple people, the inability to speak as we thought or to express ourselves in public that struck me as being so foreign to our conception of what we were fighting for.

Next day I rose early, but not before old Jeras brought in the morning *rakija*. He later took me to breakfast.

All the way home I thought it over again. The tremendous leaning on Mother Russia. Would the milk of her breasts run dry and the infants be left stranded? Would the great hopes be realized and a new era of peace and liberty reach fruition? Would all those wounded Partisans we had lived with for so long really have suffered to some end? I hoped so.

The day was fine and the sun was strong; the smell of the pines was redolent in my nostrils. I saw a young fawn lying in the sun among a heap of fern. I stopped and watched it, leaving my gun hanging over my shoulder. It smelt me, stood for a moment, then bounded away into the forest, bounded through the densest of fern, leaping high, and was lost in the great silence of the future.

CHAPTER 7

The Story of Heinrich

It was early November and the valley below us was a picture. The corn was half cut and the long strips gleamed golden all day in the sun. Everywhere the forest cyclamens were blooming, and perfuming the air like the flowers before some great silent altar. Our steps were muffled as we trod over the green moss, for the scarlet leaves still hung from the scattered oaks and beeches that grew on the fringes of the dark green pines. Every day there was fighting just a few miles away at Kocevje. Every day and night we had our patrols out watching and guarding us. Every day, as Bill and I tramped around to our scattered hospitals, we watched each turn of the path, and at the slightest sound we would creep off the track into the forest and hide until the voices passed. For who knew who they were? Chetniks had arrived in Slovenia from the south, all the worst Chetniks, those wanted for war crimes. They swelled the ranks of the Domobranci and patrolled the forest in battle dress, often wearing a Red Star. Every third or fourth day the Germans came out from Novo Mesto with their guns and tanks and shelled Poturin and Podhusta below us. The forest rang with the crashing of mortar shells, the valley echoed

with machine-gun bursts. Every night more wounded came to
our hospitals. Some days we would be completely surrounded
by the enemy. Then we received no patients and all day we
kept watch, with loaded guns and grenades at the belt. No
sound of chopping, no singing or shouting, no smoke to lead
the bloodhounds the enemy patrol used to find us.

Bill and I had a little cave not far away where we took all
our possessions and hid them, the most precious sealed in a
box covered with waterproof paper. Are they still there, I wonder, wet and rotted? The Germans found our last cache in
Bosnia, for when we caught those German officers near Drvar
and searched them we found a description of us and a photo
of me sitting at a table talking to some peasants. It was an
amusing description.

> An old man of fifty, with gray hair, thick set and clean-
> shaven. Educated in New Zealand and served in the African
> campaign. . . . He must be taken alive if possible.

I always appreciated the "alive if possible" touch, for I alone
knew where all the stores were hidden and doubtless means
would have been taken to make me talk. I wasn't taken "alive
if possible," but I did become much more careful about the
place I hid our personal belongings.

Heinrich was just sixteen, such a thin, small, adolescent boy,
with great big dark brown eyes which looked up at you as a
rabbit caught in the iron jaws of a trap looks the moment before death. He spoke in the dialect of one of the northern
valleys of Styria, soft and running like a river. His long, taper-
ing fingers grew thinner and whiter every day he stayed with us.
He came in the snow one evening about dusk, the old Italian
blanket covering him white with flakes, and as they laid him
down outside the hospital door, the crude stretcher sagged to

the rough ground beneath. He moaned a little and lifted the blanket from his face. It was Vinco and France who had carried him in, and as Vinco took off his hat and shook the snow from it, he told me that at times he thought that little Heinrich would die. He would moan and then lie so still that even Vinco, who had carried hundreds over the steep forest tracks, thought that he was dead.

I felt his pulse, or rather I felt where it should be, and couldn't feel anything. His nose was cold and his hands lifeless. We carried him straight in, without the customary washing and delousing, and laid him on a special bed. Then we covered him up and got hot stones wrapped in parachute silk and put those around him. Ivitsa, the nurse, was on duty and she brought a cup of hot glucose and lemon to him and with a spoon she gave him sip after sip.

Many wounded came in that evening, but because the way was long through the forest and because it was dark they came all night long at intervals. And all night long Bill and I and Ivitsa worked with them while José, the Italian from Trieste, and Leanna did the washing and the delousing. In the morning I went to Heinrich's bed and felt his pulse. Just a flicker now, the eyes were more curious and alive and the lips and nose were warm. We decided to take him to the operating theater and look at his wound. So, with a small dose of morphia, we carried him in and then took off the blankets and saw his left leg wrapped up in splints and his right leg in bandages. We took down one of our precious plasma bottles, frozen hard, and warmed it on the stove. Then Bill started the transfusion, and after some difficulty, for the veins were so collapsed it wouldn't run until we placed a hot stone against his arm, he put into the running plasma a small dose of pentothal. Heinrich went to sleep and quickly we took off the bandages. One knee was shot away with the popliteal artery gone, and the other leg had a fracture of the tibia and fibula and a great gaping hole. I looked at the first leg again and felt the foot. It was cold and dead; Ivitsa, watching me, went and put out the saw and instruments, for she knew as well as I did what was to be done.

Quickly we amputed the leg above the knee, turned the flaps back with a stitch of parachute silk, and powdered the whole with sulphonamide powder and did it up with Vaseline gauze. The other leg we extended with a stout silk cord behind the Achilles' tendon. Then we did a debridement of the wounds, put a catheter down to the wound, and sewed it up. Rapidly I put on a plaster cast of the whole leg, with Bill extending it on the silken cord. Then when we had finished we pulled out the cord and sealed the holes. The Thomas splint came next to support the limb, and finally Heinrich was carried back to bed. Through the catheter every four hours we injected penicillin and into his veins we kept the slow transfusion going all day.

It was not till long after that we heard Heinrich's story, for as the days slipped by, sometimes I thought Heinrich would slip by with them. But no, he slowly got stronger. We sewed the flaps over his amputation stump later. We pulled out the catheter from the other leg and gradually he came to know us. Every day when I stopped by his bed he would seize my hand embarrassingly, but in true Slav fashion, and look at me and say, "How will I live again? How can I work on the farm with only one leg? Where can I go?"

The great problem was, where could he go? For Heinrich's father and mother had been shot by the Germans as hostages from their village. A German corporal, who had been raping the women, was found dead one morning, knifed, and as a reprisal fifty from the village were shot by noon. Among them were Heinrich's parents. He ran into the marshes and lay all day long up to his neck in water, and when evening came he started off into the woods and joined the Partisans. Bitter was his hate. As he spoke of the *"tedeschi"* (Germans) his eyes would burn with fire, his long white fingers would clinch tight, and his pink lips would close hard like rocks rather than soft flesh. He became a sniper and for days would lie near where the German officers slept in the peasant house on the outskirts of the town. He watched their every move: when they came in at nights, which rooms they slept in, which room they ate in, when the sentries were changed. He would put on the velveteen trousers of the village boys and pass for a boy of ten or eleven, and play with them. At night back he would go to his patrol and get grenades and learn how to throw them. Then, when the wind sang loudly around the German-occupied house and the guard was huddled in overcoats with glowing cigarettes behind the shelter of the maize house, he would sneak up to the lighted window where the officers sat at their wine and their song. Crash through the window went the grenade, and another and another. Feet ran into the dark, and before the guard had turned, a terrific explosion and the German officers would be no more. In three districts he had done this and each time the night had swallowed him and he had returned safely to his patrol. At nights he would lie around the campfires planning new attacks and the Partisans called him "the little one." Heinrich would smile and accept his glass of red Slovene wine and was proud to be a Partisan, one of Marshal Tito's Partisans.

Then the patrol moved and the valley was full of Germans, of German tanks, and trucks and guns, all going northward to stem the Russians who were advancing into Poland. He knew that they wouldn't be there for long and so he must work quickly. With little preparation he stole through the snow, his white parachute cloak hiding him in the white gloom. He waited until the sentry had stopped and was trying to light his cigarette against the cold wind which flowed through the valley. Then he threw his grenades. He heard the glass crack as he ran up the hill toward the forest edge. He saw the explosion, a bright flash which lit the sky, and the flames start from the dried wooden house. But against the snow his moving outline showed, and within a minutes the German guns were searing the snow with bullets. He ran for the forest, he was in the forest, and just above him his patrol was waiting. But even as he ran he felt a sudden cracking of his legs. He fell, and felt a hot rushing to his head, and a hot stream of blood mushing down his leg. He cried out. The patrol, who had been watching, came to him and carried him far into the forest, into safety, to the hospital called Ajdovec. And there Heinrich lay, bravely facing the new world.

CHAPTER 8

Hospital Life

The forest was changing rapidly now. All the living things had gone; the squirrels that stole the hazelnuts, the snakes that sunned themselves on the hot rocks, the beautiful *srna*, or deer, that browsed among the fern of the hollows, the huge wild bear and her young one near the burnt-out mill of Pogaritza. The only living thing we ever heard was the lonely, howling wolves at night. I was frightened of them. Many stories centered around the lonely crying wolves, stories of lost couriers, of wounded soldiers who had been left waiting their turns to be carried into safety but who were never found against, stories of peasant women who wandered in the snows, and in the morning all to be seen were the great footprint of a he-wolf. Yes, I was frightened.

One day a horse died toiling up the hill to the *javka* where the outside world left their stores for the hospitals. He was loaded with beans, beans three years old, hard and insipid, but food nevertheless. Two bags hung over its saddle and the snow was deep and the track steep. This faithful Partisan horse had many times toiled up that track. The Germans had found him once but despised his thin legs and his saddle-sore back, and when the Partisans returned to the burnt stables, all they found left was this one horse. But he had a strong heart and he still worked in "the struggle." From Stara Zaga he toiled every day up into the forests above. Then this day he stopped. He tried hard to reach the top where the track forked and they threw off the loads and hid them under the fern. But he couldn't continue. Not that the saddle sores hurt where the ropes chaffed; it was the constant falling and slipping in the fresh snow that did it, snow that looked firm but that often covered a crevice between the rocks and the heavy foot would slip deep down so that the bags of corn rested on the snow on either side. The horse knew that there was only one more great bend, and then the load would be lifted off and they would rest awhile before going back, down in the night to Stara Zaga. But for him the day was over. He slipped and couldn't get up. The Partisan boy saw that something was wrong. He lifted the heavy bags from the saddle and bared the great raw sore. He grasped his head and said, "*Hajde, hajde, hajde.*" The horse staggered, his dilated nostrils showing the shining red flesh inside. His breath came in two great streams of quickly frozen steam. He got his feet on the firm ground underneath and the boy helped him up. He stood and shivered all over. The boy led him quietly off the track, and under the pines he lay down. The boy kicked the snow away and found some grass, but the horse was lying on his side, his breath coming fast and deep like a mighty engine. He lifted his head. The two eyes seemed alight in the gloom. A mighty neigh resounded through the empty forest, then he turned and died.

Next night I too was toiling up through the snow from Toplice to Ajdovec. Already I had lost the track a dozen times and had fallen face-first into the soft and powdery snow as my feet slipped from under me. I could feel the bumping of my heart against the chest wall, bumping and thumping as I hurried to beat the darkness of night. I knew that once night fell I should never find the hidden paths, and would have to go back down to Poturin again. A shot rang out in the twilight, a shot somewhere down below me, and then the usual rattle of machine-gun fire. I reached the last great bend before the conspirated track to the hospital and suddenly became conscious that I was not alone. I stopped and listened. I could hear a soft, muffled padding on the snow, then a crack as a branch snapped. I looked for some place to hide and found a deep hollow between two snow-covered rocks. I lay down and covered myself with snow and waited for the enemy to pass. But no one came. Then into the night, coming from the hill on my right, went a great howl, the howl of the hungry he-wolf. The soft padding ceased, and slowly it dawned on me that the sound was caused by wolves, not men. I got ready my grenades and rifle, pushing the magazines in and pulling back the bolt release. I got up and went a few paces forward and there saw the carcass of the dead horse, just bones now. The ribs were sticking high into the air like dead branches and around and around, as if on a greyhound racing track, went the wolves. One great gray brute was tearing at the straggle tendons of the horse's leg. It would tear a piece then shake its head and tear off another. Five wolves kept running around and around. I could catch the glint of light in their eyes, and as they turned and faced me I could see their bellies fat with

the feed. Slowly and silently I turned and made my way back
in the form of a great circle around them. Every minute I
could hear the padding feet follow me and I would catch a
glance of something gliding through the trees. The sweat was
dripping from my armpits; I slipped, snatching at a dead
branch. It snapped and I fell. The silent forest echoed with
the crash. I stood with my back to a tree, awaiting the on-
slaught. But nothing came . . . no eyes, no more padding
footfalls, just the ever-deepening gloom and the last ridge
ahead of me.

When I reached the hospital the snow continued to fall,
not like it does at home in Otago in great white flakes which
suddenly turn black against the light as they reach you; it was
a fine powder, like silent rain drifting through the trees, and
we became more and more isolated. The shooting and the
fighting in the valley below had died away, and in our log-
cabin hospital, now completely under snow, we had only
routine work to do. It was much too far to go to the mission,
so we got no news at all from the outside world except from
an occasional courier bringing tidings of the great Rdeča
Armada. The days were short. We had no lights except the
firelight and two electric torches we kept for emergencies.
We made a few tallow soaks to light the hospital for the last
meal of the day.

Sometimes in the evenings we would have a concert. Stanko,
a boy commissar, already twice wounded, was excellent at
organizing these. We would carry all the patients into one hut
and then rig up a curtain of blankets and parachute cloth
and away we would go. First of all it would be "Hej Slovenia"
the national anthem, and a great singing and feeling would
pierce those thick wooden walls and echo to the stars above
the song of liberation, of the end of the struggle, of the new
world. "God," I used to murmur, "I trust it all comes true."

Then we would have a long poem or dialogue, produced in Moscow, always with a strong political bias, but nevertheless excellent. They would fling themselves into it with a zest and a zeal with which I was proud to be associated, even if it was the *Polish Mother and Her Daughters Rescued by the Red Army*. They were our allies, after all.

Perhaps all this emotion was only incidental to the struggle for the new world. Then Zita, our political agent, would give a long recitative about Tito. I could never believe that the Tito I had met and spoken to was the Tito of the theme. He was in it everything possible, from a "snow-white flower" to the "Father of us all." Somehow I never liked Zita. She was the only Yugoslav woman I did not like. Was it the fact that she had been sent to "keep an eye on us," or was it the fact that she spent hours closeted with my abominable commissar, who was always so dirty, or was it the fact that she was too proud to take out the bedpans, such as they were? I never knew. But she was a Secret Police agent and when the revolt in Greece was in progress she used to go around smirking at us and I always felt that she was saying: "Think you capitalists can do that here? Why, you haven't a chance; we will fight you to the end!" "With British arms," I would add to myself.

Nevertheless these impromptu concerts were always Zita-inspired and were excellent. They would sing, sing, sing. Different songs from those of the Bosnians. Not so tragic, not so filled with the subtle, haunting, tragic melody which always made us cry, inside if not without. Here the songs were fuller of life, fuller of love, and the bravado of war. *"Na Jurish"* was one we always clamored for, and then the lovely, lilting melody of *"Počiva Jezero v Tihoti"* recalled the happy days of my own youth in New Zealand beside the still lake. At the end we always asked for more, and they always pressed for

Bill and me to sing some cowboy songs. Not strictly political, I know, but we did. Bill had a good voice, but when he sang and looked up to heaven in a soulful kind of way I couldn't help laughing. Usually he was pretty tough. I suppose singing brought back to him Pittencrieff Park and the weekends spent in the Highlands. We would sing "Old Faithful." My God, how that swept me home. Days at Lochindorb in Otago, with the wind sweeping over the tussock-clad hills like ocean waves, nights ambling home full of happiness, singing gently to the horse. Kim, he was called.

They would demand more and we would sing "Riding down the Sunset Trail," and again I would see myself swinging down the long road from Tapanui to the Pomahaka, where the river slides over the silver stones and the gold of youth was sought and never found. Then we would say, "*Laku noc; dobro spavajte*" (good night; sleep well), and open the door and walk silently to our own hut. Bill would kick the fire into a blaze, draw up his stool, and without asking would fill the two glasses with *rakija*, and in the glow and the silence we would drink, each of us far away, so far away that even the brave new world had become a mere myth, floating among the castles of our imagination.

One night when we were sitting around our fire, huddling closer to it than ever, for it was December and the snow was deep and frozen, Vinco came up the track, kicked the snow from his boots as he stepped onto our veranda, and then walked along to the beam of light which shone from our door. We heard him, and thought it was the commissar come up for a chat, but it was Vinco to tell us that fourteen patients were lying down in the *javka*, some very bad. They had been carried down from the Sava and some had already died. We got up. I realized that here was a difficulty, for we had no lights whatsoever except one torch now and several fat soaks. I hoped that they would be able to wait for morning and, after all, after fourteen days' trip in the snow, they should be ready for a night's rest.

Bill went over to the hospital to get the operating theater warm, for the roof was leaking and already the icicles hanging down inside were as thick as your thigh, and the Vaseline gauze was so hard you could chop it with an ax. I sat by the fire, glancing every now and then through the window, watching for the light coming down the steep slope of the *jamba*.

It was 11 P.M. when the first two arrived. The covering sheet was white, and frozen to the stretcher handles so that we couldn't lift it off. Vinco pulled and pulled and eventually we got the two wounded inside. One had gunshot wounds of the chest; I remember his name, it was Gregorich. His boots were frozen so hard we couldn't get them from his feet. He had a wound in the chest, high up about the second interspace, a great open wound sucking in air with every breath, and when he turned on his side the pus poured out as though from a bucket. We put him to bed, boots and all, gave him hot drinks, and let him thaw out through the night, a night spent in deep sleep, the first sleep for fourteen nights.

The other boy was an interesting case. One of his legs was frozen dead in his boot; the black line of demarcation came to about halfway up his leg. In his thigh, which was swollen like a drum, was a foul discharging wound, with the smell I knew so well, and the crepitating subcutaneous tissues extending right up to his abdominal wall. He had gas gangrene. Somehow or other, in spite of the usual virulence of the organism, the extreme cold seemed to have limited the infection. I decided not to amputate the leg straight way, but in the light of a torch held by Ivitsa, and helped by Bill, cut down through the pink dead muscles, opening up the intramuscular

spaces and liberating the tense collection of gas. We left the
lower part of his leg alone. I fully expected him to die next
day. But next day he was still alive, his pulse stronger, and
his tongue a trifle moister than before. We again gave him
plasma and serum, and kept the rectal drip going, for all patients arrived in a state of great dehydration. The gas had not
spread upward, and the smell, though still putrid, was not as
all-pervading as it had been. In three days' time gas began to
appear in his lower limb where the living flesh met the dead.
We took him to the theater, and almost without anesthetic
took off his left leg through the knee joint. Next day he had
considerably improved, and in two months he was hobbling
around singing and laughing with Gregorich, his friend.
Gregorich was interesting too, for we drained his chest at the
bottom instead of at the top, where his wound was, and in
about ten days, as soon as the large hole in his second interspace had healed, we rotated a flap to cover it, and he was up
and about, tending to his friend as though nothing had
happened.

Among those who came in that night was France Hrovat.
I remembered him well from Valla Vas quite near Novo
Mesto. He had a great wound of the thigh, from which we
extracted a piece of 88-mm. shell. Someone else had operated
on him before he came to us, and had cut away such a large
amount of the skin that fully two hands would not cover the
gap. Once the shrapnel was removed, the wound stopped
discharging and started to heal. I told France that it would
be necessary to skin-graft it and explained how it would be
done. He didn't really mind, for Ivitsa, the night nurse, slept
alongside of him and I guess that France was the same as any
other lad of nineteen, despite Tito's promulgation. Ivitsa was
also the operating-theater nurse, and to have a big operation
would make him a double hero. We did him one morning

with a razor, and with three slices of moderately thick skin we got the area covered. Then we waited and on the third day took off the bandages, again in the theater, and found that two had completely taken but that one had sloughed, all except one corner. France was really very proud of his trips to the theater, cold as it was, and I thought that after the war he would certainly marry Ivitsa. She was a charming girl, a ballet dancer from the Ljubljana ballet. She was excellent at her work, and the boys told me that when she was in the brigades fighting she was the bravest of the brave. She quickly learnt to swear in English, for the Slovene language is particularly barren in profanity, and Bill and I would constantly break out with some good British oath.

It all happened so suddenly and so unexpectedly. One night Bill and I were sitting by the dying fire. We had just finished our good-night *rakija* when Bill looked up and said in a loud and unnatural voice, "I want to marry Ivitsa, sir." I was taken aback. In a flash came an explanation for the time Bill used to take in the theater cleaning up after a day's operating, and for his extreme willingness to make unnecessary trips over at night to see this one or that. It was all clear. Those knowing looks at one another while at work, the eagerness he exhibited in helping Ivitsa with little things. The fervor with which he would sing in the concerts "My Bonnie Jean," his rapid progress with the language, and so on. I realized that throughout all these months Bill had been singing not for the wounded Partisans but for Ivitsa alone.

I gulped down my *rakija* and rose, put a log on the fire, and filled the glasses. Goyka's blond hair and smiling face rose from the flames, and I recalled the days in Vis, and the difficulties that sprang from nowhere over these affairs of the heart. I turned to Bill. His fair hair was wavy and long in front, hanging over his high forehead. His face, flushed by the heat of the fire and the release of his pent-up emotions, was turned toward me, and all I could say was: "You bloody old bastard!"

"Well, I'm going to marry her, Partisans or no Partisans," he said, and I saw that no power on earth would change his desires. "I love her and she loves me" was his simple statement, and on that rested the whole argument.

"Bill," I said, "how many know about this affair?"

"Oh," he said, "there's Hrovat, but he's all for it; he likes Ivitsa too." (I could hardly imagine his being all for it under such circumstances, but I let it pass.) "Then there's a commissar patient who tells her all day she ought to be ashamed associating with an Englishman. 'Why don't you get a Yugoslav,' he said to her, 'if you must have man?' I'll bash him one soon," and Bill and I knew that he would.

It was late when we ceased talking and I started in the first gloom of morning to go to the *glavni stab* in the forest to see Chief Commissar Kidrich of Slovenia and get in first. British permission would require some tactful handling too, I thought, but at least there would be no shootings or sudden disappearances of the parties concerned.

The snow was still thick as I fell down the mountainside, and I was indeed happy to reach Podhusta, where the *kola* had worn a track along the snow, and skiing was easier. Then came the long walk up the valley past Stara Zaga until I reached Crnosnitza, where the Medical Headquarters had retired for its winter quarters. I called in and saw Natasha, Natasha famous now in the book of Louis Adamic as Bozha. No, she hadn't been killed, as Adamic thought, but here she was fighting and working in the great struggle. Her mountain dreams with Bahtch had come true, for here had come the opportunity and Natasha was doing her share as chief administrator in medical affairs for the 7th Corpus. We had lunch of polenta and stewed beans and I pressed on up the valley toward Packa.

CHAPTER 9

The Problem of Bill and Ivitsa

It was good to get back to the mission and see Owen Reed still smoothing back the few odd straggling hairs across his forehead, and to see Peter Moore sitting down with glass in front of him and cigarette burning itself out while he played around at writing a signal. Then Raffles, always cheerful, turning over the well-thumbed leaves of the code book. The mission staff was never complete without stolid Jack Wick, in his khaki beret and boots, coming in kicking the snow from his boots and saying that it was a good day, despite the fact that it had been a hell of a day. He saw me in the corner. "Hullo, Doc," he said. "For Christ's sake look after our stores, Raffles; Doc's here. Have a *rakija*, Doc," and he poured out a liberal portion.

Peter in the meantime quietly fills up his glass. "They're bastards," he mutters, and goes on writing the signal.

I gather that things are not going too well in the mission and I seek Owen Reed and inveigle him into a corner and hear all the latest restrictions and insults. Apparently several officers had arrived at the mission from different parts of the country and all had the same story to tell. Almost identical; spying, restrictions, and insults seemed to be the same everywhere. No wonder Peter was lighting cigarette after cigarette, each one quietly burning to the end on the nearby ash tray.

It was a birthday party that night. After six o'clock, when darkness shut out the cold, bleak, white landscape, we got rid of the servants, who went off to report to Majore Bor, the chief spy (in other words, chief of the liaison staff), that I had arrived and, what was more, arrived without a courier. José, my courier, lived in a village on the side of the valley opposite to Packa, and I had let him go home instead of walking a further three miles up to the mission and back again.

The party warmed up. They actually had chicken. Where Raffles got these things from I never knew, but the mission always did better than we did. They were near the dropping ground, and when stuff did arrive for them, they always got it, whereas our supplies, an equal quantity pro rata, ran the gamut of many a Partisan route and everyone helped himself. While in Slovenia I lost about 65 per cent of stores that were dropped for me. Luka, of Medical Headquarters, acquired many of them and when I tackled him with it he explained that owing to a German advance it was necessary to divert the stores to other places. Well, one accepted that, but when I suggested sending them along to me when the German patrol had gone, it was a different story. They would see no dishonesty in appropriating my stores, and I wouldn't have cared much if it hadn't been that, in addition to taking mine, they sent in huge requests for more and yet more. The requests were always unreasonable, even had they included the whole civilian population in their calculations. They wanted far more drugs than the whole combined British and American forces would use in Italy. It was especially unreasonable at that time because we were taking all their wounded out to Italy and treating them ourselves.

I well remember being asked about the stores that UNRRA would bring in. I offered to tell them what stores would be available from British and American sources because many of the drugs they were in the habit of using were not used by us but were manufactured on the Continent for Continental

users only. The list was produced and the first request was for
an enormous number of trucks for hospital use. It was completely unreasonable. I counted up the number of hospitals,
the total populations, and tried to make an estimate, and I
discovered it to be less than one eighth of the quantities they
asked for. I pointed out that the number seemed very large,
but Luka assured me that they had already been promised,
so I marveled inwardly and said nothing. Then came instruments and X-ray sets. Again the figures were astronomical. I
quietly pointed out that it was better to ask for what was really
necessary and get it than to ask for enormous amounts and
have their request hung up while adjustments were being
made. But they assured me that S.N.O.S. had already asked
for these requirements from the American sources, and if they
were not forthcoming the Russians had promised them. Now
the British were being asked for the same things. This method
of indenting went on all the time. The Yugoslav Mission in
Italy would go to the Army direct, asking for stores, the various
corps in the field would ask our "firm" for the same stores,
and then the commands would again submit a list. Conse-
quently everyone got heartily sick of the order and it was
inevitably delayed. Just after I came out of Yugoslavia, I met
a brigadier who was with our troops who landed in Montenegro. He told me he had had the same difficulties and indeed
if he had not personally slipped the stores up by night to the
hospitals which needed them badly, the commissars would
have them whisked away in the morning to the bunkers of
Belgrade.

The party went on while I sat down with the usual list the
glavni stab had presented to Peter Moore for ordering. I carefully worked out their needs according to British requirements
for an attacking force, where casualties were much greater than
in a guerrilla force. Then I multiplied by two, to be sure that

no person would have the faintest possibility of being un-supplied, and rewrote the list.

Meanwhile the party was going well. The meal was cleared away, the wireless schedule was finished, and we were all listening to one of the sergeants singing a rather low sergeants' song, when in walked Florian.

Florian was the best interpreter in the liaison staff, and, though an ardent member of the Communist party and the new scheme of things, yet he had a sneaking feeling for us that we were not being treated exactly as welcome guests in the land. One could tell from his dry smiles, when we chaffed him about the couriers reporting our every move and conver-sation, that he felt for us. But he never went so far as to say so. He had come to say that one of the British sergeants had gone to the dropping ground on the motor bike without a courier and the *stab* wouldn't allow it. The position was be-coming absurd. They wanted completely to control the drop-ping ground and not even allow our R.A.F. chaps to guide the planes in.

At midnight old Jack Wick got me a sleeping bag and I turned in on a spare bunk. It was an uncomfortable mess, that. While the Russians lived in state in the best house in Crnomelj, the British lived in the worst in Packa. I wouldn't have tolerated it had I been in Peter's place. What a contrast to the silken parachute material over the walls and on the divans of Majore Bor's house, which the boys used to call "The Brothel"! The *stab* also lived pretty well in new wooden huts, but the people of old British Mission, which was respon-sible for almost all their total supplies, were allocated the dirtiest house in Packa.

Next morning Peter Moore and I went to the *stab* to inter-view Chief Commissar Kidrich. As Peter did not seem very interested in Bill's desire for marriage, I decided that I would conduct that side of the conversation myself. We took the jeep, for the *stab* was about three miles away just off the main road, and when we arrived, complete with courier (lest we lose the way!), we went into the interview room with Florian as interpreter. But there we met not Kidrich at all but Colonel Lark, the chief fobber-off. I began by saying that I took a dim view of the constant pilfering of my stores, and trusted that in future I would receive them untouched; that I ordered only what I considered vitally necessary, and as I was doing the surgery for five of their hospitals, I would appreciate some safeguarding of my stores.

Lark replied that Dr. Luka had made a new rule that all my stores were to be taken over by him and distributed as he thought fit. This was a bombshell. I reminded him of our original agreement with Dr. Luka, that the British would supply the stores and the surgeon, and the Partisans the hospitals and food. We had done our part and we expected them to keep to the agreement. General Jaka came in at this stage with Chief Commissar Kidrich. I liked Jaka. He was always a gentleman, and in spite of the fact that his attack on Kocevje was a failure he was a good general and was adored by his men. When General Stane was unfortunately killed by a premature explosion, it was thought that Jaka would take command. But it was otherwise. General Keder, a young man, came and Jaka disappeared "down south."

Things didn't go too well. Peter was just as fed up with the pinpricking reactions of the Secret Police as I was with Colonel Luka's decision to take all my British stores. Everywhere they placed petty obstructions in our way. They didn't like us; that was the beginning and end of it all. They mistrusted us and were making it quite clear that we wouldn't get our hands on anything now for postwar exploitation. I stated quite clearly that if they didn't stick to our agreement I would pack up and go, and Peter said equally bluntly that they were not making much attempt at fighting the Jerries, and where was the ammunition going to, anyway? This pretty straight talking did some good, for afterward things improved slightly.

Peter then left me with Kidrich, and stepped out of the hot room into the snow. We drew our chairs up beside the wood fire, Kidrich produced the *rakija* bottle, poured me a liberal one but refrained himself. He asked me how we were getting on with so many German troops only a mile or so away. I told him that we had already made plans for immediate evacuation of our wounded if we had time, and that a large cave had been found and most of our valued equipment had already been hidden there and the entrance covered with dead branches and snow.

He laughed with his small eyes and said, "*Majore*, you are a good Partisan." Then, turning to me with one of those quick furtive gestures he was prone to make, he asked, "And how is your boy, Bill?"

"Ah, Bill," I replied. "He's well, working hard. He's a good fighter."

"Yes," said Kidrich. "We all like Bill. We'd do anything for Bill."

"Well, that's exactly why I came to see and talk to you, Kidrich," I said. "Bill wants your permission to marry the Partizanka, Ivitsa."

Kidrich's face clouded over, and, looking slowly into the fire, he replied, "That is a matter entirely for the party, *Majore*."

"But surely you, as Chief Commissar, are the party?" I rejoined.

"That is a matter entirely for the party," he reiterated, and I knew that conversation had ended, and rapidly switched to another topic. We finished the *rakija*, or rather I did, smiles again twisted around Kidrich's face, and after shaking hands I saluted him Partisan fashion and opened the door into the snow. My security watcher was still waiting. He picked up his rifle and followed Florian and me back to the British Mission. I felt thwarted and disgruntled.

They were having tea when I arrived. Peter was raging at some fresh annoyance. It was so clear that they mistrusted us. Not only my stores were being spirited away but also general military equipment. At that moment our whole effort seemed wasted. It was depressing, after all we had done. They were difficult to understand. One day they made glowing speeches about you and the next were raising all kinds of petty obstructions from a political standpoint. Our usefulness had lessened, and our mana (as we New Zealanders say) was waning. It was no use getting disgruntled over it, but it was clear that the cause was the ever-mounting Russian influence. I didn't give a damn about their politics. I admired from the bottom of my heart the great desire for something better. Nothing could have been worse than the previous regime. The only point was, would the new system be any different?

Next morning, just as I was preparing to go, a courier arrived from Kidrich asking if I would please go and see him.

There he was, the same immutable Kidrich, yet despite his ferocity, his Calvinistic fervor for the new regime, his Slav subtlety, and his obvious ill-health, he attracted me. He was one of those courageous evangelical people so rarely met in real life.

With a sweep of the hand he invited me in, poured a *rakija*, and we sat down.

"I have consulted the party," he said. (I knew it was a lie, for there had not been the opportunity for him to do so.) "Permission is granted, subject to formalities."

I thanked him and said good-by, and, joined by my ever-

watchful courier, we tumbled into Peter's jeep with our few
stores and started back for Ajdovec, some thirty miles away.
The winter of 1944–45 was drawing to a close; already the
snows around Semic had gone and the spring flowers were
throwing their brave heads up from every mossy bank. We
arrived at Toplice, which was quiet, and had a grand swim in
the deserted warm pools, then hid our stores in a bunker, said
good-by to Peter, and started walking across the valley of
Podhusta.

It was afternoon when we reached the village of Podhusta
and there we found, seated on the road, a German patrol re-
pairing a broken-down truck. Luckily we saw them first, and
made a detour across the road and hastily sought the shelter of
the forest. But they too saw us and amused themselves by
firing off about a hundred butterfly bombs which fell uselessly
into the forest. At close range they sound terrifying, but they
do little harm unless by direct hit, and that was almost impossible under the shelter of the trees.

It was night when we reached the top of the *jama* of
Ajdovec and there was Bill, his machine gun ready, for he had
heard us coming, waiting for news. I told him all, though
realizing after those years that it meant nothing. But it gave
him hope and encouragement, and we sat and talked by the
glowing fire far into the night.

CHAPTER 10

A Party—Partisan-Fashion

I always felt better when I left the mission and was back again
with the Partisans. The peasant boys' knowledge of politics
was so one-sided that it had by this time toppled over, but

their bravery and communal friendship had proved to be vital
to us. When I think of them all and what they suffered!
There was Franz Gregorich, our intendant, or quartermaster.
When the war started he had been at high school. Every day
he rode his cycle through that forest lane from Poturin to
Crnomelj, crossed the river by the bridge, and toiled up the
hill into the township. School had been wonderful for him.
His father (he had no mother), his brother, and sisters had
that little patch of ground at Poturin, and, up on the hills
beyond, a strip of vines. It provided the means of existence,
but that was all. After school it was work, work; bringing in
the ripened cobs, hoeing the potatoes while his father went
to the vineyard to prune and tie up the grapes. His eldest sister
kept the house, just a two-room cottage with thatch roof, and,
behind, the shed with the hay for the winter feed, and the
corncobs tied together, shining golden, as though poured from
a cornucopia. In one room slept his sisters, while in the other
was the table and chest of drawers, and on the walls a faded
little picture of the Holy Virgin with a few flowers in a jar
beneath, and there the father and the boys slept.

One day the Italians came to the school and took Franz
away. He was seventeen then. They took him to a concentration camp on the island of Rab. There he stayed. Months
passed and he watched the daily floggings and the daily tortur-
ings of the unfortunate Jews. He witnessed the dead being
thrown into the sea every morning, and once a day he had
his plate of beans and so-called coffee water. He became thinner and thinner. They made him work, but how could he
work when he was so weak? They flogged him and threatened
him, but still only one small portion of beans daily. He saw
new faces come and old faces disappear. In the summer he
watched the dim, dun-colored Velebit Mountains blue against
the peaceful azure sky, and in the winter he saw their dark,

bold shapes gradually whiten against the gold of the setting
sun.

His legs and arms became thinner and thinner. He could
hardly move about the camp, let alone work. At night he
would creep into his hole in the ground, trying to keep warm
under his one blanket, trying to keep dry under his old piece
of canvas he had taken from someone's bed, someone who had
just disappeared. And all the time thinking of his home in
Slovenia, the grapevines, the little Madonna on the walls,
and his aging father and his sisters.

One night he escaped to the mainland. Free again, he
walked over the mountains, hiding by day, until at last he
reached home again. Thin and weak, he was filled with a burning desire to help rid the country of the invader. He joined
the Partisans, but he was useless for fighting, and they sent
him to the forest to help in the building of hospitals where
his wounded comrades could recuperate. Slowly he got better,
his legs filled out, his chest became broader, his face plumper,
and in the end Franz became my courier.

Both Bill and I liked him. He was so honest, and so eager
to work, which was more than you could say for some of the
comrades. If we asked Franz to go here or there, he would go
at the run, and come back laughing when we told him that
running wasn't really necessary.

One night he came up to our hut to ask a question. Bill
and I were reading by the fire. Bill said, "Come on in,
Franz, and have a vino," and Franz came very shyly in
and had a drink. Then he picked up a magazine which Bill
had put down and looked at the pictures. We went on reading and then Franz looked up and said, "I wish I could speak
English," and that was how we started teaching him. From
seven to eight every night Franz came for his English lesson,
but it didn't last long. He was too friendly with the British.

One day he came with tears in his eyes to tell us he was going in the morning and would not come back. He went, and we never saw him again.* We knew that he stayed at the *glavni stab* for interrogation for a day and was then sent "on," to jail.

I got a new courier, called José, José Murun; he was an old man who couldn't climb the mountains with speed, but he plugged along slowly behind us, with frequent drops from the *rakija* flask he always carried with him.

He worked his vineyard in the days of peace and one day when near his village we called in and spent the night there. It was one of those villages spread out all over the mountainside; each house built like a Swiss chalet, for the snows of winter were deep, and for months the vines lay protected by this thick blanket. José had been to America and there, by hard work, had amassed enough to come home and buy this strip of mountainside. He had one daughter about twenty, and three younger children born after his return, aged from five downward. It had been a long day's tramp for us, for we had carried not only our own stores for operating at a hospital en route but also a parachute for his wife to make into clothing for the children. It was almost night when we reached the foot of the mountain where he lived. I looked up and said, "Joe, I can't make it without a spell." As we sat down and rested, the day became lost in the mountains. Then we trudged on in silence. Up we wound, the track slippery and steep, and as I panted I wondered how they carried down the barrels of wine from the slopes to the valley below. We stopped again. Then suddenly the whole valley below was flooded with a new light, the light of the pale moon. The freezing snow crisped under our feet, shining like thousands of diamonds. Every branch arched

* He now lives in New Zealand.

over the track like a crown, and our nail-studded boots rang
clear on the hard, shining surface. Up and up we climbed.
Old Joe, as Bill and I called him, panted and grunted beneath
his load and the steepness of the track.

"My God Jesus, I wish this bloody war would end," said
Joe. "I want to get home to my joint and my kids. Could my
kids come to New Zealand after the war, do you think?" And
I saw old Joe sweeping his somewhat bleary eye up the hill
over the vineyards he loved and had labored in.

"Yes, I think so, Joe, if your country will allow them."

"I've had enough of this political life. I'm too old and you
know I want my kids to live in peace."

"Yes," I replied, and my mind switched back again across
the ocean and I saw my own country. True enough, we had
our political thugs too, especially during the war. Why, after
I left New Zealand and was working in the Western Desert
day and night, some enterprising fathead of a New Zealand
medical colonel reported to the Medical Section of the War
Office that I was both a nazi and a communist. The charge
was investigated, I understand, to everybody's satisfaction.

"Yes," Joe," I panted out. "New Zealand is a great country,
despite its political drawbacks."

"What, has it political drawbacks?"

"Oh yes," I replied, "but only mild ones. We are too busy
living to dream of killing." And we let it drop.

The *rakija* bottle was empty. Away high up we heard a
woman calling loudly, calling to a Partisan patrol which I had
just seen coming over the horizon. How black they stood out
with the moon behind! What a shot for a Domerbrand with
a Schmeisser!

There were two rooms in the house. In one José and his wife
were closeted, for it was long since he had seen her. In the
other with the stove I sat down at a table with a large flagon

of good black wine in front of me, resting half asleep in the warm room. On top of the stove the young children slept, and sitting by the warm bricks was José's eldest daughter, hanging her head coyly and pretending to read a paper. How could I help looking at her? She was strikingly dark, with black hair and full, dark-skinned face, almost like the Bosnians. Her fiery eyes furtively looked at me as I refilled the glass and I saw that she was as interested in me as an "Englishman" as I was in her as a girl of great beauty. Her lips were full and dark in the flickering light, and she was wearing a crude dress, made from an old Italian ground sheet, that fitted her figure and showed her full virgin breasts. She wore thick white stockings, knitted from unraveled parachute cord, and the strength of her legs gave one the feeling of good country lustiness, while her hands were white and smooth in spite of the arduous work she doubtless had to do. I realized that this was the daughter with the wonderful voice José had told me so often about.

There was a knocking at the back door, a kicking off of snow from the boots, and in came a Partisan and a Partizanka. They stood still when they saw me, but I rose and spoke to them and shook them by the hand and they both knew who I must be. José and his wife followed, and more wine was produced.

"You must try the white wine," José said. "I like it the better."

"Thank you," said I, for resistance had sunk to a low ebb after the hard day, and the warm room and the warm stomach had brought on a phase of politeness my colleagues did not know.

The girls disappeared into the kitchen and we three Partisans sat by the table, glass in hand. Luckily I had cigarettes and we pulled our chairs from the table to the stove. Mirko, who had just entered, told us how they had been attacked by a German patrol on the way over to the valley about three hours ago. They had all escaped into the forest and left three dead Germans lying freezing on the white shroud.

The girls and José's wife came in with food—such food as I hadn't tasted for a year. There was beautiful pickled pork, gray bread, and pickled mushrooms. We ate it slowly, for the pangs had long since subsided. Then we gathered around the huge stove and prepared for the usual Partisan "congress," which I saw would last far into the night. We talked of the Partisan advances in the south and the reverses in the north; we talked of the German atrocities everywhere they went, and the worse Chetnik and Domobranec atrocities here at our door. "Just the other day," said Maria, "the Domobranci were in Metlika and stabbed to death three women because they were Partisan sympathizers."

I couldn't take my eyes from Maria. She moved with such quiet freshness in spite of her heavy boots. Her eyelashes were like drooping willows over still pools, but when José spoke to her. I saw her face light up and her eyes shine as she ran to do his bidding.

The plates disappeared, and only the half-empty flagons of wine were left on the bare white table boards. Maria and her mother moved to the stove and sat down, watching us, ashamed of their poor clothing. The Partisan boy was silent, looking at the girl who had come in with him, a thin, white-faced girl with fair hair and blue eyes. Sitting in the best chair, an old horsehair one, José was relaxed, though the chair looked uncomfortable and impossible to rest in. He asked his wife for the piano accordion. Maria, a smile lighting her dark face, jumped up and disappeared through the door. She came back with the piano accordion, and José played. For all the day's hard walk and his gnarled fingers, he filled the house with music. No one sang, but the girls hummed the tune shyly, with downcast eyes.

Then José said, "Sing, Maria, sing, and let the *majore* hear your best." She looked at him, and then, eyes flashing, she sang a wild gypsy song. I forgot the bare, drab room, and saw horses sweep in wild abandon across the plains of Hungary. The mood changed suddenly, sad and haunting, and I heard the wind soughing through leafless trees beside the troubled Danube. The song ended, and emptiness and reality swept back into the room.

I looked at Maria as she stood by the stove. "Please, Maria, please. Some more."

"Yes," she said softly. "I will sing and sing and sing."

José emptied his glass and poured another. The wine shone and sparkled, red as rubies. He filled my glass and there was silence again. The mother in her black *ruta* whispered to the girls; the thin girl with the blue eyes moved toward Maria. Suddenly they looked at each other and sang, Maria's voice rich and deep, the other soaring above. And I sat there and listened, silent, enthralled. It was a Bosnian folk song, about the sighing of the forest and the bird singing on the topmost branch as the last flush of the dying sun touched the trees with fire. I looked across at the stove. The children slept on. The old mother steeped in the tragedy of her people, her head bowed, was singing too; three voices, singing as one. I closed my eyes and was conscious of soaring; soaring home, wrenched back, back again to all the beauty and the yearnings of youth. Once more I climbed the mountain peaks and sang with them, everyone was singing. Then slowly the voices died, died sweetly, with the last deep notes of Maria echoing in the darkened valley below.

José was asleep, his head on his outstretched arm. Maria said, "Will you sing for us now, *Majore?*" I knew how much they wanted to learn a song José had heard once in the States—he was always asking me to write down the words. So I sang it to

them, "Ye Banks and Braes o' Bonnie Doon." It sounded weak
after what I had heard, but they asked for more, and I remembered dimly "The Mull Fishers' Song" and sang that.

"How like our songs," Maria said. "What is it about?"

"It's about a Scottish boy from the islands, Maria, sitting in
his boat that rises and falls with the swell of the sea. He is
watching the hazy islands, his home, and dreaming of his girl."

The mother went into the next room and put more fuel on
the stove. The door opened on her return and again she stood
by the girls. They looked through the uncovered window, and
as I watched her, I saw Maria's eyes grow tender. She spoke to
the pale, thin girl, and again they sang, a song to the moon.

> *Sijaj sijaj bleda luna*
> *Kakor si sijala do polnoci.*
>
> *Saj si lepa saj si mlada*
> *Drugega fanta dobila si boš.*
>
> *Saj sem lepa saj mlada*
> *Drugega fanta ljubila ne bom*
>
> *Pojdi doli bleda luna*
> *Samo za mene ne boš*

Shine, shine, pale moon,
Shine on thro' mid of night

I hear thee, that my beauty,
That my youth, will lead me,
Other loves to find.

Shine, shine, pale moon,
My youth, my beauty and my love,
Is all for him who is no more

The pale moon shines, the pale moon wanes,
For me it never more doth shine.

The Partisan boy looked up and, like me, through the window. The moon was shining on the frozen snow, changing the gloom of the valley to shadow and light. Through the window it shone into the room, lending its light to the flickering tallow soak. Maria, her head high, the thin girl's hand in hers, looked out over the snow. Her voice was smooth and sweet as the nightingale's, her mother's the accompaniment of running water. The thin girl looked up, her mouth rounded and her lips quivering, and I saw her eyes fill with tears. The sadness of the song was over us all; it filled the house and flooded out to the cold snows beyond.

José was awake, and I looked at him. Tears ran down his face unheeded. The voices were stilled, and it was like waking in a vast, empty hall, the choir gone, the orchestra fled and the spell broken.

José turned his bearded face to me. "My God, that was wonderful. She can sing, my girl!"

Next day as we toiled home with rucksack filled with wine, the crisp frozen air, the sparkling hills, and the forest beyond filled me with joy and the speed of youth. We climbed over rocks, we slithered into crevices hidden by the snow, the bottles chinked and rattled in the heavy rucksacks, but there was something exultant in the air. A great fleet of American bombers flew high overhead. I looked up into the glare of the sun but couldn't see them. I turned and saw José toiling up, far behind me, sweat dripping over his dark face and shoulders bowed with the heavy load he was carrying. I stopped, kicked some snow from a dead fallen tree, and waited. He came up panting, sat down beside me, and took the wine from his pack, silently handing it to me.

"Well, how did you like my place?" he said.

"José, I think Maria had the finest voice in the world," I replied. "She swept me away, away to the clouds of desire and the islands of peace; away, away. I haven't listened to anything like that ever. Why don't you send her to America to your relations and get her trained for the stage?"

"You remember the last song she sang?" he asked.

"Yes, I do, 'Sijaj, sijaj, bleda luna.' "

"It happened this way," said José. "Maria had a boy friend. Is that what you call them? He was a fine boy, as blond as she is dark, as gay as she is serious, and as active and healthy as the young fawn. They had known each other since childhood days, when his family came from Styria to live down in our valley. Every day they would meet when they went to work in the fields below, and every Sunday when they had heard the Mass, they would sit under the linden tree and play and sing and dance until evening came, and her mother and I went home up the hill, leaving them, Maria and Stane, to come home through the woods. I never knew what happened on those walks home through the woods, but I would see them when they came into the open path walking arm in arm and whispering and laughing all the way up the steep slope home. We old people envied them, for we knew what was coming to the country. But they together had no time for anything but the look in each other's face. We liked Stane, he was so fresh and young and Maria was such a good girl.

"Then the Germans came and Stane ran away into the woods and joined the Partisans. We heard nothing of him for months. Maria used to ask all the bands that came by night through the forest and over the hill, 'Do you know Stane. Where is he now?' But no one knew.

"One day a passing courier stopped at the house and gave a note to Maria. It was from Stane. He was coming back into our valley. He would come and see Maria. He was a sergeant now, and asked to come and see us again.

"The house was transformed, Maria sang all day long. She did not heed the German planes that flew so low overhead every day; she just sang in the vineyards. When they all went down into the valley to pull the beans and peas, she sang until everyone in the village knew that Stane was coming home. Days passed and he didn't come. Every patrol that climbed the hill, she would look and wait, but no Stane. The moon flooded the valley every night and the wind would sing in the trees, but no song came from our house. She still hoped and hoped, but now the sounds of the fighting were very near. She knew he could not come. She heard the German tanks droning up the valley, she saw the steel-helmeted swine climbing the mountain tracks, and she ran into the forest. They went to her house and asked for wine. Her mother filled their barrels full and as they left she turned and spat on the ground. In the dusk Maria crept home and prayed to the Virgin. In her hand she brought some wild cyclemens and put it in front of the Blessed Mother and looked at her and again prayed for Stane. Firing broke out in the night over the hill; she crept up on top of the stove beside the frightened children and kept on praying. Still the moon shone and she couldn't understand why the Blessed Virgin did not answer her prayer. The firing ceased, and the night sounds again filled the valley.

"In the morning they found him, lying face down in the snow. Face down in the snow, his clothes stripped from him, his limbs frozen, his blond hair flowing into a deep footprint beside him. His young lithe legs white and stark and his long strong arms crucified and stiff. Like Christ, she thought. From his belly a frozen dribble of blood had tinged the snow red, and beside him were three empty brass shells. Her mother cried a little, but Maria's eyes were dry. Slowly she took off her dress of green ground sheet and covered him over. They carried

him down to the house and buried him there, under the pear
tree on the hill slope. Next day more snow came and covered
the fresh earth so that nothing remained.

"That is why Maria sings that song," said José.

We put on our packs again. The bottles chinked and we
made more fresh imprints in the snow.

CHAPTER 11

A Chapter of Difficulties

It was night when we reached Ajdovec. Bill had a great fire
going and hot soup ready. Where and how he made it I never
asked, but I guessed that Anitsa from Toplice had helped Bill
in the way of some extras which she always stowed away in
secret places so that the Germans could not find them when
they raided her house, which they did almost daily. We sat
down and I washed, and then Bill said that he had had a message from our fracture-femur hospital to say that some of the
men were ill and would I go over as soon as I could. I couldn't
start out that night, for the snow was too deep and the moon
was hidden by great snow clouds which had been gathering
all day.

Before daylight we left, with rucksacks on our backs and Bill
with me this time instead of José. We left Ajdovec still asleep
and in darkness and climbed out from the *jama* across the
conspirated paths. In winter we had a different method of
conspiration from the steppingstones of the summer. In winter,
with the soft snow lying feet thick under the trees, every foot-
mark made its telltale sign. We would make dummy tracks
in great circles leading back again to the forest roads; but at
some point, at right angles to the dummy track and preferably

in the lee of a huge block of limestone or behind a fallen tree, we would hammer the snow down hard with the backs of shovels, then micturate over the hard-beaten snow until an ice surface formed. From behind the shelter of a rock or tree we would step carefully from the dummy track, and sieve fine snow over the frozen path as we went, thus obliterating all footmarks and camouflaging the track completely. Doing this three or four times at mile intervals made it impossible to follow our tracks to the hospitals. Naturally the German Alpine patrols who sought us out were alive to this, and they counteracted the method by using great police dogs to get the scent of the wounded. At all costs we had to beat the dogs, and this we did. We had no meat to use as bait, and necessity forced us to adopt grisly but effective tactics. Amputated limbs were dragged along the dummy tracks and thus the dogs were thrown off the scent. Only by employing such desperate methods of conspiration were we able to continue our work and protect our wounded from murder.

By the time we reached the road, dawn was streaking across the mountaintops. It was bitterly cold and a wind was blowing which threw the loose snow against our faces and dislodged the snows from the boughs above, so that unless we took extreme care we would be showered and completely enveloped by a hundredweight of snow. Struggling through drifts and falls kept us warm, and as we walked I told Bill the story of Maria. We sat down in the snow for a spell before we started climbing the steep slope which led into the fracture hospital. I saw at once that it was the wrong thing to do to tell Bill this story, for he then began telling me about Ivitsa. For everything had gone awry. First of all, the paper forms didn't come, then, when they eventually did come, they were filled in incorrectly. New ones were procured and completed, but the courier taking them back was allegedly killed; and so on, until it was obvious that permission granted by Kidrich was only a fraud. "Why, why is the world like it is?" he said. "I want her more than anything in the world and I can't have her because of the communists. To bloody hell with politics," he muttered. "I didn't come here to wrestle with politics, but to help Partisans to fight the Germans. Why can't I have Ivitsa?"

"Bill," I said, and I looked at his face, red in the cold, and his scarf frozen hard with his breath, frozen hard and white, binding him tight like a hangman's rope. His blue eyes so clear and honest-looking; old Bill, I felt sorry for him and realized a little what he was thinking. "Well, Bill," I said again, "I'll do all I can to help."

"I know you will," he replied, "but it's these bloody communists. Have they no soul, no feeling, no time for human emotions or human desires?"

"Plenty, Bill, but only in as much as they are concerned."

I pictured Kidrich sitting in his office, with his thin, steely eyes and his pleasant smile. Smooth is what we would call him. I wondered why he was so against all of us trying to help in the struggle against the German swine. I wondered if he really cared for all these peasant boys and girls with their happy homes and villages, with their loves and their joy of living. Was it just that the great state machine drove him on, crushing all humanity underneath its great communist roller?

"Well, I don't give a damn for Kidrich or anyone else," he said. "I'm a Scot and I'm going to marry Ivitsa, communists or not!"

I thought that it was time to get moving. The wind was singing in the trees, singing over the mountaintops, singing, singing, singing, and I heard the echo:

> *Pojdi doli bleda luna*
> *Samo za meme ne boš.*

We arrived at the hospital door, kicked the snow from our boots, and went in. Ceslav the Pole was in the first bed, and I saw at once that there was something wrong. I went to where Leanna the nurse was standing, talking to a patient, and took her with me to the little theater at the end of the ward. Then she told me it all. The cold had so swept into the hospital and the blankets were so thin and only one per man that five of the patients had frostbitten legs and toes.

So we started and had a look. Five had gangrenous feet. While they lay in bed, with bad food, practically no vitamins, and poor vitality, the cold had stepped in and frozen their poor feet. Already the toes were black and in two cases the limbs were dark purple up as far as three inches below the knee. It had happened only within the last two days, Leanna said, so we took them to the theater and did what we could.

We injected the deep nerves of the lumbar region with anesthetic to paralyze the nerves which cause dilatation of the blood vessels below. It was a simple procedure and within ten minutes we could see the flush of blood surging down the legs and feel the heat gradually returning. The two legs which were purple and numb gradually became pink, pain returned; with satisfaction I saw that the parts were not really dead. But the toes which were black stayed black in spite of everything, and we wrapped them up in cotton wool and tilted the head of the bed high to promote a surging of fresh blood to the part below.

This was a major tragedy. I had often asked for more blankets; I had often suggested that blankets were better on the wounded than being cut up for pansy uniforms to encase the members of the staff. Here was the result. There was a knee joint that I had hoped to save, but it had gone wrong in my absence. It was a perforating wound involving the bone ends. We had washed it out, filled it with penicillin, and left a catheter in the cavity for four-hourly penicillin. But the catheter had been pulled out and couldn't be replaced and the joint was full of pus with a deep abscess extending up into the thigh. Here was the everlasting problem—to treat conservatively and drain the joint, or to amputate? How often did that problem crop up. So easy in British hospitals, where every hour some- one is available to watch the leg and to watch the patient. But here in the forest, without a trained nurse and with a doctor who could come only once in ten days, what could I do? Infec- tion so well established, open bone ends in the joint, and Germans a couple of miles away. We amputated the limb above the knee joint, getting rid of the infected bone, and left skin flaps lying open, unstitched, to allow the abscess to drain. It was a depressing day. Then just as we were about to get into our coats again, Maria, the party member nurse in charge, took me aside and asked me to look at her breast. "There is a lump, *Majore*," she said. "But you have been so busy with all these wounded boys I have never liked to talk about it."

I can see Maria now. Her husband was a judge in the old regime and one of the Jewish faith, I think. They had led a quiet, refined life in one of the large towns. I could imagine Maria entertaining her friends at tea, with all the dainties ob- tainable, her gray hair done up meticulously, her long, shining fingernails, her serious gray eyes, which always seemed to be questioning and asking, "How much longer? How much longer?" Her quiet resignation when the nazis took her hus- band away; her final flight into the forest when they came for her.

She lay down on the communal bunk and undid her tight blue blouse. With difficulty I persuaded her to take it off com- pletely. She seemed abashed at her nakedness and put over her chest a clean white towel. I could smell cancer as soon as she took off the blouse. I gently lifted off the piece of lint she had over it and there was a fungating growth of her left breast, fixed to the chest wall, and in her armpit were hard, stony, fixed red glands already terribly infected with secondaries. Over Maria hung death.

I spoke to her gently and told her that I would dress it for her and take her into the larger base hospital where we lived. "No," she replied. "I know it is cancer and I will die. But all I want is just to work quietly here with these Partisans who are freeing our country from chains." It was better so. All through the long winter Maria worked on, in the stifling silence of the forest snows, until spring came. Spring with its rushing waters and the singing of birds. Spring with its green buds and the trees again with uplifted branches, spring with a fresh hope and new life soaring down the sun-splashed valleys. And in the spring, I thought, Maria would die.

CHAPTER 12

"Doctor Bill"

It was January 1945. The Germans were being swept from Bosnia and Dalmatia, and we all felt that soon, very soon, the war in Europe would cease. Our hospitals were all full again, for during the long winter with thick snow it had been impossible to carry out air evacuation. Indeed we had been fairly isolated from all British news, and had lived a life playing hide-and-seek in the forest. We had had nothing to read, no lights to read with anyway, but Bill and I had learnt a lot of each other during those months.

It was January 15 and I had just returned from a long journey to another hospital called Yelen Brig. Bill was not yet home; he had gone over to our femur hospital to see that everything was satisfactory. I kicked the fire into life and put on water for him to wash with, for it was getting dark and he would be home any minute. The fire was blazing and there came a knock at the door. I got up and a courier was standing there with a letter for me. It had come from the mission. I opened it and read.

*Dear R. We have had a message saying return Serg. ———
immediately for repatriation under the long service scheme.*

It had come, as I had asked. Every time we had asked about his marriage, there was always some excuse delaying it for a few more days. Bill was getting more and more difficult and I did not wonder. But as the weeks passed, I saw that he was determined to take the law into his own hands and marry his Ivitsa with or without the sanction of the party. And I knew what sort of trouble that would bring. I had to get him away.

I pushed the letter in my pocket and sat by the fire. Of course I was sorry now that it had come, for our association through danger had been of the happiest, and during the two years we had been together there had hardly been a word spoken in anger.

I remembered the day I had chosen Bill in Cairo. Colonel Buttle had said, "You won't find him trained or as quick as your R.A.M.C. boys in the C.C.S., but he's a good chap and one you can trust in all circumstances."

That recommendation appealed to me. Firstly because it came from Buttle, for whom I had a tremendous regard, and secondly because it was so devoid of bull's-wool. It was that night I met Bill at Rustum House in Cairo. He had just come in the door and doubtless had seen the snake of Asclepius on my beret and guessed who I was. He stopped in his path and said:

"Are you Major Rogers?" And I said, "Yes."

"I believe you want someone to come with you into occupied territory. Can I come?"

I looked at his young, boyish, smiling face; I saw his two prominent incisors cleaned and as white as snow; I saw his hands and nails, clean-looking and fine; his shoes polished and his slim, tough stature. He appealed to me straight away.

"You're Sergeant ———?" I asked.

"Yes," he said. "Can I come? I've had no experience in operating rooms, but I'll learn."

His voice was Scottish, soft and running like a mountain stream, and he recalled the days of my youth, when I had heard many similar voices in Otago.

"Yes, you'll do," I said. And that was how we met.

He did learn all about operating theaters, and very quickly. In those days on Vis, when we worked probably harder than we did anywhere else in our whole two years, he was a great strength to me.

It was a long time before I heard all about Dad and Kate and his home, for these Scots are reticent until they know you. But sometimes over the fire at nights he would talk about Dad, whom I pictured as a severe and self-made man, whose struggle through the days of bitterness following the 1914–18 war had not been easy. He told me about Granny in an affectionate way and how his mother had died young, leaving Dad to bring up the children with the help of Kate, his sister.

Kate had married recently, and I pictured her, the good Scottish housewife, whose admonitions to Father and Bill about dirtying the floor she had just scrubbed being passed on now to her, I did not doubt, dutiful husband. There was in that family a devotion which in New Zealand is missing, or at least is not evident on first sight. The old bond between parents and children is a loose one in New Zealand. We are not brought up in the hard school and home life is almost lost in the maze of outside contacts.

The Yugoslavs liked Bill. He learnt their dialects quickly,

with no book and no teacher, and everyone called him "Doctor Bill." Often they asked for him in preference to me. It was Bill who gave the enema which brought so much relief, it was Bill who gave the penicillin which caused the painful arms, it was Bill who sat on their beds at night and spoke to them of the homely things they wanted to speak about, it was Bill who adjusted the splints, who gave the drinks, who injected the morphia. And it was Bill who had fallen in love with Ivitsa.

Ivitsa was my best nurse. At nights the two of them used to sit in the operating theater cleaning the instruments and Bill would take each one and teach Ivitsa the name in English and what it was used for.

Then he came to me and said, "As I'm going to marry Ivitsa, can I bring her to our hut at nights for an hour to teach her English?" That sounded all right to me, as good an excuse as any. I said, "Yes, I'll talk to the commissar about it for Ivitsa's protection." So I went to the commissar and told him that I thought it would be a good idea if Bill taught Ivitsa English, so that she wouldn't be stranded in a strange country when they got married.

He smiled at me and tactfully agreed.

Our hut had two rooms. Hitherto we had used only my room, with the large open fire, and at nights we would sit there until it was time for sleep, when Bill would retire to his own cold room. But now I always found a fire burning in Bill's room and a constant hurry to get cleaned up early. We would sit and drink our last *rakija* beside the fire. Bill would glance every minute or two at his watch until finally we would hear on the snow outside the little steps of the ballet dancer and a timid knock at the door.

Ivitsa would come in. Bill would draw up a stool to the fire, for friendship's sake, I suppose, and then in a minute they would go off, and I would hear a vast stoking up of his fire, then, for a minute or two, "I am, thou art, he is . . ." Gradually the sounds would grow fainter, and then silence. A silence broken by an occasional laugh or word, while I sat alone, wishing I were ten years younger.

At ten o'clock, being a good father, I would get up and shout, "Time, Bill," and they would emerge, looking sheepish but joyously young, radiantly happy, and as the footsteps died away in the snow and I sat waiting for Bill's return I envied them in their new-found whirlwind of happiness.

When he came back, we would sit by the fire as it died. Often in silence. Then Bill would look up at me and say, "By God, I'm going to marry her, even if I have to wait years."

And now he was to go. I was just working out how to tell him, when I heard the familiar kick of his boots against the steps and in he came. "By God, I've had a hell of a day," he exclaimed. "I lost my way in the snow and didn't arrive till after the meal, and there was none left, and then I found the Russian was growling about his bandage, and the Pole about his extension, and that commissar chappy—you know the one that's always causing trouble—well, his plaster was too tight and he'd started to cut it off himself."

"And what did you do, Bill?"

"I just told him it was going back, and I put it back. And I told him that if he did it again you'd give him hell."

"Did that satisfy him?"

"Yes. I don't think he'll do it again!"

By this time Bill was stripped in front of the fire, and was busy washing himself from head to foot. In between he said, "What kind of a day have you had?"

"Oh, full of disappointments too, Bill," I replied. "That skin graft we did hadn't taken at all due to an acute infection, and they took off the extension from a fracture and now the bone ends have slipped back into the original displacement."

"All in the day's work," he said, and began to put on his warmed dry socks. Then we pulled up the stools by the fire and the usual silence intervened while Bill got down a little *rakija*, which we had on returning from long trips.

We started sipping it. Suddenly Bill said, "What's on your mind tonight?"

"Bill, I've just got word that you're recalled immediately, and that means tomorrow, to go back to England on repatriation."

"But I can't," said Bill. "How about Ivitsa?"

"Well, you'd better go over to the hospital and tell her," I said.

He drank on in silence, then got up and went into his own room and stoked up the fire. In ten minutes I heard the two of them come quietly around the track, open the door, and go into his room.

I started writing a letter, but the words wouldn't come. I picked up a book and started to read, but it all seemed unreal and stupid. So I poured another *rakija* and lay on the bed watching the dying end of a cigarette.

Curious how attached I was to him. There was something about him just blown in from the hills, fresh and redolent of youth, so honest. "Jesus," I murmured, "I'll miss him." Not that we could go about much together, for one of us usually stayed at Ajdovec in case of trouble, and we had both made our own friends. But just the sense of reliability he gave, someone to talk to about the Secret Police, someone to laugh with when I displeased the commissars, someone to tell the stories to I heard when at the *glavni stab*. "Jesus, I'll miss him."

No sound came from the other room. I started a new cigarette and watched it disintegrate into ash. It was better that he went straight away, without too much time to think about it all. Besides, the enemy were all around and for days we had been expecting an attack. I put the billy on the fire to brew a cup of cocoa for us all, and when it was made I tapped gently on Bill's door and woke them up.

Bill came in first and sat down, pulling up a stool for Ivitsa. Her eyes were red with tears and she sat beside him saying not a word. From her breeches—she wore an old pair of Bill's —she pulled out her handkerchief and dried her eyes. Bill tenderly put his arm around her and they disappeared out of the door into the night.

Next morning we had early cocoa and robbed our store of a tin of bully beef. He got dressed, burnt some old letters of Dad's and Kate's, showed me a bundle of clothes he was leaving for Ivitsa, and together we left Ajdovec.

Firing had already started down in Podhusta, about a mile away, and the Germans had begun mortaring the village and the forest above.

"Bill, you'd better not go down into the valley," I said. "Go the forest path and avoid the valleys like hell."

We came to the forest road and there I stopped.

Bill turned and said, "Well, cheerio, sir. Thanks for all you've done for me. Look after Ivitsa. I hate going." And he turned on his heel after clasping my hand and I watched him, walking slowly with his rucksack on his back and his gun over his shoulder, until the trees parted us.*

CHAPTER 13

Conversation with the Commissar

I was alone now, for they had conveniently removed my second José from Ajdovec because he was too friendly with us and

* He married the first Scottish lassie he met on his return, and now he and his family live happily in New Zealand.

I had been to his house. At least that was the supposition, and, following the usual rule, that was the cause. I worked all morning in the theater with Ivitsa. She called me *"Stari Papa"* or Old Father, and every now and then she would look up at me and both of us knew what we were thinking. We were thinking of Bill, walking solitary along the forest tracks. She was wondering, Will he ever come back to me? I was thinking of all the grand chaps I had met in these five years, our paths had crossed, and then we moved on, never to meet again.

The same day orders came for Ivitsa to go down to Croatia. I had a talk with the commissar about it and managed by most strenuous exertion applied through Colonel Luka to get the order reconsidered. So Ivitsa stayed—for that day.

That afternoon a penetrating wound, three days old, of the abdomen arrived. Already thin pus and feces were pouring from the wound. I made up some glucose saline from snow water and that helped him a little. Plenty of morphia in these cases was the only thing you could use.

Next day I gently explored the wound, mainly for the purpose of excising some dead abdominal wall. As I irrigated the hole, I saw in the bottom the inner wall of the cecum, and, lying in it, a piece of mortar bomb and a piece of his tunic. We gently removed these, and after four perilous days of gastric suction and copious morphia he gradually recovered. Finally, when the blow did fall, and the Germans found Ajdovec after I left, I was told that he walked out of hospital with a fairly large cecal fistula, but alive.

We had to maintain day and night patrols, for the Domerbrands were camped only a couple of miles away from us on one side, and on the other were the Germans less than a mile away. One evening Marko the commissar and I were on a patrol, for the firing had been very close to us all afternoon. We came out of the *jama* and down the conspirated track. Just a few hundred yards down we saw the glimmer of a fire, and the forest was reeking of smoke. We crept near, very near, and saw five Germans and a Chetnik sitting around the fire. It was just too easy for words. The forest rang with the music of victory, and five of the hospital-hunting hunters had gone. We dragged them away from the track, behind a great rock, and covered the bodies with snow until a more propitious time should come for their disposal.

Next day I went to the hospital at Yelen Brig alone. It was a long way. Three times on the track I hid in the forest behind a bush and waited until an enemy patrol passed. I began to get anxious about Yelen Brig, for the doctor in charge was just a nurse, really, and he had quite a number of bad cases to look after. When I arrived at the conspirated track I found no sentry. I approached now with extreme caution, thinking that the Germans had found the hospital. But no, the hospital was completely empty. Nobody left at all. I looked for tracks but knew how useless that would be. They had gone off in the night, and were probably hiding away in the depths of the forest. I sat down for a while and read the *Sten Cas*.

Every hospital had its *Sten Cas*, or wall newspaper, and here I read for the first time about the German rout in Italy, and how the Germans had surrendered in places and elsewhere were streaking up into Carinthia via Trieste. Then I saw a little drawing of Tito. Someone had written under it "*Smrt fascismu, sloboda narodu*" (Death to fascism, freedom for the people). I hoped that *sloboda narodu* would be a reality. How the fire of liberty had seized these Partisan boys! To think of our own officers' messes in the Eighth Army, listening to one of Churchill's great feats of oratory, when *fascismu* was on our very doorsteps. Why, they would just turn from the wireless, and resume their game of cards without the faintest trace of emotion. Someone had written a story of the Red Army's liberation of Poland. It was punctuated throughout by many "*Zivio Marshal Stalin,*" "*Zivio Rdeča Armada,*" and alongside was a little love story of a Partisan commissar and a Partizanka from Carinthia. Not one word of the other Allies in the fight for freedom.

I turned and walked home. That night I felt bloody lonely, so I called the commissar to come up and have a drink by the fire. I was never quite sure whether he was a communist or not. If he was, he was a most liberal one.

Before the war he had been a schoolteacher somewhere up in Styria. He had a good knowledge of our literature and sat and discussed Galsworthy, Jack London, H. G. Wells, and Conrad. Yes, he had read them all in translation, some in German, some in Yugoslav. He asked me about Van Loon and had I read James Jeans? And so the conversation gradually veered around to the present situation. He asked me what I thought of communism?

I replied that my real knowledge of Marxism and Leninism was extremely limited, like that of most Britishers, but I respected any country that had, in the brief space of twenty years, practically wiped illiteracy from the land. What I didn't like in what I saw around me was the dishonest propaganda, the distrust of the British as allies, and the fear which was all-pervading among the peasantry. I didn't like the method of ruthless progress exemplified by Kidrich in the Ljubljana assassinations, and I didn't agree with the exclusiveness of election of party members.

"Yes," he replied. "Those are difficult points to answer. But you must realize that we are passing through our birth pains, and birth is always associated with pain. The intolerance of nature in producing a healthy child sometimes gravely damages the mother, you know."

"Yes. That is so," I replied.

He broke in, saying, "We don't want the anesthetic of capitalism in our birth—even though it is from a so-called democracy."

"But you have had it already," I retorted. "Think of the thousands of tons of British equipment that have been flown into your country by our pilots; think of the thousands of tons that have been sailed in by our Navy. Why, your very gun, your uniform, your boots, are British anesthetics, if you like to call them that."

"Yes. So they are, so they are."

"Another drink, tovarisch?" and I poured a glass of Anna's best *rakija*. "What do you think will happen in the future?"

"It is very difficult to surmise," he said. "Very difficult, for we are apt to forget the great numbers of Yugoslavs who have taken no part in this struggle, or have been actively associated with the other side. Look," he went on. "Our Partisan Army was only three hundred thousand out of sixteen million. What of the Chetniks, the Ustashi, the Domobranci, the thousands of townspeople who stayed safely in the occupied towns? What will they think of it all? No, I don't think they will agree with us, and for the immediate future we must be very strong."

"Well, aren't you?" I retorted.

"Yes, but strong not only in arms, but in purpose. We must be ready to take our place in the world as a competitive nation, not as a Balkan backwater. I have seen much in the struggle for liberation. I have lost all in the struggle. But out of it I see youth, filled with a relentless desire for a better land, and for peace."

"That is it—peace," I said. "With that before us as our beacon we will do much."

But would peace reign? I wondered, as the fire died.

CHAPTER 14

The Story of Milica

It didn't seem the same at Ajdovec now that I was alone. The nights seemed longer; there was no one to talk to. That was depressing enough. Then came the horrible tragedy of Leanna's fracture-femur hospital. I set off one day on my usual fortnightly visit. The hospital was so well hidden that even I, who alone knew where it was, could hardly find it underneath the great dark pines of the forest. But the Germans and Domobranci found it. Perhaps the ringing of an ax against the hard wood; perhaps the drift of smoke led them to it. Perhaps someone else knew. When I arrived late that afternoon, and fired the warning shots from the ridge to tell them who it was, I heard no answer. The forest was silent and dead. Climbing down over the rocks and roots, I smelt fire, and then suddenly I knew all. Among the ashes, white as a shroud, were the dead bones.

For a long time, ever since the failure to take Kocevje, it had been apparent that actual offensive operations by the Slovenes had been at a standstill, and in consequence my work was slackening. True enough, we got in a fairly regular supply of patients, but few of them were recent casualties. Most of them came either from the far north across the Sava or else from around the Istrian Peninsula. Then odd people used to arrive from the headquarters. I remember receiving no less than four arteriovenous-aneurysm cases in one week. They were all old cases who had been able to carry on with their work until such time as they could be spared. Most were caused by machine-gun bullets which had by some curious chance passed between a large artery and vein in their course through a limb, and nicked a piece from each in their passage, thus forming a short circuit in the vascular supply of the limb.

How different is the actual work of the surgeon in the field to the ideal technique one finds described in the books, often written by someone who has never been in the field. I knew well the accepted technique for the repair of this shortened circuit; it was to repair the artery and restore its continuity. But how difficult it is in most cases. The whole area is a mass of dense fibrous tissue and the artery is reduced in caliber to that of a quill; very often making repair impossible to the ordinary worker. We managed to break the short-circuiting by tying off the vessels above and below the connection, thus sending the blood around by different channels.

One of these cases was a Partizanka, and when I went around the ward in the morning and saw her lying there, I stood a minute and thought, Surely it is Milica! Just a flash through my brain; here was Milica again. But Milica lay under some rocks down in the Bosnian mountains. Her fight for liberty had died over a year before. But it was a grand fight she had made, and somehow that morning I missed Bill to talk to. I wanted to tell someone that I had seen the very image of Milica again.

I first met Milica when I stayed with a sabotage group who were operating on the Split–Bihac road. She was young and yet old, for the enemy had been hard on Milica. Her parents had a house near the main road and pleasant plot of land which sauntered down to the river, bathed in sun, and flowing smooth, so that the corn grew six feet high and the cobs were full and luscious, and the tangled beans stretched their arms far above the supporting poles as if determined to climb higher and reach the sun. Milica had two sisters, one nineteen and one seventeen, and all the happy summer days they worked in the fields with her father and mother, planting, hoeing, and weeding; and, in the autumn, picking. Her village was a mile away from the farm, and on Sunday, with her father and mother and sisters, Milica would walk to Mass along the white twisting road up the hot valley. And then in the afternoon, in her beautifully embroidered dress, she would wait for her brother Marko and his friend, who came on cycles from Banja Luka, where he worked. Milica had great yearnings and stirrings in those days, for in the summer sun, after the feast of chicken and potatoes and the glasses of red wine, they would sit under the trees and she would watch Marko's friend, the young lawyer, who talked of the towns he had seen and the future he hoped would be his. It almost seemed to her that he was saying, "That will be ours," for she knew, as he knew, why he came so often to the valley. She knew what he meant when they sang those songs and she caught his brown eyes looking at her. In the *kola* he tried to get next to her and hold her hot hand, while the accordion played away and they danced in the never-ending circle. Yes, Milica was very happy in those far-off days.

Then came the rumblings of war or revolution. The boys did not come so often now, for in the cities there was fever and discontent. New groups among the students; some with the crusade of fascism tingling through their veins, speeded by the promises and the visions from students in Germany; some spurred by the fiery revolutionary doctrines which came from Mother Russia. The gymnasium—the university—seemed split in two. Some were already wearing uniforms when the blow came. So swiftly did the Germans come; so swiftly did they seem to know all those who, in the months before, had spurned the new ideal. And those were soon imprisoned, or killed, and few escaped. In a flash the country, which before had seemed peaceful to Milica, became a seething fire of murder, rape, and imprisonment. Her brother never came home again, nor did her lover. Every Sunday she watched the road for the two cycles which had to free-wheel with such speed from the village to their home, but every Sunday the road was empty. The meetings under the linden tree on the hot afternoons when dinner was finished were no more, and in the fields there was much murmuring and whispering against the new regime.

True, the Germans passing along the road in an unending stream never interfered with her people—they all seemed to be hurrying southward—and the corn ripened slowly in the sun and the grain was scythed and gathered in. Then winter came. But this winter was different from any others, for while the roads were still open, great German trucks came and stopped at each little farm demanding corn and grain, wine and beans. "You will be paid later," they said. But the peasants knew better.

The light which sometimes burnt before the Virgin in the old days was always lit now, for the priest had told them that many souls had perished throughout the land and evil stalked among them. Her mother, still waiting for her son to come home, went to Banja Luka to ask for him. But the office where he worked had been burnt to the ground and no one knew her son. She went to the police and there found a German Gestapo man talking to the head of the office and she crept out, frightened to speak. She walked to the cemetery and scanned the graves. So many new ones with no names on them. She wondered, Could he be there? No one knew; the town seemed unreal to her, not like the Banja Luka she used to know, with its streets filled with streaming, happy peasants, this one with a duck under her arm and that one with a couple of chickens. True it was, some people seemed happy, talking to the German officers who came and went in their motorcars. She came home. The mile from the village to her house seemed a long way. She remembered her boys, one dead long since, playing in the fields, so happy, pushing their little cart of hay home in front of the heavily laden *kola*. She saw the cart lying in the long grass, its wheels half hidden. She heard them laugh . . . but that was long ago.

The door was open. Milica was inside, grinding some corn in the old stone mill they had used years ago. Funny where the men from the power mill down the valley have gone, her mother thought, and she turned to Milica.

"Milica, I haven't found him. No one knows, no one."

Then she sat down in the shadows, and, seeing the Madonna above her, she crossed herself and prayed that he might come home. And Milica, seeing her mother deep in care, ceased grinding the corn, and sat down beside her, cried a little, then rose and, taking a bucket, went out toward the cow byre. The cows were chewing the new hay and when they saw her shadow through the door they stopped, turned their heads, then went on chewing. She sat beside one and slowly milked it. Each squirt of the fresh, bubbling milk hit the bucket and ran down the side. She stopped, pushed her head into the soft, warm cow, and cried until dark came.

Next day a German truck stopped at the house, and they came into the great shed where the golden corn was stored in wooden bins. They asked for her father, but he was down in the fields near the river. One German came up to Milica. He spoke to her and looked at her soft eyes, and saw her shuddering with fear. He told her that they had come for corn and wheat and hay, but Milica, with fear rushing through her veins, knew what was making his eyes shine and his fat, podgy little fingers open and grasp the empty air.

She went toward the open door to escape and to call her father and mother and sisters, but he was quick. He stood there in her way and seized her by the wrist. She wrenched it away, her whole body in a fever of fear. She could feel her heart thumping, her hands trembling, and where he touched her she felt red and hot and unclean. She again attempted to seek the fresh open air, but he seized her and flung her on the soft hay, and sprawled his fat, gross body over hers, his lips open and covered with foul German slobber. She kicked, she bit, and his companions stood laughing on the other side of the barn, watching every movement and waiting for their turn. The hay got in her eyes and up her nostrils. Then they heard another car stop on the road and steps coming to the barn. He got up from her, disheveled, and with the leering look of thwarted lust still blazing from his small eyes. She ran from the barn, ran and ran into the open fields where her father and sisters were gathering the dried beans, and then she fell on the grass beside them and burst into tears, sobbing and wiping her lips, and burying her head in the grass beside her.

When they returned to the house, the barn doors stood open. They went in and saw only the empty bins, and pinned onto the hanging door was a notice written in German, which none of them could read.

That night as they sat around the stove whispering and weeping and praying, they heard cars coming down the valley road. Quickly Milica rose and went out into the night to see what was there. But at the same time the cars stopped at the gate. She hid behind the empty *kola* and watched four steel-helmeted figures go into the house. Then came the sound of shots, then more shots. She ran across the fields into the darkness, ran and ran until a small hillock hid her from view. She lay down in a hollow and wept, and even as she did, she saw a tall flame shoot into the sky, and heard the crackling of dried timbers burning. She crept to the hilltop and saw her home blazing high, and around it on the road stood the four helmeted figures. The car moved away into the night. Already the flames were sinking, and the rosy-red sky was again turning into the deep blue of the night. She walked slowly homeward and stayed the night by the dying embers.

So Milica joined the Partisans. Dull, lifeless, the bloom faded from her cheeks, and the roundness of her face, the youthful sweetness twisted into hard-lined furrows deepened by the beating of the cruel winter, and sallowed by the bleaching of the soaking rain. It was a small band she joined, a band who every night trudged in silence over the mountain passes, carrying their arms and their grenades, their small bags of food, their hearts burning with revenge against the invader. The hate Milica bore was perhaps the deepest of them all. As they hid high up behind the rocks, watching the German transport twisting and turning down the Split–Bihac road, she would remember her blackened home and her dead father and mother. Yes, they found them, shot, and lying between the barn and the burnt house. Her sisters they never found, and sometimes Milica used to wake and think of that fat, gross German swine, who had caught her wrists and breathed his foul breath over her lips. She never knew what happened to her sisters, but she often thought.

One night they stole a great supply of Molotov bottles and grenades from a German truck which had broken down. They killed the guards. Now life was easier and revenge was sweeter. Her companions had two machine guns. In the early morning they would lie and watch the convoys streaming down to Split and the south. Soon they got to know which convoys returned in the evening. True, they always had tanks to guard them, or troops or mounted guns, but the Partisans would choose a piece of road which bent and twisted down to the straight valley road beneath. At first they would lie above and machine-gun the trucks, if the convoy was small, then run into the mountains above. A certain satisfaction would fill Milica as she watched the trucks lying smoking below and the German dead sprawled out on the road. But she wanted more and more. She wanted to destroy the tanks which guarded the lorries as they sped back and forth. But what could twelve do against armored trucks and tanks? At night she would lie thinking about it all. She would hear her companions sleeping near her, tired and dead to the world, she would see the silent sentry standing, guarding them in the shadow, then she would turn and say, "How can I kill more and more and more?"

One day she dressed as a peasant, and, flinging a black *ruta* over her now silver head and taking in her voluminous dress two grenades and two Molotov bottles, she went down to the road. Far below them they saw a German convoy coming up the valley. Her companions hid just above the road on each side, their machine guns ready and loaded. Milica began walking down the road, spinning her wool. The German convoy started climbing and twisting and turning. The front armored car was near her. She hung her head, bowed like an old woman. It swept past her, breathing its fumes of death and despair. It turned the corner. Then came the convoy. It too passed her as she stood on the side twisting the wool from the stick. The last tank came near her. She bent down, seized her Molotov grenade, and as the tank passed she hurled it under the track. Immediately flames leapt from below the tank and started climbing over its iron sides. The Germans opened the turret. She threw in her grenades, and as they started shooting, a stream of lead from the Partisan guns shot them down. The tank was on fire. Milica scrambled up the hill behind the rocks. The tank was abandoned, the Germans shot. The column ahead had halted but could see only the smoke. They couldn't turn on the narrow road. A mine laid far ahead exploded and blew up the road, trapping the column. Shots filled the air. The Partisans began to escape up into the forest.

The German tanks by this time were filling the hillside with shells, but where were the targets? Milica had reached her companions. Soon they were all together, running through the forest to their hiding place. Evening came and they rested, then in the darkness set off walking some thirty miles to start all over again.

Yes, there was satisfaction in that, and at each vehicle she blew up or burnt she smiled and thought of her mother and sisters. She would pray to the Virgin to forgive her, and then in the next minute plan and scheme again. But at last the Germans got to know the old woman walking along the roads spinning her wool. When she was carried in to me and I lifted the blanket thrown across her and saw the clothes, her heavy black skirt soaked with blood and smelling of feces, I knew the end had come. We lifted her into bed and undid the clothing and there across her white belly, twisted, contracted like giant worms, were the coils of short intestine, which no mortal man could ever replace.

We gave her morphia. Her face seemed to change as she lay there, the furrows smoothed out, and a bloom came back again to her cheeks. Her Partisan cap lay on the pillow beside her, the Red Star shone against her silver hair. Her hands, pale white and sweaty, lay still against the gray blanket. I lifted her head and gave her a drink. She whispered, "You English are so kind and I am happy now." Ten minutes later I came back to her, and she was dead. But no one would know. For when the forest, great, green, and living, had swallowed her up, she became alive again, beautiful in the new-found liberty.

I looked again. No, this wasn't Milica.

CHAPTER 15

Spring Comes to the Valley

Spring had come and the snow of the valley below was fast disappearing. Perhaps it was a good thing, for now we could get our patients up and away more easily; perhaps it was a bad thing, because with spring the Germans began to squeeze us in that little valley, squeeze us from both ends. Every day now there was shooting on three sides of us; every day I crept through the forest to our lookout point and with glasses scanned the valley below. I could see the tanks streaming along the Novo Mesto road. I could see the trails of dust behind the lorries filled with infantrymen, hurrying up from the south to stem the tide of the Allied armies in the west and the Russians in the east. We heard little news. It was much too dangerous to go to Packa, where the British Mission had been. We saw nothing of the Yugoslav medical officials. Indeed Bogdan had never been to Ajdovec since the day it opened, and Luka had been only once since.

There was throughout the peasantry a feeling of tension, of apprehension. No one dared speak in anything but a whisper about the rapidly changing political situation. Fear was everywhere. In the night groups of men would appear at someone's door and next morning the owner of the house would have disappeared. Where, no one knew. Secret Police, they told me, were everywhere. I did not need to be told that, for I had an almost permanent watch on my movements and found it increasingly difficult to move without being followed by couriers. Everywhere I went, everything I said, was reported to the proper source. Everyone with whom I was thought to be friendly was interrogated.

Indeed fighting the Germans had become almost a secondary part of the policy, and as far as one could judge politics, the maneuvering for postwar power had become the major part of the Slovenes' life. True, they fought when pressed, and we were pressed now on all sides, but the good old days of 1943, when offensive action and guerrilla warfare were the whole of the struggle, seemed to be dead. More and more equipment was coming into the country and less and less fighting was going on.

It was apparent from the odd snatches of conversation I heard all over the country, and from talking to my patients, that behind the Communist party there was another group of politicians working, working fast for its own ends. When I spoke to people in the district, it was plain that they did not favor a Russian communist regime. Among the many peasants I knew the percentage of communist sympathizers in their own district was about 5 per cent. Among the Partisans, from whom I had ample opportunity to get the facts, the percentage was about 10. But among that 10 per cent were all the people in authority and all the people with power.

Most of the Partisans were heartily sick of politics. The one question was: "Why don't the English come and occupy our country until we settle down? We can't trust our politicians." When I replied that the Allies had decided that Yugoslavia should be a Slav zone of influence, and that the British couldn't come, they said, "Well, I hope the Russians come soon, for we are frightened of what is taking place."

What was taking place one could never find out. It was very much behind the scenes, anyhow. The magnetism of Tito seemed to be diminishing. The spontaneous loyalty that had surrounded him in 1943 had gone, and now, though he still exerted considerable influence in Slovenia, it seemed to be slowly evaporating. And that was a bad thing.

The one thing that still gave me hope for postwar stability was the dual control, or what I hoped was dual control, of Commissar Kidrich and President Vidmar. And I remembered Vidmar's humanity, and I remembered Kidrich's ruthlessness, and I wondered how long that dual control would last.

Since Bill went, the emptiness of the hut depressed me. One Sunday I decided to go down to Toplice and talk to Anna, a villager we had befriended, have a good swim in the hot baths, more talk with Anna, a little wine, and then home.

After going around the wounded I set out with a rucksack on my back to bring home anything I could get hold of in the valley. Sometimes the peasants would give me eggs, sometimes a piece of pork, sometimes a bottle of wine, and I in my turn gave them pieces of parachute to make the clothes they so badly needed.

On the road down a lot of firing started around Podhusta and up on the hills behind Novo Mesto. I stopped, hesitated, and wondered whether it would not be better to return. But the sun was shining and I decided to wait. More firing, but this time farther down the valley toward Valla Vas, and as I watched I could see the German heavy guns in their usual positions on the edge of the forest, just above the temporary bridge over the Kerka. The machine guns added the staccato to the foul music of the whirring mortars. Then, quite suddenly, it all ceased. I started digging up a cyclamen to take back to our garden around the steps of my cabin. I couldn't reach the roots and just as the corm was coming loose, it split right across. I stopped in disgust, disgust at not getting the flower, and disgust at breaking it and destroying it.

No more firing. I moved farther down toward the valley and stopped again. I could see streaks of dust along the Novo Mesto road as the German gun lorries went home. The machine guns had stopped too, so I decided that I would go down and be very careful before I went into Toplice. Podhusta was deserted. A Partisan patrol was winding its way up the valley toward Poturin, so I crossed the flat and reached the river by the bridge. No sentry was there, but I met an old woman slowly walking along the road. I stopped her and asked if Toplice were safe.

She did not know, but the German barbarians had taken her two cows away that morning, and now she had nothing. "Maria Madonna," she murmured and crossed herself. I left her and continued over the low hill which separated Podhusta from Toplice. Just before I came out of the woods by the old bombed mill, I stopped and watched the village. I could see no one. Then a church bell started ringing down Dvor way. How incongruous, I thought. Christ in the midst of all this. It tolled and tolled and tolled and the echoes sped up the valley until a continuous note was sounding. I went down to the bombed mill and crossed by the swing bridge. Immediately I saw on the road the marks of motor vehicles, German vehicles, for I knew that the Partisans had none as close as this. I walked along the road past the school and entered the village. Just at the church I saw a group of peasants talking to the village priest. Two were crying piteously and wiping the copious tears away with their black *rute*. The priest was wearing his vestments and was anxiously looking along both roads and up on the hill beyond. They stopped momentarily when they saw me. I knew that they thought I was a German. Fear swept over them and one old woman hid her head beneath her *ruta*. I spoke to them and heard the priest say, "It is the English doctor," and I passed on to Anna's house.

At the door was Gruno, the Alsatian. He growled as I approached, and as I went to push open the iron gates, he snapped dangerously at me through the bars. I said, "Gruno,

Gruno," and he stopped and slunk away. I opened the gates
and Anna met me at the door. "Go away, go away," she cried.
"The Germans have just left. It's been terrible." And as I
looked up the lane I saw four dead Partisans lying on the road.
I went inside. The old man, Anna's father, was walking up and
down the kitchen muttering, "Maria Madonna, the swine,
Maria Madonna, the swine!" I sat down, and as I did fresh
firing started again up the hill behind the village. "Quick,
quick!" said Anna. "Get in here, they won't look here," and
she pushed me into a secret place, damp and musty and dark.
I heard Father go out to the front door and call Gruno inside,
then I heard Anna lock the door and walk back to the kitchen.
More shots flattened themselves on the walls of the house.
Somewhere I heard an airplane and then the dropping of
bombs. I knew that the Beaufighters or Hurricanes had arrived
and were making their daily Dvor–Novo Mesto sweep. More
bullets and machine-gunning, but farther away. I crouched
and tried to bend my knees and sit, but it was impossible.
Then I heard a hammering at the door and a window on the
second story opened, and I heard Anna talking to them. They
asked her to open the door for them to search the house. She
replied they had just searched it an hour ago and what did
they want to search it for again?

They kept kicking the door. I heard her go downstairs; I
heard Gruno barking in the hall and Anna telling her father to
lock him up. Then the door opened and the Gestapo entered
the house. They went into the kitchen, four of them, their
heavy boots echoing along the uncarpeted corridor. They
looked into her cupboards and took all her glasses and knives
and forks, and then came upstairs and went into the bed-
rooms. I pulled back the magazine of my automatic pistol and
put down the safety catch, expecting every moment to be
found. They opened her wardrobe and found some sheets and

pillowcases. They took them, they took her clothes hanging on the hooks and her old opossum-skin coat, and then marched out of the house. I breathed again and changed position and put up the safety catch. Anna was filling up the range with wood, for I could hear the door open and then close. The old man tottered down the stairs and relocked the door. Everything in the village was deathly still. Not a sound.

I was getting hungry and was very stiff. I stood up straight, banging my head on the roof, and then crouched down again. Firing started again, but far away. It must be nearly midday, I thought. Someone walked along the road outside. It was an old peasant. He walked along until opposite Anna's house and then went into the *gostiona*, or pub. I could hear a great talking going on. Then Anna went to the front door, opened it, looked along the street, and disappeared into the *gostiona*. A Partisan boy came down from Poturin with his gun in his hand and he went into the *gostiona* too. Anna came out, I saw her through the chink in the broken plaster, she opened the door, and came to me and told me they had gone. I came out and we went downstairs to the kitchen, where we could watch the road through the window. But all was quiet. The German patrol had departed to Novo Mesto.

Then Anna told me the whole story.

In the early morning a Domobranec and German patrol had come to the village in search of food. "There is no food," they were told, so the German officer began a house-to-house search, and found some hidden supplies. They made a heap on the ground in front of the *gostiona*, then began systematic looting of everything of value in the houses. They next took fifteen old men and women as hostages for having Partisan sons or being Partisan sympathizers. They took five young women and kept a guard on them. Then they found hiding in a loft two Partisan brothers who had come home for the night to see their parents. They took the fifteen and the two Partisans to the cemetery on the hill just outside the village, and commanded the boys to dig a grave. One of the boys threw his shovel at the German officer and immediately he was seized and they chopped off his hands with an ax against a tombstone. The other brother, terrified by the piteous cries, was seized and beaten, then thrown on the ground and with the sharp edge of a shovel they chopped off one of his arms. Blood flowed freely. He lay still. The women and the old men standing there called on Christ and Maria to save them. The cries echoed to the village below, but time was pressing. The Germans swung a machine gun around and in the burst of fire and smoke all fell to the ground. A swift knifing followed for those who were not fortunate enough to be killed.

The Germans then turned on their heels, left the dead behind, and walked down to the village again. They gathered up the loot they had taken, put it in a wagon, and with the five young girls they left the village.

No sooner had they left than a peasant who was hiding near the cemetery came running down and told all he had seen. The priest hurried to the cemetery and saw the brutality. A few of the old people struggled up the street after him, but hardly had they gotten around the corner when the Germans came back again. They heeded not the frightened old people but came straight to Anna's house, where they had left the loot, and it was at that instant that I had to hide in her secret place.

I listened to the story and then went outside, followed by Gruno. In every house I heard quiet sobbing and many prayers. Everything now looked so peaceful. The green hills across the valley, a *kola* coming along the road, and the bees droning among the hedgerows. The church with its little cemetery was full of bitter tears. Old women in their voluminous clothing, their hair disheveled, were standing in a huddled group around the bodies. The priest was already burying them and the two boys, lying one across the other with broken limbs half chopped off, looked like the crucifixion of everything young and clean and healthy in the world. I turned and walked down under the lime trees lining the road. Broken shadows moved across the road as a faint breeze stirred the trees. The bell in Toplice started to toll. Slowly, monotonously it rang; the running river groaned as it sought the liberty of the great Kerka beyond. The green hills crouched and crept nearer, hiding us in deep shadow; night slipped over the mountains beyond. I reached Anna's house beside the river. Not a light showed in the village. Just as I stopped to enter the gate a nightingale sang.

CHAPTER 16

"You Will Come Back to Us"

The war in Yugoslavia had ended. The night before I left was a sad one. As the evening whispered down the *jama* through the trees, I looked out the window of my hut and saw Ajdovec at my feet. The men of evening patrol were just climbing the other side with their guns over their shoulders. I had watched many people climb out the *jama* opposite me. Franz, my courier, where was he now? Down near Trieste in jail, I heard. Simondia, the vivacious wife of Jeras; yes, she had panted and stopped many times climbing up through those pines. And the great hordes of young Partisan warriors who had been led away, blindfolded, from the hospital which had befriended them and made them whole again. Yes, blindfolded, so that no torture could ever make them reveal the secrets of hidden hospitals. I had watched them as they were led away, one by one, out of the *jama*, through the forest, over logs and stones, through drifts and icy steeps until any idea of situation had been lost. Then they were left on the roadside to await others who came from the fighting below and took the bandages from their eyes, and back they went to battle.

I remembered José Murun, toiling up; old Joe, whose daughter could have commanded the world of music at her feet, yet was still driving the horses and feeding the pigs at Packa. And Luka and Bogdan, my two colleagues; Luka, inspired by the party and never trusting anyone, Bogdan, just a little tight as he climbed among the trees and stones. There was Vic, from London, freed from the prison of shade and silence, and Bill still quietly dreaming of Ivitsa. Poles, Russians, Checks, Bosnians, Slovenes, and Dalmatians—all had passed that way. I called the commissar.

"Come up, Ivanovich, and have a chat before our meal."

He came up and brought with him a bottle of good *rakija*. He laughed and said, "For you, *Majore*."

"No," I replied. "For us." And we sat beside the log fire talking. He said that the patients all wanted to say good-by to me. They were having a concert for me. Our food would come up to the hut, and then we would go to another hospital, Yelen Dol, over the mountaintop, and then return for the concert.

We spoke of the future. He was filled with the enthusiasm of the recently converted. "Yes," he said. "We have been born in blood, and fought in blood, but now for the first time we have our country freed and united. Never again will we be bound by capitalist chains. We have found freedom."

I looked at him. The firelight shone through to his retina and for one brief moment I saw there into the very back of his eye; further, for I saw into the heart of young Yugoslavia.

Through all these years of occupation it had been a battle of youth. It was the seventeen-, the eighteen-, and the twenty-year-olds who had won the fight, and the great hope of the future was in their hands.

But behind it all who was there? Was Comrade Kidrich going to be content to hand back his country to the peasantry who had freed it? Or would the politicians still wrangle, scheme, plot, maneuver, and plan bigger conquests? Would the tension, the fear, and the apprehension, blowing in every wind across the mountains from the north, die away and give peace? Would the Church, whose part in the liberation was in some cases far from commendable, catch up with the new ideals and the new outlook, or would it strive to maintain the status quo? These heavy thoughts sank down through the *jama* with the oncoming night.

Perhaps the greatest difficulty of all, as I saw it, would be the cleaning of each person of his hate. What a river it would take to wash it all away. But the commissar, Ivan, was already filling the glasses again. He said I would be asked to sing all the songs Bill and I had sung throughout the long winter nights. "Ye gods," I replied. "Alone? Never!"

We got back to the main hospital about ten o'clock. All the patients had been moved into one ward and when I came in with the commissar they shouted, *"Zivio Majore Rogersau! Zivio!"*

I waved and replied, *"Zivio Demokratska Federativna Jugoslavija! Zivio Marshal Tito!"* And then we settled down.

I sat on the bed of Ceslav, the Polish medical student, now almost better. Truly I didn't pay much attention to the concert. They sang all my favorites for me. *"Počiva Jezero v Tihoti," "Teško Je Zaboraviti Tebe," "Na jurish."* And then I sang the Maori song of farewell, *"Haere ra."*

One of the patients made a speech, followed by one from

the commissar. I didn't listen to the speeches. I looked around on all the beds in the firelight, and I saw again all those who had been in those beds before, the ones who had died, the ones who had left us and rejoined the fight, and the ones who would still be lying in bed for months to come. The speeches ended.

I couldn't speak to them. Why, they called me Stari Papa, Old Father, and when a father says good-by forever to his children, can he make a speech? In the twilight of the fire I went around to every bed and shook them by the hand. A word to this one and a word to that. When I reached the end, it was little Heinrich, tears flowing freely down his face. He seized my hand, and, shyly dragging it under the blankets, he looked up at me and said:

"You will come back to us, won't you?"

GLOSSARY

bolničarka	nurse
srna	fawn
Chetnik	Serbian Quisling
komanda mesta	communist head of village soviet
corpus	division
devedeset	ninety
Domobranec	Slovene Quisling
drug	comrade
drugarica	female comrade
Demokratska Federativna Jugoslavija	Democratic Federated Jugoslavia
glavni stab	headquarters
gostiona	pub
hudič	obscenity
hajde, hadje	gee-up
javka	hidden place for collection of wounded
jama	deep depression in forest
"Kako se kaze?"	"How do you say it?"
kola (1)	wagon
(2)	cartwheel dance
kuna	crown coin in Croatia
"Laku noc; dobro spavajte."	"Good night; sleep well."
"Na jurish"	"Let us fight"
Nasa Borba	*Our War*—Partisan newspaper
Nasa Zena	*Our Women*—Partisan newspaper

omladinski dom	youth hall
Partizani	Partisan fighters
"*Partizani Nasi*"	"Our Partisan Fighters"
Partizanka	female fighter
pecina	cave
"*Počiva Jezero v Tihoti*"	"Rest beside the Still Lake"
polenta	stewed maize or beans
polje	polje
Rdeča Armada	Red Army
ruta	black cloth worn over head
sigurno	certainly
"*Sijaj, sijaj, belda luna*"	"Shine, shine, pale moon"
Smrt fascimu, sloboda narodu	Death to fascism, freedom to the people
S.N.O.S.	Parliament in exile (Slovene)
Stari Papa	Old Father
Sten Cas	billboard news
stoj	halt
tedeschi	German (Italian)
"*Téško Je Zaboraviti Tebe*"	"It Is Very Hard for Me to Forget You"
tišina	comrade
"*Triglav, Moj Dom*"	"Triglav, My Mountain Home"
Ustashi	Croatian Quisling
zdravo	greeting
"*Zivio . . .*"	"Long live . . ."

AUSTRIA
ITALY
DRAVA R.
SAVA R.
Ljubljana
Ajdovec
Novo Mesto
Zagreb
Toplice
Podhusta
Poturin
Metlika
Trieste
Kocevje
Semic
Karlovac
Crnomelje
KUPA R.
Fiume
Susak
Topusko
Glina
UNA
Slunj (Sluin)
Dvor
Otocac
Plitvice
Bihac
Udbina
Petrovac
Ostrelj
Martin Brod
Mazin
Drvar
Ticevo
Zadar
Knin
DINARIC ALPS
DUGI OTOK
KORNAT I.
Sibenik
ADRIATIC SEA
Ancona
ITALY
Vis
VIS I.